Inhabiting Stone

Celestin Büche

Contents

Overture

Thus, instruction that is supposed to educate an artist could consist at most in helping him to listen to himself. Technique, the means of art, will not help him. This ought to be, wherever possible, occult knowledge, to which he alone has access who finds the way himself. He who listens to himself acquires this technique. It is a route different from that of the curriculum, by roundabout ways perhaps, but with unerring certainty.
—ARNOLD SCHOENBERG | *Theory of Harmony, 413*

This book is inspired by the teachings of Nirman Cain. But the essence of Nirman's teaching is that he has no teaching, which leaves to question whether these first two sentences already contradict each other? But when writing about art, one is always at the cusp of contradiction. And this book is full of them.

I met Nirman on a sunny spring day in early 2020. I was out for a run in Amsterdam Noord when my eyes met a shiny egg-shaped sculpture resting on some pallets at the opposite end of a public parking area. I immediately sensed something special about the sculpture and the place surrounding it. Somehow, it contributed to its environment so that the whole area made sense. Just like a Japanese Zen Garden can evoke a sense of stillness, the sculpture gave its surroundings a suspicious degree of balance. This was surprising because the area was filled with cars, old ship construction machinery, run-down boats, overly stuffed litter bins and other cues that would usually suggest the opposite of a well-balanced environment.

I stopped my run and approached the two men sitting in front of the sprayed container that seemed to serve as the sculptor's studio. It was immediately obvious which of the two had fathered the sculpture that had drawn my attention: in a way it looked just like him.

The white marble stood around half a meter in height and had some lines drawn across it that made sense of its underlying form. But it wasn't the form *per se* that kept my gaze glued on the sculpture. Rather, the stone seemed "active" or "online" in a way untouched stone does not.

But no matter where I looked, I found no cues that would help me explain the mystery: His hand tools were warped, his workbench provisional, and his stones rough. Most of the stones he works with, he told me later, are stones he finds, stones he receives as a gift, or stones that are abandoned by other sculptors because they do not live up to their respective quality standards. "They are like street dogs!" he sometimes likes to characterize them.

Throughout our first exchange, I further noticed that one temple of his spectacles was missing, that the chair he was sitting on was rickety and that the hammer he was working with was loose on the stalk. And yet, none of these things *appeared* broken. Equally, his caravan —though full of worked-through benches, worn-through jackets, dusty drinking glasses and unsorted firewood— did not deserve to be labeled *dirty*. Even the glass of wine that spilled onto the concrete floor I did not perceive as *wasted*...

I think I knew immediately, but we still took our time to arrive at the core that had lingered from the moment I met him, namely whether I could start as his student?

Even though I did not have any previous training in art, Nirman agreed to take me on as a full-time apprentice. From the very beginning onwards, however, he made clear that he had nothing to teach me. He even refused to call me his student, for the stone, and not him, was to be my teacher. His role was only that of a "translator," he maintained.

Over the following years I spent sculpting at his workshop, Nirman did not instruct me much nor did he want me to take inspiration from him or any other artists. Like any great teacher, he wanted me to come to an understanding myself. And whenever he did catch himself being instructive or judgmental, he immediately corrected himself by stating that I should never listen to him. Or do the opposite of what he was suggesting.

Whenever Nirman does improvise a "lesson," as he likes to call it, he seems just as curious, just as surprised about the words he utters as anyone who cares to listen. And indeed, sometimes I did get the impression that my questions were used but as alibis for him to continue instructing himself. So what he is really exploring when he teaches, it seems, are the boundaries of his own understanding, not anybody else's. Arnold Schoenberg once remarked about his experience as a teacher:

> *Perhaps the pupil is only an outward projection of the teacher.*
> *The teacher speaks to himself when he speaks to that pupil…*
> *He instructs himself, is his own teacher, his own pupil.*[1]

And in precisely this manner, Nirman conveys his actual teaching sideways, namely that it is **the search** that matters and not any of the answers arrived. Schoenberg continues:

> *Had I told them merely what I know, then they would have known just that and nothing more. As it is, they know perhaps even less. But they get to know what matters: **the search itself!***
> *I hope my pupils will commit themselves to searching! Because they will know that one searches for the sake of searching. That finding, which is indeed the goal, can easily put an end to striving.*[2]

So what Nirman provides is not so much a set of techniques for how to make sculptures as it is something more fundamental: an enduring approach to art. Or shall I say: to life.

After I had been sculpting for a while, an urge to write started to build within me. I did not know what book I wanted to write, or what book wanted to use me to write itself, but without giving it much thought, I simply started to write.

Because I knew that every attempt to put Nirman's teaching into words was destined to fail, I decided not to die trying. So, instead of writing about Nirman's approach to sculpture, I started to reflect on what I had to come to understand myself. This might be wildly different from the account of any other of his students, for what the search reveals is unique to every person. I, therefore, do not claim that any methods or conceptions presented in this book resemble any of Nirman's viewpoints, nor do I claim to have understood any of his teaching (if he has one, that is). Also, the sections on the psychological and metaphysical implications of this way of working, as well as its relevance for the development of sculpture as an artform, are entirely my own. Should you, however, in reading this book find anything truthful for your own creative process, then all praise shall go and belong to Nirman, for it was him who held the space for me so that I could experience what came to be the foundation of this book.

Soon after I began to write, I grew curious about what others had written about this ancient artform. Not much it turned out: When I went through the available literature on sculpture, I was surprised how little of it there was, and even less so about its underlying craft. This surprised me because I always considered sculpture in its most basic form —using hand tools to give form to a block of stone— to be amongst the most prestigious of the arts and thus expected that every book that could be written on the subject had already been written. But when I compared the size of the library section on how to make sculpture against the sections on writing, painting, or making music, I could not help but wonder why this artform seemed to have largely escaped linguistic characterization.

And what is more, none of the books I encountered described the craft in a similar way as I got to know it working alongside Nirman. The literature seemed to limit itself to describing stone types, techniques, ways of achieving specific outcomes and other aspects I learned to be of secondary importance. To offer a comparison: If the literature on how to write were in the same state as the literature on how to make sculpture was, then all available books would have been about grammar and building vocabulary, both of which are of secondary importance for the production of good writing.

Why sculpture has remained somewhat forgotten in the how-to literature can only be speculated about. One reason might be that working in stone is often conceived of, or framed as, too difficult compared to other art forms. The implicit assumption many seem to hold, or perhaps even promote, is that other art forms like drawing, working in wood, bronze, or clay must be mastered before one should dare to fiddle with stone. The literature further facilitates this elitist image by overly focusing on figurative sculpture and by presenting sculpture as an institution that is distinguished by rules that must be adhered to, laws that must be respected and techniques that must be mastered before one is entitled to call oneself a sculptor. In such a framing, then, there simply is no room, nor a need, for a guide on how to make sculptures.

It thus seemed as if the curious who have not found a master, or have access to a workshop nearby, had to choose between two extremes: Either they could pick up a book by, or about, some of the great sculptors of the past —Auguste Rodin, Constantin Brancusi, Isamu Noguchi, Jean Arp, Gaudier-Brzeska, Barbara Hepworth, or whoever— and somehow try to distill their insights backwards into their way of working. *Or* they could pick up a book with *Technique* as part of its title and study step-by-step guides on how to best carve a snail out of a block of stone. Both wouldn't get them very far in terms of producing art because what remained missing is the *in-between*, the description of the actual process: And indeed, when I went through the available literature on how to make sculpture, I could not find a single book that lays out how one can move from carving a snail following a manual —an approach that can produce decoration at best— to participating in the creation of art. "Sculpture is the least understood of all the arts," Brenda Putnam writes in *The Sculptor's Way*, "and the student must frequently grope his way unaided along a dark and unfamiliar road."[3]

There exist, however, a few books from other disciplines that have accomplished this feat of describing how a craft is turned into an art form, how some raw material can be turned into a work of art. *Ensouling Language* by Stephen Buhner is one of them. *The Natural Way to Draw* by Kimon Nicolaides is another. But such works remain obscurities; yetis of sorts.

What unifies such works —*The Fine Art of Cabinetmaking* by James Krenov is another one— is that they originate from a similar climate of mind: Their authors understand that, in the production of art, feeling comes first, technique second; that the process is primary, the result secondary; that development counts more than does completion. They further understand that artists are bound by a certain way of relating to the material, by a certain *ethos*. That is, by the desire to make things right. Not for the customer, not for themselves, but for the material itself. Because it deserves it . . . and because they must.

When I encountered this deserted literary landscape on how to make sculpture, I got a suspicion about where the urge to write this book might have been coming from. And following Toni Morrison's call, "If there is a book that you want to read, but it hasn't been written yet, then you must write it," a book began to take form that describes an *underground* way of sculpting. That is, a way that isn't concerned with the outcome, but the process; not with surface, but with meaning; not with technique, but with feeling; not with form, but with essence.

This book, then, is equally *underground* in flavor. By that I mean that, during my writing, I was not concerned with anything outside the material, which is to say, outside the words, sentences and paragraphs that make up its text. What I *did* care about was whether each word enjoys inhabiting the line I put it in and whether the writing came to reflect my experience of working with stone. In that way, besides being *how-to* literature, this book is probably best understood as poetry. Or perhaps, as a form of diary.

I always considered this book a sculpture, not one made of stone, but of words. And just like the form of a sculpture only serves as the container for the meaning that it holds inside, the meaning of this book is equally to be found beyond the words that make up its text. The words lying on these pages are thus to be seen like the chips and dust the sculptor took away. Judging the book by them would be as meaningless as judging a sculpture by the pieces lying around the workbench. For what counts is not what the sculptor took away, but what they has left. This, of course, is delicate with the medium of language because that which has been left out is not visible, as it is in sculpture, but remains invisible behind the text.

Just like every sculpture, this book has twists and turns, rough edges, smooth transitions, holes, shining parts, surfaces that have been polished and others that have been overlooked. But I invite you to look at this book as a whole and not as something comprised of individual parts. Much like when listening to a piece of music, focus on the flavor, rhythm, organization and depth rather than on individual sentences or the arguments provided. To use Christopher Nolan's phrase from *Tenet*: "Don't try to understand it. Feel it!" And whatever you feel *is* the instruction and not any of the concepts described.

To give an example, Stephen Buhner's *Ensouling Language* is not a great book (only) because it contains exercises that will develop your writing, but because it *is* a great book in-and-of-itself. And *that* is the manual. Similarly, what makes Kimon Nicolaides' *The Natural Way to Draw* an excellent starting point for developing your drawing abilities are not (solely) the exercises he provides, but the orientation of mind he drew from when he wrote it.

So then, this book does not seek to illuminate the *dark and unfamiliar road* by offering exercises, illustrations, work plans, or other specific instructions for making a sculpture. If anything, it seeks to encourage you to walk into the dark yourself.

Part I
On Art

Chapter 1

On certain mountainsides in the far west where one might want to build trails, an obsidian rock sheath is found, glassy, impossible for horses' hoofs to get a grip on. So smaller rocks have to be laid on it, but carefully. So he thought that words might be used that way, one slipped under the end of another, laid down on the glassy surface of some insight that one couldn't stand on otherwise.
—ROBERT BLY | Reaching out to the World, 49

Take any tree and look at its shape, its structure, its power, its marvelous expression of form. Nature gives rise to such forms without effort, knowledge of technique, or the guiding hand of a textbook. It just does it. And even though many tree trunks appear similar, no one is ever quite the same.

When I look closely at such a trunk, such as from a silver birch, for example, I can sense an outward pressing force inhabiting the stem. It is this force that infuses and creates the continuous and shifting forms that can be found everywhere in nature. Such forms are never perfectly straight, round, or closed, but always fluid, moving and in transition. They are, in every sense of the word, alive. Things infused with this force radiate a beauty that, if one takes the time to look, cannot be negated.

One can sense the presence of this force most clearly in the animal and vegetable kingdom, but it can also be found in realms often defined as inanimate, such as in stones, books, or canvasses.

When I first saw Nirman's sculptures, not only did they bear the same characteristics of form that can be found in the natural world —they were distinguished by a sense of wholesomeness, movement and fluidity— but they also appeared to be infused with the same life-giving force that can be sensed in the trunk of a tree.

Nothing can be said about this force in and of itself because it only exists in-between and inside things and thereby escapes all measurement attempts. Calling it a force is actually already misleading because it creates a conception and image of something that is inherently conception- and imageless. But calling it a force probably comes closest to hinting at what it *does*. Calling it potential probably comes closest to hinting at what it *is*. Paul Klee writes:

> *The power of creativity cannot be named. It remains mysterious to the end. But what does not shake us to our foundations is no mystery. We ourselves, down to the smallest part of us, are charged with this power. We cannot state its essence but we can, in certain measure, move towards its source. In any case we must reveal this power in its functions just as it is revealed to us. Probably it is only a form of matter, but one that cannot be perceived by the same senses as the familiar kinds of matter. Still, it must make itself known through the familiar kinds of matter and function in union with them. Merged with matter, it must enter a real and living form.[1]*

To aid this force into *familiar kinds of matter* —into canvasses, stones, books, etc.— is, always has been, and always will be, the true quest of the artist. The experience of co-creation, of channeling the life force into a material, is the attractor, yes, the secret, that lies at the heart of all artistic pursuits.

The creative force must be understood in the same way as the force in *Star Wars* has to be understood. What it is or how it can be mediated into an artwork cannot be explained or put into words. It has to be done. Or, to be more precise: allowed to happen. It is something that is done actively, but the experience itself is passive in nature. Like when you let yourself fall asleep. Or when you are actively relaxing a muscle.

And just like you cannot force yourself to fall asleep, you cannot force an artwork to come "alive." About all you can do is make yourself available for it to happen *through* you. "You cannot govern the creative impulse," Nicolaides writes in *The Natural Way to Draw*, "about all you can do is to eliminate obstacles and smooth the way for it."[2] And on some days it will come and on others, it won't. All one must be is open, trusting and patient. John Steinbeck provides this wonderful analogy for the realm of writing:

How can the poem and the stink and the grating noise - the quality of light, the tone, the habit and the dream - be set down alive? When you collect marine animals there are certain flat worms so delicate that they are almost impossible to capture whole, for they break and tatter under the touch. You must let them ooze and crawl of their own will onto a knife blade and then lift them gently into your bottle of sea water. And perhaps that might be the way to write this book - to open the page and let the stories crawl in by themselves.[3]

Paul Klee uses the analogy of a tree to describe how the creative force, once accessed, finds its way into an artwork. The artist, Klee invites us in his analogy, can be viewed as the trunk of a tree. With its roots, the tree extends into the ground —into oneself— to suck in the sap —the creative force— that flows beneath all and everything. The sap nourishes and powers the tree and, when the conditions are right, will result in the growth of a crown. The crown, then, he emphasizes, will show little resemblance to the trunk of the tree, for it is a synthesis of these two. He writes:

The creation of a work of art —the growth of the crown of the tree— must of necessity, as a result of entering into the specific dimensions of pictorial art, be accompanied by distortion of the natural form. For, therein is nature reborn.[4]

There always remains something lacking when somebody copies, even when the form and the texture are indistinguishable from the real. This is not only true when copying organic nature but also when existing works of art are reproduced:

If you took one of Nirman's sculptures and brought it to a stonemasonry to be replicated even to the millimeter, the result is still bound to be without artistic value. In the original, the sculpture is the result of a unique coming together between a man and a stone, whereas, in the replica, the result is imposed from the outside. And because the replica is not the result of such an intimate meeting, it will never possess the hum that clouds the original. For the process always leaves traces, as every detective knows, no matter how thoroughly the villain sought to clean up.

The same can also be reasoned towards from the opposite end: Had Nirman worked with the stone the replica was inflicted upon, he would have arrived at a different form. Or else again: Had the stonemason listened to the stone they inflicted the copy upon, they, too, would have arrived at a different sculpture, for each stone demands its own process with its own unique outcome.

So only those who allow themselves to merge with the material create the necessary space for the miraculous to occur. Those that remain with the outside, those that copy, might capture all but what made it grow. "If one has reproduced nature realistically it is not creation," Constantin Brancusi writes. "An artist must create. A reproduction of a horse in marble or bronze is a corpse of a horse."[5][6]

Kazimir Malevich took the notion that artists must not copy one step further, if not to say: to its logical conclusion. Because what Malevich asserted is that, even though the distortion of the natural form —which Paul Klee asserted as necessary for the production of art— is a good starting point, it is not enough. That is because nature not only never copies, but it also doesn't take inspiration. In nature, no form is tied to any other form but everything represents itself. Everything *is* itself. So, if we truly want to create, Malevich derived, our artworks cannot be tied to anything external —images, ideas, stories, or whatever— but they must be allowed to represent themselves. To *be* themselves. He writes in *The Non-objective world:*

> *In copying or tracing the forms of nature we have fed our consciousness with a false understanding of art [. . .] The artist can be a creator only when the forms in his picture have nothing in common with nature [. . .] Forms must be given life and the right to individual existence.[7]*

According to Malevich, any notion coming in from the outside is thus *in the way* of an artwork acquiring individual existence. Because as long as an artwork is tied to something external —be this through modes of imitation, inspiration, representation, conception, influence, abstraction, or whatever— it is not allowed to represent itself and, therefore, not truly creative. So *anything* within an artwork that is not essential to itself, any meaning not to be found in its material, is distorting its artistic value.

Jean Arp also supported this view that artworks must be kept free from outside influences to come fully into being:

> *Art is a fruit that grows out of man like the fruit out of a plant or the child out of its mother. But whereas the fruit of a plant acquires completely independent forms and never resembles a balloon or a president in a cutaway suit, the artistic fruit of man generally shows a ridiculous resemblance to the appearance of other things.*[8]

When looking across the landscape of contemporary sculpture, one rarely finds a sculptor whose work would qualify for Malevich's criteria. Or formulated more sharply: When looking across the landscape of contemporary art, one rarely finds a sculpture that qualifies as a work of art.

When speaking about the origin of their forms, most modern and contemporary sculptors assert that their works were inspired *by* something or are meant to represent something. When speaking about their sculpture's meaning, they equally assert something from the outside, such as by clouding them within a story, or by offering an explanation about why they made a certain form. Implicitly, these sculptors view themselves as separate (or above, to use a more forcing metaphor) from the material they seek to infuse (or impose) their ideas with.

This split between the material and the meaning conventional sculptors seek to impose it with becomes further apparent when we pay close attention to the inherent implications words like *inspiration*, *representation*, or *abstraction* carry. Because as long as an artwork is inspired or influenced *by* something, meant to represent something, or abstracted *from* something, there exists a split between the material that makes up the artwork and the place it derives its meaning from. As a matter of fact, these are all still modes of copying, albeit hidden or distorted ones.

This dualistic split between the material and the place a sculpture derives its meaning from also becomes evident in the way conventional sculptors develop the form of their works: Most still first cast a model in clay, plaster, or bronze, or make a miniature version before they go on executing their idea in stone. This makes their resulting work nothing but copies and, thereby, a priori disqualifies them from being of artistic value. Some might counter that many contemporary sculptors no longer deploy this intermediary step but develop the form directly in stone. But even though *direct carving* seems to have superseded sculptures from being mere copies of previous casts, most sculptors still impose the form from the outside, such as by first sketching it on a piece of paper or by drawing the outlines of their aspired figure onto the stone. So rather than having freed themselves from imposing themselves on the material, they simply pushed back the act of imposition —much like the panpsychists pushed back the "problem of consciousness" by claiming that every atom is conscious to save themselves a materialistic worldview. These sculptors, like the panpsychists, have not yet had the courage to take the jump into the unknown by giving up the desire to know what their sculptures, or reality, are about.

So even in contemporary approaches, where the form is directly developed in stone, there still is an idea, a model, a form, an outside, which sculptors seek to impose, rather than them having the courage to let the sculpture arise from the inside out. Harold Rosenberger, who coined the term *Action Painting,* once remarked fittingly:

> *To work from sketches arouses the suspicion that the artist still regards the canvas as a place where the mind records its contents—rather than itself the 'mind' through which the painter thinks by changing a surface with paint.* [9]

Another metaphor that many sculptors like to draw upon when speaking about the development of their sculptures is most succinctly caught in the phrase, "Every block of stone has a statue inside it and it is the task of the sculptor to discover it," which is often attributed to Michelangelo. This metaphor implies that there already is a finished form inside the stone that

waits to be freed by an artist. This is, of course, nonsense because there is no finished sculpture inside a stone, just as there is no finished tree inside a seed. The stone, just like the seed, exists in a state of pure potential, and to come into being, it needs to be developed and grown. So more often than not, this metaphor, just as the metaphor that sculptors use the form of the rough stone as a starting point for their development of form, is used as a Trojan Horse by which sculptors cover their act of imposition upon the material by clothing it up in more romantic language.

Friedrich Schiller made a similar observation in *Letters upon the aesthetic education of man*. Because what he observed is that most artists deceive the spectators, as well as themselves, by making their work look *as if* it was created in a cooperative approach with the material. But behind the image, he noticed, always lays an act of violence, in which the artist imposed themselves on the material. He, however, does not render this problematic, for he maintains that stone does not feel and therefore does not care. Only in human education, he proposes, can an approach work in which artists (teachers) do not impose themselves on their material (the children) because only humans, as opposed to stone, have agency.

Schiller clearly never got intimate with stone because such a misguided conclusion following such a profound insight can only come from a thinking mind and not from the hands of a caring artist. Because, in my experience, stone presents itself as anything but an innate material upon which violence can be performed without repercussions.

Anyway, almost universally, sculptors speak about the curves in their forms as being "inspired by the human body" or by "forms found in nature." Almost universally, sculptors say that "they only set the angel free that was already within the marble." I, however, propose that the time is ripe to move beyond such associative talk; that the time is ripe to free sculpture from any sort of outside; that the time is ripe to free sculpture from having to stand in relation to something beyond itself.

So this approach seeks to liberate sculpture from all dualisms, making notions like inspiration or representation meaningless at best. It aims to free sculptures from their makers and instead seeks to give them *the right to individual existence*.

In that way, sculptures developed in light of this book's approach do not need to be inspired by anything, neither by a concept nor by the stone itself. Like the crown of a tree, they are the synthesized product of the stone's DNA and the environment they are born into. And just like the same tree would give rise to a different crown depending on the environment it grew in, so will each stone result in a different sculpture depending on who, where and when it was worked on. Meaning, those who work in light of this approach will never know what form their sculptures will take; until they arrive at it.

The forms that spring out of this process might appear unlike any the world has ever seen. In fact, as long as they resemble an existing style too closely, chances are that their makers did not fully surrender to the process. Because when they fully submit themselves towards having an artwork emerge on its own, something novel, something revolutionary, something contemporary is bound to be revealed. Malevich writes:

> *The works of such artists [those who copy] are always comprehensible to the public (the majority of people) because they represent nothing new, whereas the works of the creative artists contain new solutions to the eternal conflict between the subject and the object and bear little or no resemblance to accustomed reality.*[10]

In many ways, this way of sculpture stands diametrically opposed to the traditional way stone sculpture is understood:

Traditionally, stone sculptors carve a form *into* a stone. They seek to reveal an image by removing excess material. They seek to create form from the outside in —think of ornamental sculpture or someone sculpting a bust. There, the artist uses the stone not unlike the clay modeler uses a heap of clay: the material itself is secondary, the image, the final form, primary. The traditional approach focuses on the outside of the artwork: what it signifies is what matters.

This approach, by contrast, aspires to discover form from the inside out. Those following it *search* for form inside the material rather than applying it from the outside. The material is primary, and the image, or the form, is secondary. The focus is on the inside of the artwork: the pursuit for meaning, artistic value, for life itself, is central. What it signifies is irrelevant. What it *is* is what counts.

Comparing what constitutes a mistake between these two ways of working further helps us understand the difference: For those who encounter the stone with a pre-defined idea, a mistake is any kind of divergence from the ideal they sought to realize. Whereas for those following the gist underlying this book, an unintentional occurrence is simply an invitation, a starting point to continue exploring the form from.

Notice how the conventional approach is bound to fail on both ends: If a sculptor somehow *manages to* impose the ideal onto the stone they had in mind, the result is destined to appear machine-like, lifeless and cold —it remains a copy, after all. And if the person *fails to* impose the ideal, every divergence will be identifiable as a mistake. Everyone will then see what they tried to do, and it will be visible where they have made a mistake.

Sculptures developed in light of this book, on the other hand, cannot have such shortcomings. Since there is no idea the sculptor works towards, no one, including the artist, will know what was intentional and what occurred by chance, what was deliberate and what introduced itself by accident. And whatever forms arise from such a process will, all on their own, be reminiscent of the forms found in nature, where the distinction between what is a mistake and what is intentional is equally insignificant. In nature, all is luminous, liquid and alive, even when it's broken.

Chapter 2

Identifying some as "artists" endangers art.
—*WILLIAM STAFFORD* | *Writing the Australian Crawl, 47*

Responding to what this approach to sculpture could be called, I once said: *Exploration of form.*

Exploration, because there is nothing but the act of exploration this approach is concerned with. The outside, the image, the appearance, yes, even the form, are all of secondary importance. So is the stone the sculpture is made of, the tools used in the process, the time spent crafting it, etc. All that is of concern is the act of exploration, of searching, of listening, and not that of realizing anything brought in from the outside.

Some might suggest adding an *abstract* into that definition because my sculptures do not depict anything "concrete." But when looking at the notion of abstraction, we must wonder whether it means anything at all? Since can it not be said that *no* sculpture is abstract just as much as it can be said that *every* sculpture is abstract? Because if it can, we can dispense of the notion of abstraction in the same way a mathematician can dispense of values that arise on both sides of an equation:

The former can be reasoned towards when we consider that all sculptures manifest in the physical and are therefore concrete. Calling a sculpture "abstract" would thus represent a confusion about its ontological status as a material object. The latter can be concluded if we consider that even a photorealistic sculpture underwent a process of abstraction by which the artist chose to exclude certain aspects of reality. So *every* sculpture can be coined abstract. ~~Abstract~~ = ~~Abstract~~

Not so fast, some might counter. Because another understanding associated with this notion is that *abstract art* refers to works whose content does not correspond to objects seen in everyday reality. But this conception does not provide much to stand on either, because what is seen in everyday reality is such a thin slice of what *can* be seen and what *is* seen by different people: If I ate some *Stropharia cubensis*, two hours into the experience, my environment would turn into a Van Gogh; twenty minutes after taking some Ketamine, my visual field would appear as if it were sketched by Cy Twombly; and twenty seconds after inhaling some 5-MeO-DMT, I would be (looking at) a Malevich. So what kind of everyday reality is this notion built upon that can reliably be dissolved through the ingestion of a tiny bit of matter?

I further prefer not to call my sculptures *abstract* because it suggests a dichotomy between the artwork and its maker. As I've outlined before, when we say something is abstract, we imply that the artwork stands *in relation* to something else. This can be something external —an object— or something internal —an idea— which the artwork is meant to be *abstracted* from. But this approach doesn't know any sort of outside. It is direct. Like drawings made by children, which we don't call abstract either. After all, we understand that the concept of abstraction is meaningless to a child, for a child simply expresses what it feels. In fact, even this description does not quite do it justice because it suggests that a child expresses what it feels. But this distinction a child does not make. A child does not feel something and then decides to express it. Witnessing, feeling, expression, all is just one happening. And because children do not have this intermediary step, the lines drawn by children are so powerful and difficult —if not impossible— to reproduce by an adult. I think it was Picasso who once said, "It took me four years to paint like Raphael but a lifetime to paint like a child."

I became particularly aware of the redundancy of the notion of abstraction when I made a furious drawing with my eyes closed. Because when I opened my eyes, what I was looking at wasn't some less precise, condensed, or simplified depiction of some idea, nor was its content a mediated, adulterated, or translated depiction of something previously existing. No, the drawing was direct.

It is this direct contact, this direct transmission, that this book is ultimately after. And just like children, who, up to a certain age, cannot help themselves but to draw in this direct manner, need not know anything about representation, technique, perspective, or figuration to reveal a line that radiates life, we also do not need to know about any of these to manifest a work of art.

That is why anybody can make a sculpture regardless of whether they have an inclination for art, possess drawing abilities, or regard themselves as uncreative. Creativity is not, as it is often said and believed, a skill or a personality trait one can possess, but a place, an experience, a state of consciousness that anyone can tune into. It is, as the writer William Stafford put it, "a natural activity for one not corrupted by mechanical ways."[11] And similar to drawings made by children, sculptures made by the uninitiated often possess a roughness and an authority that academically derived and "correct" sculptures lack. They possess a liveliness that sculptures made in a paint-by-numbers approach never will, no matter how technically advanced the sculptor who connected the dots.

A related assertion that persists in popular thought is that one must possess some secret faculty of mind called imagination to be creative. That is, one must be able to imagine what something would look like in the physical before one makes it manifest. And if one does not have this imaginative capability, one is not a creative person and, therefore, disqualified from making art. What nonsense! To me, my imaginative capacity is meaningless for making sculptures. Since when I sculpt, I am concerned with the material as it is and not with what it could look like in some hypothetical future that will never arise anyway.

People also often assert that sculptors must have a lot of patience. I equally disagree; I don't have any patience at all! But to make a sculpture, I don't need to have patience because when I am in the trenches of the Now, I automatically understand each chisel beat to be critical, to be cutting edge, so there is no room for the notion of patience to arise. And if it does arise, it only indicates that I wasn't present with the stone. For as long as I am present with the stone, I am always walking on a cliff's edge. With gravel under my feet. In the dark. Rain pouring.

Most sculptors, if they deserve to be called that, work through an enormous amount of stone in their quest to realize their predefined ideas. And they don't do so sustainably so that the excess pieces could be used for other sculptures. No, they unconsciously slice the stone with an angle grinder and then bang the excess pieces into unusable fragments. I say unconscious because nobody working with awareness could ever treat stone like that.

The fall into unconsciousness happens because they mistake the image for the sculpture. They believe the outcome matters, not how they arrived at it. So as long as there is a lot of material between them and the form they aspire to reveal, they see no point in working through it attentively.

Those working without an image in mind, on the other hand, automatically know that they have to be attentive to each chisel beat because they never know where they are in their sculpting process.

Let me emphasize the significance of this: When a mason carves the nose of a bust, they understands that each action will show itself in the result. They understands that every blow will influence the figure's appearance. But it is only then that they realizes this. While carving out the figure's rough shape, they doesn't realize that how they do this will also influence the feel of the work. The true sculptor understands this. They understands that *every* action co-determines the final sculpture. So for the sculptor, *every* beat with the chisel has the same immediacy as when a mason is carving some delicate feature of a bust.

People also like to use the phrase, "even a single blow can break the work," when characterizing the craft. But those who find themselves agreeing with these sorts of statements should equally know that something in their way of working is off. Because when one is present with the form, there is no such thing as "breaking the work." All there is are new directions to work towards. Artists like Paul Klee, Jean Arp, or Jean Dubuffet understood that unintentional occurrences, or what some might call mistakes, do not mark the end of a creative journey but, if they have any significance at all, new beginnings. With almost all stones I worked with, the process had me take surprising turns because something unintentional happened. But more often than not, such happenings led me into directions I would otherwise not have ventured into.

Sometimes, children came to draw on the concrete around the studio while their parents enjoyed a drink at the nearby restaurant. On one such occasion, a girl drew a pigeon that often sat with us at the studio.[12] The pigeon had hurt her foot and often watched us for hours throughout her recovery.

I wasn't there when the girl drew that pigeon, but I only saw the image afterward. While I was admiring her making, Nirman told me that, after she had finished her chalk drawing, her father came over and, instead of celebrating her masterpiece, showed her how to make a *more accurate* drawing by moving chalk around his fingers. The truth being, of course, that nothing could have ever been more accurate than the girl's drawing. And even though the father was probably well-meaning in his unconscious intentions, interventions like these marked the beginning of the girl's ability to draw freely. A few months later, she probably already pushed chalk around her fingers, hoping to please her father's eye.[13]

We all once had the ability to perceive and act directly, to see and hear authentically, but most of us got out of touch with it during our upbringing. Ideas about how something is supposed to look like, what something supposedly is, were poured into us, distorting or blocking our ability to experience reality firsthand. And what came naturally to us as children, we have to rediscover painstakingly as an adult. So let's not waste any more time moving chalk around our fingers but let's draw some pigeons instead.

To sculpt from such a place, we must first realize that we constantly impose ourselves upon our environment. Because only when we have become, at least in part, aware that we are constantly projecting concepts upon all and everything can we begin to fathom what it would mean to move beyond them. And since the mind is a master in camouflaging itself, it is often easier to spot the mind, and its mechanisms, in other people, which, in turn, can help us spot it within ourselves.

One way I became aware how most people are fully occupied by their minds was by noticing how they seek to label and categorize my sculptures. To make them known. The thinking mind cannot exist in the unknown —in experience— which is why it does not like shapes and forms it cannot give a name for. So it immediately tries to fit them into a category by projecting something concrete onto them. One of my sculptures, for instance, was labeled a fish, a surfboard, a spoon, a shell, a feather, a phallus, a finger, a pole, a harp, a tongue, a rocket and a helmet, even though I was not inspired by any of these things. But once the strangers found a fitting word that approximated what they were seeing, they usually eased up, reassured themselves that what they were seeing was "indeed a tongue!" before happily walking away as if they had solved a riddle.

People also frequently want to know the name of my sculpture. When I respond that they do not have a name, they are often disappointed or even bewildered. "What is the meaning of it when is has no name?" they seem to wonder. This reminds me of my grandmother, who lamented that she "could not find me" in her prayers because my parents had not decided on my name until the day of my baptism. Before I was given a name, to her I did not exist.

It is difficult to appreciate an artwork without immediately giving in to the impulse of wanting to categorize or label it. But the act of labeling takes away the opportunity to experience its naked meaning. Since when the labeling has occurred, we are no longer perceiving the artwork through our senses but through a superimposed concept. "How difficult it is, though, to refrain from replacing the thing with its sign, to keep the object alive before us instead of killing it with the word," Goethe once remarked.[14]

But when we see authentically, we can feel the meaning inherent to an artwork directly. We can directly perceive what the artist put into it because the entire process is, in some way or another, reflected in the outcome: The tools used, the artist's understanding, the attention and care present during its making, all are imprinted within the material. But if we immediately jump to the label or demystify the work in some other way, we rid ourselves of the opportunity to experience the artwork for what it is: an artifact of the process that led to its creation.

When I began working at Nirman's studio, he said that the purpose of his studio was "to create a space where animals like to come and children like to play." This utterance alone gave me a sense of what his studio space was all about. For those who do not immediately label off everything, most prominently children and animals, are often much better at grasping what a place is all about.

Another question strangers often ask is: "What stone is it?" as if they know anything about stone types. But even if they knew anything about stone taxonomy —which they don't— notice how this question has little to nothing to do with the sculpture. But usually, after I respond *Pakistani Sandstone* or whatever, they nod with reassuring satisfaction.

Others want to know how heavy my hammer is, what chisel I use, how much the stone costs, etc. But again, notice how all these questions are targeted at demystifying the sculpture. And the more it is demystified, the more the unknown is removed, the further away the spectator moves from experiencing its true meaning.[15]

A related instance occurred when a friend asked me when I would start making "real" sculptures. Obviously, this is an absurd question because there is no such thing as an "unreal" sculpture. But what he was comparing the realness of my sculptures against were sculptures by some Renaissance master, into which my sculptures, with their more ambiguous forms, did not fit. And, to his mind, the function of any sculpture that is not figurative can only serve the purpose of learning the technique and not be an end in and of itself.

"What will it be?" is another question I am often asked. Similar to my friend's implication that my sculpture somehow wasn't "real," this question also suggests the absurd notion that the sculpture wasn't already something. "But it will be more, right?" a woman once asked when I responded that what she was looking at was the finished product. "If anything, it will be less!" I responded to her puzzled face.

People also repeatedly urge me to engrave a text or symbols to make the sculpture "more meaningful." What they are comparing the meaningfulness of my sculpture against are, of course, gravestones or memorial stones. And without such an engraving, my sculpture does not fit into these categories and is therefore incomplete.

The lowest common denominator the mind can pull out when confronted with something that looks neither random nor purposeful is "art." "What are you making?" is by far the most common question I am asked. Sometimes, I respond, "I do not know!" whereupon some counter: "Oh, so you are an artist!"

The notion of art is difficult because no one knows what art is. This became most obvious to me during encounters with children and teenagers. More than once, I was asked whether what I was doing could be called "art"? I could then witness how their minds learned to classify anything that they could not put into an available box, such as "he is making a gravestone," "building a staircase," or "constructing an arch," as art.

My favorite encounter related to this occurred with a girl visiting a nearby market. I did not hear her coming, so she took me by surprise when she suddenly stood next to me. "What is the problem?" she asked. I was confused by her question and did not understand what she was referring to, so I asked her to clarify. But I could immediately see how confused she was about the fact that I did not understand the obviousness of her question. This, in turn, made me worry because I thought that I might have missed some obvious problem surrounding me. But before the conversation could unfold any further, her father —who must have heard our exchange— jumped in: "He is not fixing a problem. He is making art!" She immediately jumped back, expressed a loud "Ooh!" and a mixture of confusion, shame and ambivalence was expressed on her face. She had absolutely no concept of art and felt guilty for not having recognized my sculpture as such. She assumed I was fixing a problem.

What a pity she felt that way, for art does not like to be recognized. Jean Dubuffet captured this succinctly when he wrote:

> *Art hates to be recognised and greeted by its name. It runs away immediately... As soon as it's unmasked, as soon as someone points the finger, it runs away.*[16]

And also, not only was the girl's assertion that I was fixing a problem most wonderful, but perhaps also closer to the truth than her father's correcting statement that I was making art.

Chapter 3

Teach thy tongue to say 'I do not know,' and thou shalt progress.
—attributed to MAIMONIDES

The general public assumes that the secret to making art lies in the acquisition of technique. The common belief is that if one masters technique, then great art will follow. Of course, nothing could be further from the truth. Art does not result from the application of technique, but from the confrontation with the unknown. And because technique resides in the known, it has the capacity to thwart the creative process rather than facilitate it. That is why rules about the correct usage of a tool, or conventional ways of how to progress from a rough stone to a certain form, are the least important elements of the craft. For if one does not first learn to be receptive, to listen, to feel, one is apt to produce industrial stonemason's work, not art:

Industrial stonemasons have a clear image in mind of what the end result should look like: They want to make a sink, a fountain, or a trophy maybe. Once they decided what they want to do, they calculate how much time it will take, what the end result will cost, what parts can be done by the apprentice, the machine, and what parts they must do themselves. They then contemplate what stone to pick, what tools to use, what sculptural techniques to apply before beginning the actual carving process. Following, they sketch the outlines onto the stone before carving out the rough shape with an angle grinder before working deeper into the form with pneumatic chisels. In the end, they might sandblast the result or give the work a "high finish" by polishing it with a machine.

Throughout this process, they might use glues, screws, or metal implants for stabilization, artificial substances to increase erosive resistance, oil to make the color look "deeper," engrave a saying to make the work "more meaningful" or put the figure on a base to disengage it from its background. And even though they cannot control the process entirely, they make every effort to do so: They might clamp the stone between a vice, cushion it in foam, hang it from the ceiling, or spray water on it to prevent it from cracking. They are, after all, afraid of the stone, and the stone is afraid of them because what they are doing isn't so much a cooperation as it is an act of violence. And as a result of their encroaching act, stone often appears domesticated and tamed, like a polished Swiss rock crystal: What was once an insisting piece of nature is turned into little more than gimcrackery. Yes, the industrial stonemason's approach yields quick results. But something deep, something meaningful cannot spring out of such a process. Art can never happen.

Similarly, when sculpture is approached as an academic discipline by which artists seek to manifest a certain ideal of form, the results are equally bound to be of little artistic value. Countless hours are wasted in which students carve oloids, hyperbolic paraboloids, Moebius strips and similar academically derived forms. I say wasted because such sculptures do not arise out of the deep waters of the unknown, but are products of the narrow irrigation ditches of the linear mind. And even if they are executed with excellent technique, something about them always remains missing. It is difficult to say what that is —an unevenness of line, maybe? —a touch of the unpredictable, perhaps? — but it is evident that they are not true works of art. They remain as flat as the feeling of this sentence.

Such sculptures remind me of a dinner I once attended at a renowned cooking school: As the highlight of their yearlong training, the students had to prepare a multi-course dinner for friends and family to demonstrate what they had learned. However, even though the food was served in fancy dishes, prepared in unconventional ways and served with plenty of wine, I could not help but assess that the food did not taste. Everybody's concern was with the outside, with what the food looked like and how it appeared, not with how it actually tasted. On top of that, the air was filled with anxiety: The students were afraid that the cream on the pudding might not hold, and the parents wondered whether the £36,535 spent on their children's course was really worth a carved piece of tasteless cucumber. There was no love for the craft, not a creative impulse present, no honest smile given.

The utilization of techniques may produce technically correct sculptures, but sculptures that possess luminosity, sculptures that mean something, cannot occur from such approaches. Because even if all the steps on the menu were followed correctly, the meal won't taste if the most important ingredient remains missing.

All who follow such overbred and alienated pursuits mistake the art for something it is not and waste their time with aspects that are of no importance. They believe sculpture is a science, whereas it is closer to a religion. They believe sculpting is something done mechanically, whereas it is better thought of as a form of tantra. For whoever sculpts like that, sculpture will always remain a hobby, not a lifestyle. Something that is done on the side and not at the center. And nothing that didn't grow out of the center can ever take on artistic quality.

Typical questions regarding technique are: How should a particular tool be used? What degree has the chisel to be applied against the stone? Which direction should one be working? Where and how should one start? How does one get a surface straight? How does one minimize the risk of unintentionally breaking something off?... But instead of looking for answers to such questions in a book or even a teacher, the stone can be asked directly. Because the stone always gives feedback on whether it likes the tools used on it, whether the angle at which the chisel is applied is good, or whether it is hit too hard. Knowledge of technique really isn't necessary for making a sculpture —no, it can even be obstructive:

Paradoxically, the most hindering statements for one's sculptural development can be those that are the most true. That is because the mind always seeks to avoid the confrontation with the unknown by acquiring an understanding from the outside. It does not want to go through experience because, in experience, the thinking mind cannot exist. But acquired truisms about sculpture, such as that two convex surfaces should not touch, or that the inherent association of the material should be brought into its opposite —in the case of stone, which is associated with heaviness, rest and hardness, the resulting form should thus suggest lightness, movement and softness— are counterproductive to hold in one's head when sculpting. But the danger with studying concepts like these is not that they are misleading or untrue, but their counterproductive quality lies within the fact that there is a kernel of truth in them. And this acquired truth, which has been discovered by others, is then holding one back from experiencing it oneself. Studying theory can become like a drug then, for the mind can gorge on the truth discovered by others without having to step aside. Which it must if real understanding is to be developed. Intellectual information can thus pose a barrier to one's learning process because it can create the illusion that one has already understood something, even though one actually hasn't. Nicolaides writes:

> In learning how to draw, it is necessary to start back of the limitations that casual information sets upon you. Preconceived ideas about things with which you have no real experience have a tendency to defeat the acquiring of real knowledge.[17]

Real knowledge, as Nicolaides put it, can only come as a result of experience. And to possess real knowledge of sculpture does not mean that one knows how to hold a chisel or how to carve a flat surface, but it means that in whatever one does, there will be a certain flavor, a certain vibration, that makes itself known in the work. And this kind of knowledge cannot be acquired from studying a textbook, nor can it be leapfrogged towards. It must be worked towards painstakingly. It comes out of the unknown.

In fact, the state of not knowing is the ideal starting point for any artistic endeavor. Notice the difference: As long as I know what I am doing, I am in the known. And the known is always from the past. It is dead, unalive; no juices are flowing. Hence, I am executing. Whereas as long as I don't know what I am doing —such as when I am looking for the next step I must take— I am in the Now. And every action performed in the Now is an act of exploration, is fresh and infused with the quality of being true. Hence, I am creating.

That is why, instead of giving in to impulses that are aimed at disenchanting the unknown —studying technicalities, rules of form, the works of other artists and so forth— Nirman encouraged me to simply start and allow my way of sculpting to develop naturally. Technique can always be acquired later, but being receptive gets more difficult the more one loses oneself in knowledge.[18]

On Breaking the Rules

There exists a regrettable notion that one must first master the rules before one is entitled to break them. Accordingly, the paintings by Jackson Pollock wouldn't be worth anything if he didn't also possess the ability to paint figuratively. This is obviously absurd and makes no sense upon closer investigation, but it is a kind of thinking deeply ingrained in us.

I once made a furious drawing with my eyes closed using some charcoal from the fireplace. The power of the drawing, the quality of line, the meaning inherent to the composition were evident, not only to me but also to others who bothered to look. However, because the drawing could have been produced by a four-year-old —nothing figurative could be discerned in it— people, including myself, were hesitant to acknowledge its artistic value. "But isn't it just scribbles?" the mind constantly interfered.

The difficulty with appreciating non-representational art stems from the fact that our feeling sense cannot express itself like our minds can. Feeling occurs in the body, and because of the reigning dictatorship of our minds, we often overlook or neglect our bodies' impressions in favor of our mind's analysis. And for the mind, scribbles are not art. Or if they are, then only when somebody made them who already mastered the art of drawing figuratively and decided to *go back* to drawing scribbles. Scribbles, then, are something conceptual. They are only valid if they stand in relation to something, be it, at least, the artist's ability to draw figuratively.

Even today, many still confuse art as something that is aimed at depicting reality as closely as possible. And every deviation from this ideal is only valid to the degree that the artist would have been able to approximate *the* ideal. Again, the implicit assumption many seem to hold is that one is entitled to make scribble drawings only if one can also make a painting indistinguishable from a photograph. And because I never learned how to paint a photorealistic painting, I am, according to this line of reasoning, not entitled to call my scribbles art.

The notion that those who cannot make figurative art are not entitled to make non-representational art is a tragic one. Because of this notion, one can witness students moving chalk around their fingers at every other workshop, not developing anything authentic in the process.

Cultural strongholds like "one has to master the rules before one is entitled to break them" were all over my head, as well as the heads of others, when I started to sculpt freely. Like with everything, one is encouraged to do something different, but the entire system goes haywire as soon as one does. Like Neo gets to experience when Morpheus takes him for a stroll in the *Matrix.* And because a copy of the system exists in our heads, we are not even safe from ourselves.

In fact, I also began learning how to draw more realistically to verify the artistic value of my scribbled drawings. But soon I realized that one had nothing to do with the other: Because he who learned to get the proportions of a portrait "right" had nothing to do with what made those furious strokes with the charcoal. It soon dawned upon me that the notion that "I must first master the rules before I was entitled to break them" did not even make sense, for *I* was not even present when the scribble drawing came into being. And no amount of studying would have changed anything about that. If anything, knowledge of technique would have posed a barrier for my arm to move freely for, as Nicolaides remarked: "When you become self-conscious about rules, they impose limitations upon you."[19] In hindsight, it is obvious: Why would it make a difference for the artistic value of my scribbled drawing that I would also be able to make a photorealistic drawing when I, eyes closed, allowed my arm to move freely across a paper?

Similar thoughts plagued me when writing this book. Do I have to be a sculptor for decades to be entitled to write anything about it? Do I have to have carved a bust before I am entitled to write anything about the fallacy of technique? And even though parts of my mind would answer many such questions with a decisive *"Yes!"* I figured that it would not make a difference. At all.

Because what counts is always the present moment, the confrontation with the unknown and nothing acquired in the past. And this stays true whether I have been sculpting, writing, drawing, or whatever for one year or thirty years. Time ceases to exist when the *I* is not, making notions of age or years of experience obsolete. In fact, I assert that you, too, can tell whether these lines are fresh and were born out of the Now or whether they were dragged in from the past. And whether they are fresh is *all* that matters. Not the years of experience I have as a sculptor.

Everything born out of the Now, whether cliché, contradiction, paradox, or even falsehood, we can thus maintain, is artistic. And everything borrowed and regurgitated, no matter its content, is not. Truth has nothing to do with factual correctness, but everything with how it is brought into existence.

That is why something true cannot be transported from one medium into another, nor can it be transported through time: Something true on paper can be wrong in stone, and something true today can —or, to be more precise: will be— false tomorrow. If, for example, I accidentally deleted this paragraph and rewrote it tomorrow by recalling these words, it wouldn't be true anymore. I would have changed in the meantime: I would have had certain experiences, eaten certain foods, taken certain decisions, read certain texts, all of which would have subtly influenced who I am. And these changes, however minuscule, would have wanted to reflect themselves in my writing. They would have subtly influenced my choice of words, sentence structure, punctuation, etc. Nicolaides writes:

> *It is not that the artist is consciously trying to change his technique. He is changing his attitude to form and color — in fact, to life — and his technique naturally changes, whereas if he were bound by considerations of technique his development would become cramped.*[20]

I became particularly aware of this by noticing how a statement continually loses its energetic pregnancy when repeated. Because when I first said in a conversation that Nirman's sculptures appear closer to animals than stones, I felt I had discovered a powerful metaphor to characterize his work. But with every time I repeated this conception, it became less true. And after I had said it a few times, it appeared as utter nonsense. What is more, when I kept saying such things at dinner parties, I could be sure that, when I went back to the studio the next morning, all I could see was a man hammering on a piece of rock with no animal in sight. Repeating such conceptions increasingly began to feel like taking a drug, in which I was trading a few moments of sounding "deep" or "elaborate" with days in which the stone didn't speak. The stone called me out, questioning whether I truly knew what I was saying when I stated that stone was alive or whether I was simply recycling a metaphor I once arrived at in the past. And the further I drifted into repeating such conceptions without giving them a new form of expression, the more the stone rebelled against them.

Truth, we can thus maintain, cannot be repeated, but it must be given a new form of expression in every moment. When repeated untransformed, it gradually loses its energetic pregnancy or, at worst, turns into a lie.

Part II
Sculpting Stone

Chapter 1

Show me the stone rejected by the builders. That is the cornerstone.
—JESUS | The Gospel of Thomas, 66

There are plenty of books that discuss various types of rock and their apparent suitability for specific projects, including which tools are needed and how they are "properly" used. This is not one of them. But it is still worth spending some time with the material the stone sculptor works with:

Stone

The geological terms to describe different types of rock —marble, limestone, soapstone, etc.— provide little relevant information for making a sculpture. For to label a stone is not to know it.

Also, depending on the quarry the stone was extracted from, the same type of stone can appear in various structures, compositions, colors and formations. Limestone, for instance, which is sedimentary rock that has formed over millennia through the deposition of mussels, skeletons and other marine animals, can be anything from soft and porous to hard and dense, depending on the heat and pressure it was exposed to throughout its formation. Marble, which is created when limestone recrystallizes under the influence of heat and other geological pressures, can also occur in various colors, degrees of hardness and porosity. So, depending on where you get your stone from, you might get a stone that goes by the same name but portrays very different characteristics.

What makes choosing stone by name even more confusing is that stones are sometimes referred to by their composing minerals (quartz, calcite, feldspar, …), their geological rock type (igneous, metamorphic, sedimentary, …), their place of origin (Pakistani Sandstone, Anröchter Stein, Naxos-Marble, …) or made-up commercial names (Statuario, Azul Cielo, Monarch, …). And if the magnifying glass is put on any of these, many keep fractalizing into sub-categories with unintelligible specifications and quality standards.

But it doesn't end there: I once asked a geologist whether he could help me identify a stone I was working with. He responded that identifying rock is not as straightforward as one might believe it is. He would first have to take a piece to the lab, pour acid over it and investigate the bubbles that appear before he could make even a vague statement about what the stone is comprised of. But taking it to the lab would probably not have ended our discussion on how to properly name the stone but led us into a rabbit hole in which we ended up discussing metaphysics —for what is matter anyway?— rather than discovering anything useful for the sculpting process.

I rarely know the names of the stones I work with, and nobody else seems to know either. Sometimes I even made up a name to see if anyone would notice? No one ever did.

Thus, whenever I search for a stone, instead of spending time with aspects that are of little use anyway (the stone's name, what other artists have done with it, etc.), I approach each stone like a child would, namely through my senses: I *feel* the stone with my hands, I *listen* to the sound it makes when I hit it with the hammer, I *look* at how its surface breaks the light. When approached in this way, each stone elicits a different quality, a different mood, even when their type, or any other of their surface dimensions, are the same. These perceived qualities can be subtle and not fit any of the gross categories our language offers. But usually, there is a sense for whether a stone is *male* or *female, confident* or *shy, vulnerable* or *resistant, old* or *young, powerful* or *weak, lefthanded* or *righthanded, modern* or *traditional, hot* or *cold, heavy* or *light, elegant* or *clumsy*, etc. Some stones elicit biographical associations, reminding me of a specific dream, person, place, or experience. Others might remind me of sci-fi objects, resemble an idea, or resonate with a particular style. And it is *these* qualities that will define both my experience working with them, as well as the final result.

People always ask where to get a stone from. Unfortunately, I can answer this question no better than if they asked me how to best get a partner. Of course, I could point them to a dating platform —to a sculpting shop— but that is only the beginning of a true love story in the rarest of cases. In my experience, a stone just always turns up at the right time. Shortness of material has never been an issue.

Having said that, I still want to offer a few recommendations that lean themselves well toward this book's approach:

In the beginning, I advise against going for any kind of extremes: A hard stone like granite will break your tools, hurt your wrist and develop slowly. A big stone can also be overwhelming because it is more difficult to absorb, feel and see the form in a large stone. A stone too small can also be restrictive because it has no material to play around and have fun with. So, an ideal stone to begin with lies on the lower end of the Mohs scale of mineral hardness and is no heavier than what you can still carry.

I also recommend against starting with an overly posh material, for the more expensive the stone, the less inclined you are to work loosely. Also, with fancy stones like transparent alabaster or Carrara marble, the stone's surface tends to distract from engaging with its insides.

Another consideration is the form of the stone: It is tempting to pick a stone that already has a form. All you have to do then is adjust some surfaces. That's great, but if you never do more than just express what is already there, you and the stone remain like salt and water that hasn't been stirred into each other: separate and unchanged. So, especially in the beginning, the most "limiting" forms, such as a simple block, tend to facilitate the growth of a crown, whereas stones that already have a form tend to hold you back from it.

Tools

John Coltrane said, "You can play a shoestring if you are sincere," and the same is certainly true for sculpture. Just like you can draw with anything that transfers from one surface to another, you can sculpt with anything that takes off material from stone. The Cyclades produced the most extraordinary sculptures with only the most basic tools, so anyone who insists that without carbide-hardened chisels, electricity-powered milling machines, or diamond-laced polishing tools, you are unable to make a sculpture, can happily be ignored.

Also, the simpler the tools used, the more powerful the sculpture becomes. That is because the more technologically advanced the tools become, the less visible the artist becomes in their makings. And the less visible the artist becomes in their makings, the less artistic power their sculptures will possess.

Most justify their use of power tools because they believe it makes them faster. But not only is that not always true, but it also misses the point. It is not true because, in many cases, there is a more elegant way to remove a large piece of stone than bulldozing it off with a flex. And it misses the point because when one rushes through a lot of material, one is not really working through it, both internally as well as in stone.

It's like the difference between hiking a mountain versus taking the gondola to the top. Yes, the ladder was faster, but the person hiking covered more ground. So those who use power tools might be able to remove more material in the same amount of time, but they are apt to forget about the insides. All they sculpt is surface, is form, but not that which lies invisible underneath. They are wasting their time sitting in the gondola instead of taking real steps on the ground.

The mind will always want to buy more (elaborate) tools because it assumes they can bring about better results. But this approach is about the experience one is having *while* sculpting, not *after* sculpting. And elaborate tools tend to lead to the conclusion that sculpting is about making a sculpture, whereas sculpting has very little to do with making a sculpture, just as hiking has little to do with reaching the top. Making a sculpture, like reaching the top of a mountain, is simply the outcome of a process. The end result of an experience.

One way to prevent the constant temptation of wanting to use more elaborate tools is to move to a more technological tool only when one has gained the necessary skill and understanding to do the same with the simpler tool. Those who take jumps without having acquired the necessary understanding to do the same without technological support are like those who let themselves be carried up Mount Everest but do not even possess the necessary understanding to climb an average-sized mountain in Alpine

Style. They are further up than they should be, and not only will they be delirious due to all the stone dust they are producing, but they will also not develop any real understanding. They will, in fact, be wasting stone and time.

I further recommend against using tools like the bush hammer, files, or polishing sponges too early. Because with such tools, one can work on the stone while having a small risk of unintentionally breaking something off. But this is a bug and not a feature because such tools allow one to mess around the stone without knowing what one is doing. With hammer and chisel, on the other hand, one always has to remain vigilant and clear in one's actions. So the difficulty with "easy" tools such as the file or the bush hammer paradoxically lies within the fact that they are so easy to work with: Because they are so easy, they do not force one into knowing what one is doing but constantly tempt one into messing around, which is always to be avoided.

Meeting the Material

When I begin working with a stone, I do not immediately chart chipping it, but I take some time to get acquainted with the material: I place the stone on the workbench and start walking around it; I have my hands glide over its surface to explore its texture, its composition, its form; I lift the stone to sense its heaviness, its hardness, its body; I grab the stone with both hands and turn it, push it, move it around; I feel where it goes, what it wants, what it does, who it is. I form an image of the stone, not with my mind, but through my senses. I do this until all concepts my mind tends to superimpose upon the stone dissolve, and all I am left with is raw sensual data.

I also look at what side I instinctively rested the stone upon. The resting side must not be fixed and can change throughout the sculpting process. But for now, I simply notice which side I instinctively rested the stone upon.

The internal image developed in this way must not be coherent or concrete: The stone might feel different from what it looks like, might have a different quality when touched blindly than when judged by the sound it makes when moved across the workbench. At this stage, I simply accumulate data like a scientist would, who does not yet know what they will need the data for. "The job is to get at the truth -" Nicolaides writes, "the truth as you will be able to understand at first hand, arrived at by the use of all your senses."[1]

After greeting the stone this way, I pick up hammer and chisel and have it rhythmically glide through the stone. I am not pushing or imposing, but gently moving the chisel through the material. In light of Paul Klee's "taking a line for a walk," I simply follow the chisel wherever *it* wants to go and do not impose myself on it. I simply watch how the top of my chisel removes bit after bit after bit.

In doing so, I do not concern myself with sculpting form but only with what my chiseling feels like. I get a feeling for the hardness of the stone, for the way it pushes back against my chisel, for the way the chisel finds its way through the terrain. What I aim for is not so much a specific technique as it is a certain quality of attention, a certain poetry of motion. Barbara Hepworth provides a wonderful image of what this could look like:

> *The strokes of the hammer on the chisel should be in time with your heartbeat. You breathe easily. The whole of your body is involved. You move around the sculpture, and the whole of you, from the toes up, is concentrated in your left hand, which dictates the creation...[2]*

Whenever I sculpt, I have the stone rest in front of me on a flat surface. If I work with a light stone, I rest it in a sandbag so that it doesn't move when I work on it. I never work in a funky way so that the stone jumps around or is balanced awkwardly. Not only because I am doing myself a favor in terms of safety but also because I give the stone a clear chance to respond to my actions.

When I chisel, I let the stone break wherever it wants to and try not to force anything off it that it is resisting against. There is, for every piece of stone, a gentle and effortless way to remove it. Whenever I encounter resistance, I simply adjust my chisel or take a detour and remove that piece in some other way. The resulting trails have, at times, reminded me of the forms rivers carve into the landscape when they find the most effortless way downstream. And just like rivers do not impose themselves on the landscape but work in harmony and accordance with it, I go to the left or to the right whenever I encounter resistance. And besides creating a good result, water that is allowed to flow in this way also creates the ideal conditions for life to reside in.

Also, and perhaps counterintuitively, even a straight surface created in this whirly way will appear straighter than a surface cut with an angle grinder. That is because a straight surface revealed through this cooperative approach rests within itself, whereas the other is imposed from the outside. It is a straightness with a structure, with a character, like the surface of a calm sea, and not one flat and sterile like that of a man-made canal. "Crookedly all good things approach their goal," Nietzsche wrote in *Thus Spoke Zarathustra* and Nirman also once condensed the same into a "Never go straight!".[3]

So even though different ways of working might lead towards the same form, the quality of the form will still *feel* different depending on the journey one took to arrive at it. The journey is carried within the stone like a memory and somehow impregnates itself within the outcome. Becomes the outcome. *Is* the outcome.

When I have my chisel glide through the stone, I do not just look at the stone but also at the form and size of the pieces that come flying off, the impact my doings have on the tools and the sound my beatings make. When the bits flying off are overly large, I know I wasn't gentle enough or applying the chisel at a wrong angle. When there is only dust but no pieces, I also know I am using the wrong tools or hitting the stone too vertically. When the stone creates a dull or hollow sound, is painful to the ear, or in some other way off, I also know that I must try something different for *that* stone.

Only when the size of the bits are no larger than intended, and the beatings emit a soft ring, can a sculpture begin to absorb these qualities. So, especially in the beginning, I focus on whether my chiseling feels good, sounds good and nothing else.

One way I assess whether my technique is good is by being attentive to the impacts my sculpting has on my body: Since when my shoulder, back, neck, or wrist hurt after a session, or when I tire out quickly, I know that something in my way of working must have been off. Because when sculpting is done right, it isn't tiring, nor does it create a sore hand or a stiff neck. If I swing the hammer —or whatever tool I am using— with ease, sculpting has no detrimental effects on the body. No, it becomes a form of Tai Chi. If done right, I feel energized and centered after a sculpting session, not tired and worn out. Sculpting is a rejuvenating craft, even though —or precisely because— it involves manual work.

When my technique is good, my tools will also hardly wear off. So, if my tools break, truncate quickly, or warp themselves into weird shapes, then this is another indication that I wasn't sculpting from my center.

Stone doesn't care how much force it is hit with, how much of its material is removed, or what tools are used on it. What it *does* care about is whether the doing feels good to the stone, the carver and the tools. So those who believe they are doing the stone a favor when working in an awkward position in order to preserve a piece of the rough stone are mistaken. Stone would much rather have them work in a relaxed way, even if that means they have to blast a considerable piece. The cabinetmaker John Krenov liked to say that "there's a play between doing things in a way that feels good and getting good results."[4]

Often, the outermost layer of a stone is more difficult to control because it was cut by a machine or exposed to erosive forces. Usually, I use this layer to get a feel for whether the stone likes the flat-headed chisel, feels at home in straight lines, or whether it prefers the point chisel and wants to inhabit organic forms?

In this process, I just have come off whatever wants to come off, regardless of whether it is scaring large pieces. The wobbles and holes that occur at this stage will later serve as directional signs for developing the form. I think of this stage like the scrambling of a Rubik's cube that has to be done before one can start solving it. Because even though the arrangement that results from this random scrambling will define the journey, every starting position is as good as any other.

If you follow this approach, do not worry if your stone, after having worked over its surface this way, doesn't look like anything you had in mind or unlike any sculpture you have ever seen. In fact, what *should* worry you is when your stone takes on a recognizable form too early. This, in all likelihood, would signify that you tried to steer it in a certain direction instead of simply getting acquainted with the material.

Also, notice how the mind tends to create an attachment to the substance the stone is made of. Commonly, no matter the size of the stone, the mind will somehow be fixed on the idea that the final sculpture should, more or less, be the same size as the block it was developed from. But this is, beyond economic considerations, arbitrary. Stone isn't attached to its substance, so it doesn't mind how much material is removed. That is, because stone doesn't have a mind: a Buddha carved in stone is a tautology. So whether one grinds a huge stone into a fist-sized sculpture or barely changes the stone's original size bears no influence on whether the sculpture will possess artistic radiancy.

The mind always wants to *do* something, so it is generally reluctant to work without a clear image in mind. And indeed, it takes courage to work loosely, especially when others can see it. But executing an idea to make something pretty is easy —anyone can do that— because one remains within the confines of the conventional. But to have fun with stone by doing things that have no obvious cause or direction, that only the bravest have the courage for.

In other students' work, I often perceive their sculptures to be infused with the most artistic power when they first meet the stone in this way. Because as soon as they begin to carve form, their minds come in, distorting the stone's natural power. Whereas as long as they are just having fun, trying different tools and ways of working, they already have what they will be searching for for the rest of their sculpting lives.

This artistic flavor, or aura, which surrounds the true work of art is difficult, if not impossible, to write about. It is unknowable to the mind and cannot be photographed, pointed towards, measured, or be seen when approached with a skeptical eye. But when one is open to its perceiving, its reality is clear and unambiguous. In fact, the true work of art is characterized precisely by the fact that it is immediately recognizable as such.

This vibration that can be sensed surrounding true works of art, I believe, is the result of some sort of psychic infusion by which the stone begins to radiate whatever was put into it. Stones, not unlike minds, seem to absorb, and consequently reflect, what was poured into them. So actually, physical tools are of no importance for making a sculpture. Something else —attention, intention, or whatever one prefers to call it— determines whether the work possesses artistic quality.

Relatedly, I recall an afternoon on which Nirman, a woman and I took the time to fully appreciate a stone I randomly picked up from the ground. All three of us were mesmerized by the beauty the stone portrayed. And with all three of us offering the stone our undivided attention, the stone equally flipped over into being a sculpture. This occurred even though we didn't alter its physical shape, so our attention alone infused the stone with the same creative force.

I had a similar experience when a friend offered her singular attention to one sculpture I was working on. Because up to that day, the sculpture didn't particularly speak to me, and I always considered it somewhat of an oddity. But the sculpture suddenly made sense when this friend talked about what she was perceiving. Through her active engagement alone, she co-manifested the sculpture into existence.

Chapter 2

Listening is a search.
—*JAMES KRENOV | The Fine Art of Cabinetmaking, 23*

The technique of standing back is the only technique that Nirman did teach me. As I understand it, the technique maintains that most of the time should not be spent working *on* the stone but standing back from it, circling it from afar. This might sound like an easy and trivial technique, but it is not.

The immediate impulse is always that of wanting to do something *on* the stone rather than to stand back from it. But as long as I do not stand back, my eyes always identify something on the surface instead of allowing me to engage with the form. "Let me just fix this," or "Just let me get this straight," the voice in my head tells me, and before I know it, I find myself messing around the surface instead of contributing anything toward the development of form.

When I stand back, on the other hand, I can no longer see cracks, holes and other aspects on the surface, but all I can perceive are the stone's form and the quality with which it rests in space. And if I do not first attend to these, if I do not first attend to the metaphysics underlying my sculpture, all my subsequent research will be built on sand. So at heart, standing back is a method to get unimportant details out of my sight, which is almost the same as saying: a method to get me out of my mind.

One way I learned to apply the technique of standing back is to stand back so far that I can barely see the stone anymore. From such a distance —this can well be 20 meters or further away from the stone— I can no longer tell whether I am looking at a figurative sculpture or whether I am looking at a rough block of stone. All I can see is a vague, albeit harmonious, blob.

From there, I move a few steps closer until I can make out some basic aspects about the stone, such as where it has most of its mass or the direction it is skewed towards. Then, I start walking around the stone in a circular movement until I find an angle I like; I walk around the stone until I find an angle that, if I could only see the stone from this angle, I would not want to change anything about it. There is always at least one angle from which this condition is met; otherwise, I have moved too close already.

Once I discovered such an angle, slowly, without taking my eyes off, I start walking around again until this sense interrupts. This might be because my eyes met an edge that sticks out, because a ridge appears that somehow violates the stone's proportions, or any other aspect that makes me assess that something is "off." If unsure what part prevents the stone from appearing "right," I give myself some time and keep walking around.

When, after having circled the stone for a while in this way, I discover an aspect that interrupts the fluidity of form, I ponder what I could do so that this side, too, can be stretched, can be turned tender. It does not matter whether I discover something large, such as that I need to blast a third of the stone, or something tiny, such as that I need to round off the top: I simply look for what aspect interrupts the form.

Once I found such an aspect and arrived at a conception of what I could do to alleviate that interrupting, I walk back to the stone and do it. And once I have done that to the best of my ability, I stand back again and start over. And that's it. That is the technique of standing back.

When, after having executed something on the stone, I return to the distance from which I took my decision from, the form I initially sensed might have been lost, even if I expected that taking off *that* piece would further have helped to express it. But that doesn't matter. I simply start anew and see where the form wants to go now. And as soon as I discover something that interrupts the continuous movement of the stone — regardless of whether that is the most crucial part of the form I anticipated before— I go back to the stone and do it.

When I circle the stone, I keep moving and do not allow my gaze to freeze at any one angle. Since when I look at a stone from a point of rest, I am inclined to focus on individual aspects rather than on how they function together. But focusing on a single angle in sculpture is like focusing on a single note in a musical composition: it does not mean anything without its relationship to all the others. In music, as in sculpture, it is the relationships that make the song, so I make it my quest to discover how different elements function together; how one side relates to another, how the bottom relates to the top, how the back relates to the front. And as long as

I keep moving, I am apt to focus on these relationships instead of falling for the temptation of getting any one aspect "right."

What makes this technique difficult is nothing technical but the internal conflict it creates: With every step I walk back to the stone to execute what I have decided from afar, my head tends to provide a reason why taking off *that* bit is a bad idea. On my way back, my mind dreams up numerous forms and shapes for which the part I am about to take off would be indispensable for and suggests a dozen other bits it wants me to remove instead. It thus takes courage to follow through with what I have decided from afar because when I arrive back at the stone, executing what I have decided from afar might appear anything but obvious, if not outright outrageous.

Ideally, I could control a 20-meter-long chisel because with such an instrument, I could not mess around with insubstantial details, nor could I doubt the decisions I have taken from afar, but I would remain concerned with nurturing the stone's quality and form.

After I've worked from a distance in this way for a while, there comes a moment when the stone appears wholesome, just as it did when I first looked at it from 20 meters away. But before I move to the next step, namely moving a few steps closer, I ensure that I have considered the stone from all angles. Only when all integrates do I move a few steps closer.

Once arrived —say, I am now 15 meters away from the stone— additional depths and nuances will have become apparent. The stone will look different again. Some aspects I couldn't see from further away will now interrupt the fluidity of form. But the procedure stays the same: I start circling the stone from an angle I like; I walk around until the form interrupts; I search for a way to resolve it; and, once found, I walk back to the stone and execute. And once I have done so, I stand back again and start over.

In this process, I only walk back to the stone if I have a clear conception of what I want to do. Stone does not develop when I am ambiguous or when I take chances: it wants to be treated with clarity.

Coming back to stone is a bit like meeting a dog: When I approach them without knowing where I am at, the situation might get tense because neither knows whether the other can be trusted. But when I am clear and decisive, the dog will be equally clear and decisive in their response. They might signal that they want to be petted or that they want me to back off, but no matter what they signal, it will be clear and unambiguous. And anything clear and unambiguous has a beauty to it, even when it goes against convention.

This method of standing back, feeling the form, deciding what must go, executing it and standing back again is all I need to turn a stone into a sculpture. Whenever the stone appears harmonious from one distance, I walk a few steps closer, repeat the process, until, at some point, I arrive at the stone.

At each distance, I continue until each side functions as the center, until each side is my favorite side, until each angle is my preferred angle. If there is still some aspect that doesn't feel right, I keep circling, I keep adjusting, so that it too becomes connected, so that it too becomes inhabited. Only then do I move a few steps closer.

There is no rule for how long I spend at any one distance. Some stations might take months to reveal themselves; others might allow me to work through them in a single session. I remember one stone that kept me on the first station for weeks. With another, it took a single morning for me to arrive at the stone.

Throughout this process, I do not shy back from frequently changing the resting side of my sculpture. A good sculpture appears fluid and harmonious, no matter which side or direction it is rested upon, so I do not hesitate to rotate it around.[5]

For the technique of standing back, it doesn't matter if the form of the stone changes starkly throughout the process or remains roughly the same. All that matters is that I do not skip a distance. And if I did skip one, or if I find myself messing around the surface, all I must do is stand back and start over, just like I attend back to my breath when I lose myself in thought during a meditation. To illustrate the importance of not skipping a distance, consider the process of polishing a stone as an analogy:

Common sense has it that if you want to polish a stone, you must begin with a rough sandpaper and gradually move up to finer grits until you arrive at the polishing cloth. Now, if you overlooked a spot with the rough sandpaper, you will not get it out with the polishing cloth, for the cloth does not reach deep enough into the material (unless you spend an enormous amount of time, of course). Instead, you will have to return to the rough sandpaper and start again from there. From this, we can conclude that the key to a good polishing result is to not jump any grits and to not overlook any parts before moving on to a finer grit. Common sense, as I said.

The technique of standing back rests on a similar logic: No sculpture can appear harmonious from a closer distance that does not already possess the same quality when looked upon from further away. So, if my sculpture does not appear wholesome from a particular distance, it also won't suddenly do so when I move closer to it: Whatever I haven't resolved from a particular distance won't resolve at a later stage, just like the overlooked spot won't come out with the polishing cloth. Instead, I will drag the unresolved issue inwards and, if I do not stand back and continue from the distance from where the sculpture appears harmonious, will waste much of my time.

However, this does not mean that I cannot still alter the form substantially at any later stage. But if I cared for the stone's fundamentals, the process will, at no later stages, instruct me with something that will overthrow its balance. The stone will, as if by magic, maintain its balance when looked at from a distance, no matter what I do closer to it. So, if I arrive within 5 meters of my workbench and decide that a third of the stone needs to go, then doing so will not disturb the proportions or balance of the stone when looked at from all distances I have already passed. From all distances I have already passed, the sculpture will continue appearing "right."

Sometimes, I might have to work over the entire stone to integrate just a single aspect, including sides I previously thought to be fully resolved. But just like one has to turn all the pieces of a Rubik's cube to move just a single piece to its place, I might also have to move all sides to resolve a single transition. From the outside, this might seem like I am going in circles because, while I am turning all the pieces, nothing connects or sits right anymore. But there is a difference: When I begin working on a piece of stone, its surfaces are simply unordered, whereas the unorder arrived at this later stage contains the solved state within itself. Because just like the degree to which a Rubik's cube was already resolved remains preserved when one turns a sequence to move a piece to its place, the degree to which I already solved the form will also remain preserved when I integrate a specific issue. I do not know how this works, but stone seems to have some kind of memory in that it contains and remembers everything that was already developed on it. How it is expressed might change, but the degree to which a form was already resolved always remains preserved within the stone.

So, I do not worry if my sculpture, after weeks of work, suddenly appears as if I just started working on it. Since when I continue, it will soon become evident that the chaos was just some passing stage encountered on my way.

Throughout this process, the felt reality of my sculpture can be as fluid as mercury: Sides previously thought to be finished can suddenly stand out again; aspects previously condemned as boring can become the new center; the front turn into the back; the top become the bottom. So, I try not to get attached to my doings but seek to remain present with the Now of the form.

Most of the time when I stand back, I do not immediately find what I must do. There might be a sense that something is off, but I cannot find what that is, and even less so how to resolve it into the form. I have circled the stone for hours in this way without using my chisel once. In such hours, I have even hoped for the stone to fall off the sculpting table so that a broken edge would provide me with a direction to work towards. That's how desperate I have been. And because the mind does not like to be in this state of not knowing, it usually suggests moving a few steps closer so that it finds something to hold on to again, something clear that needs doing. But taking away material only makes up a small proportion of the work. It is that which comes last following the actual work. Which is swirling around the sculpture, unknowingly of what I must do.

Standing back is a tremendously powerful technique that I can always fall back on, no matter what stage I am at in my sculpting process. Whenever something unintentional happens, whenever I take a bad turn or carry the sculpture into a dark alley, I can *always* stand back and start anew.

∞

An immediate objection against the technique of standing back is the lack of complexity that can be imposed onto a stone when decisions are taken from afar.

Like all objections, this objection roots from the mind because the mind regards itself as complex, and it wants to see that reflected in stone. And simple or enclosed forms, which the mind (falsely) assumes this technique leads towards, do not sufficiently reflect its self-beheld intricacy. So, it would rather want me to make sculptures that have twists and turns, interlocking shapes, see-through holes, sharp edges, patterns, or other elements it believes would shock or impress. But unsurprisingly, like in the realm of language, where the mind believes that adjectives "add" expressive power, the inclusion of such "complex" elements often ends up having the opposite effect. Consider the following example:

Notice how the expression "Form is a powerful language" has less expressive force than "Form is a language," even though one might expect that the adjective *powerful* would enhance the expressive power of the noun *language*. But by making the noun explicit, it is stripped of its potential. And potential is always more powerful than anything made explicit, for it includes the infinite. So by leaving the noun undefined by an adjective, it automatically contains all potential adjectives that could be placed before it. Language is many things, *powerful* being one of them. But by settling for a single adjective, the noun is stripped from all other adjectives it would otherwise contain within itself.

So the mind thinks it is enhancing expressive power by adding adjectives —or in the realm of sculpture: lines, engravings, see-through holes, etc.— whereas they often weaken it.[6]

Chapter 3

*Speaking or writing, the words bounce instantaneously into their context,
and I am victimized by them, rather than controlling them. They do not wait
for my selection; they volunteer.*
—WILLIAM STAFFORD | *Writing the Australian Crawl, 57*

I don't have many principles guiding me throughout the development of
form, but here are some that have proved useful:

Overall, I seek to accentuate the stone as it is. This accentuation process
can be anything from quick and superficial, to long-lasting and penetrating.
With some stones, I barely remove any material; with others, I work away
most of the substance until I find that the stone is sufficiently expressed.
However, my overarching maxim is always that of doing as little as possible;
every action must be justified by a necessity.

In this accentuation process, I make the expression of the quality my
primary, the development of form my secondary and the shaping of the
surface my tertiary priority. Of course, all of them are interrelated and
dependent upon each other, but when I sculpt, I maintain this hierarchy of
prioritization. In practice, this means that if I perceive something to be off
on the level of form, but which does not interfere with the perceived quality
of the stone, I do not rush changing it. Or the other way around: If I have a
well-developed side that does not feel on par with the stone's quality, I do
not hesitate to adjust it either. Quality comes first, form second.

The same goes for the relationship between the form and the surface:
If there is an irregularity marking the surface, I let it come out as part of the
natural development of form. As long as I focus on exploring the form, all
irregularities will eventually come out as a result of this underlying search.
And they do so in a perfectly logical manner without me having to attend
to them actively.

Whenever I ignore this order and try to remove an irregularity directly,
my doings seem to hurt the stone. The result appears as if something was
amputated then, not naturally resolved. The difference can be compared
to the molting of animals: They also dispense with their skin, fur, or

exoskeleton in a perfectly logical manner, and if the molting process is allowed to unfold naturally, everything takes care of itself. But if the animal grew impatient and tried to force off its molting parts, it would hurt, if not kill itself.

And in the same way, the development of form and the smoothing of the surface take care of themselves as long as I maintain this hierarchy of prioritization. I do not know why this is so, but that is the first joy of working with stone: I do not need to understand how the form develops; all I need to focus on is accentuating the stone as I perceive it. The rest takes care of itself.

And even if some irregularities remain, then so much the better. Sculptures are surprisingly forgiving in having broken parts and other irregularities marking the surface. And more often than not, such aspects turn out to be the most interesting parts of a sculpture. So, as long as the surrounding form is developed and the theme of the stone is fully expressed, broken bits, cracks and other such aspects are never in the way of a sculpture taking on artistic quality.

Besides standing back, another way I avoid the tendency of constantly wanting to attend to the surface is by using rough tools as much as possible. With fine tools, such as the file or polishing pads, I am tempted to mess around the surface instead of remaining present with the stones' quality and form. Contrary to rough tools like hammer and chisel, which constantly force me to remain present with these underlying dimensions, fine tools tend to pull me away from them. That is why I switch to a finer tool only when I did everything I could with the rougher one.

As long as I stick to this principle, I will also not conceptualize a fine tool as an instrument to treat the surface with, but as a tool that allows me to explore the form to a finer degree. And that is what a tool is for. A finer tool is simply an instrument that allows for a deeper exploration of form, not something to treat the surface with. So when I use a polishing pad, for example, I do not circle it across the stone's surface, but I use it to get deeper into the form. I am still exploring the *form* when I use the polishing pad; I am *not* polishing the surface. The polishing happens as a side effect, just as the development of form happens on its own when I focus on expressing the stone's underlying quality. The difference is subtle, but substantial.

To me, a good sculpture is one in which there is a balance between the degree to which the stone's quality was expressed, the form developed, and the surface polished. So a sculpture polished with the 3,000-grit polishing pad (a grit used for polishing glass) better has its form explored to the micrometer. Because when the form is only half-heartedly substantiated, but the surface is polished like glass, there exists an imbalance between the degree to which the form was explored and the degree to which the surface was polished. The sculpture will appear unnatural then, as if it were a human artifact and not a piece of living nature.

So, as long as I do everything I can with the rough tool before moving to a finer one, my sculpture will always maintain this balance. I will always have a sculpture that feels and *is* natural.

A related aspect concerns the order in which I develop the form: Conventionally, sculptors start by defining certain *points* and *lines*. They start by defining the top, bottom, outlines, collision points and so forth, from which they start to develop the form. But by doing so, they force the stone to comply with these predefined points. I, on the other hand, focus on developing the *form* and have these points and lines appear on their own. I allow the top, collision points, edges and so forth to form by themselves. So, when I have two sides coming together, I do not define where they meet but instead focus on exploring the form of both surfaces. And soon, a line will appear between these two surfaces all on its own. A line not artificially defined but a line that arose naturally because of a coming-together of two forms.

Not only does this inside-out way of working result in more fluid forms, but it also makes the development of form much more dynamic. After all, it is difficult and against the material to force a form to comply with a predefined line, but it is simple and cooperative to have a collision point move of its own accord to comply with a form. Therefore, counter to the conventional approach, the top, edges and collision points are the last aspects I attend to, if I attend to them at all.

When John Coltrane was asked what he was trying to achieve musically, he responded: "Starting a sentence in the middle, and then going to the beginning and the end of it at the same time … both directions at once."[7] And in precisely this manner, I treat my entire sculpture as one and do not develop any parts isolated from any other parts. I move in all directions simultaneously and try to ensure that no part gets ahead of the rest. I do not first carve the front, then the back, then the top and then the bottom, but I do all at the same time… all directions at once.

Pissarro once shared with Cezanne a wonderful impression of what such a process could look like in painting:

> *Do not work bit by bit, apply colour everywhere and observe the tonal values closely in relation to the surroundings. Paint with small brushstrokes and try to record your observations immediately. The eye must not concentrate on a specific point but should absorb everything. . . Work on the sky, the water, the branches and the earth simultaneously and keep on improving what you do until the whole thing works. Cover the whole canvas in the first sitting, and work until there is nothing more to add . . .*
>
> *Do not follow rules and principles, but paint what you see and feel. Paint boldly and without hesitation, because it is important to get your first impressions down. . . You must be bold, even at the risk of going wrong and making mistakes. There is only one teacher: Nature…[8]*

I do not conceptualize the sculpting process as being comprised of different stages, like setting the proportions first and solving the details second. Because once I conceptualize, I am bound to produce industrial stonemasons' work, not art. For when the process is conceptualized and dissected, the result is also bound to be conceptualized and dissected.

Mimicking the Stone

One way to get movement into the sculpture is to express what a stone is *doing*. This has to be done through the body because, to the mind, the stone isn't doing anything. To the mind, the stone is just a lump of matter passively resting on a workbench. But every stone always does something, just like every human always does something, be these restful actions like being seated or being asleep.

To get an understanding of what the stone is doing, I mimic the stone with my body. Children do this automatically when they try to comprehend someone or something. They act out what they see with their whole bodies: They become it. Children understand that when they imitate, they automatically feel what the imitated thing or person feels like from the inside. Nicolaides writes in his chapter about life drawing: "… if you do not respond in like manner to what the model is doing, you cannot understand what you see."[9]

In addition to mimicking the stone with my body, I draw gestures into the air to suggest or dramatize its movement. This might look funny to a bystander, but it is a highly effective technique.

If I am unsure how to best mimic the stone, I try throwing different gestures at it to see which ones fit: Do I best represent the stone when I punch karate kicks into the air or dance eurythmy around it? When I proclaim Beethoven's *"ta ta ta taaa"* or Britney Spears *"I'm not a girl …"* towards it? This does not have to be the same for any two persons because no two persons are the same. So I do not try to figure out the correct movement. There is no such thing. I simply search for whatever feels true and nothing else.

I remember a day when a stranger asked me what form I was aiming for. I responded by making a gesture in which I furiously formed a fist in the air and pulled it towards my body. I don't know what the stranger thought of my description, or whether my response made any sense whatsoever, but I felt I had accurately communicated my affairs with the stone. Words don't operate in this realm, and I often lose my connection with the stone when

I try to express what I am after. But as long as I refrain from the impulse of wanting to label it and just let myself be one with the form, there is no doubt about my affairs with the stone.

Drawing on the Stone

Another way to come to an understanding of the form is by drawing lines across the stone. Conventionally, sculptors like to draw the outlines of their aspired figures onto the stone so they know from where they must develop their desired image from. This is not what is meant here. Rather, the lines I draw across a stone are meant to accentuate its underlying quality and form. I like to think of them like the lines drawn with eyeliner: Ideally, one should barely see that they are there because their purpose lies in highlighting and accentuating what is already present underneath.

The lines drawn across a stone in that way are perhaps best conceived of as invitations, as possibilities, as potentials, as trails from where the surrounding form can be discovered from. I must not follow or abide by any of them because their purpose lies in helping me to comprehend the stone. They are *not* meant to give me a starting point from which to develop the form, but their function lies in helping me to make sense of what the stone is doing, where the stone is going, how the stone is moving.

Drawing lines across a stone is a tremendously powerful tool because lines can quickly create order and clarity within the form. They help me discover where different sides come together, or where the form starts moving in a different direction. In effect, it becomes much easier to see, and feel, what parts are interrupting the stone's continuous movement.

By drawing on the stone, I am also sorting the stone into comprehensible segments. A sculpture is usually too complex to be comprehended at once, so if I do not first organize it into different parts, I am developing my sculpture in the dark, hoping to find form by accident or luck, which, of course, will hardly ever happen. But if I resolve one aspect after the other, I always know exactly what I am doing. And wherever there is clarity of action, clarity of form will follow.

Drawing lines across a surface is a bit like searching for the origin of a bodily emotion. And just like an emotion dissolves once its origin is located, so will I see what I must do once I comprehend the form by the lines I have drawn across it.

There is no standard for how to draw on stone, for the perception of what makes a good line differs from person to person and from stone to stone. When I do not know what lines help express the stone's form, I draw random lines across it until I find some that work. There is always an immediate sense whether a line contributes towards the expression of the form, or whether it appears applied from the outside. One way to think of it is to compare it to the parting in one's hair: It is difficult to define what makes a particular line work, but it can always immediately be sensed whether it does.

Because most of the action happens at high- and low points, highlighting them is almost always a good idea. To find these points and lines, I often utilize natural light. I turn the stone and wait until the shadow turns in a different direction: This is the highpoint. When I utilize the light this way, I also don't need a ruler or any other measuring device, for the light is 299,792,458 precise.

My ability to create simplicity in the form by drawing lines across the stone tends to develop at the same speed as my understanding of form. And that is no coincidence, for drawing and sculpting are like mirrors to each other: an advance in one will be reflected in the other.

Interlude I

The human being knows himself only insofar as he knows the world; he perceives the world only in himself, and himself only in the world. Every new object, clearly seen, opens up a new organ of perception in us.
—*GOETHE* | *Scientific Studies, 39*

It is not one's knowledge of technique that is decisive for the outcome of a sculpture, but one's ability to feel. Technique, like science, is simply a means to an end, but not an end in itself. Applying scientific methods does not equate to generating knowledge, nor does mastery of technique equate to generating art. It is that which comes before, or that which underlies the application of technique, of science, which is decisive for whether art, or knowledge, is produced. "After all the investigation," John Coltrane once concluded, "all of the technique doesn't matter! Only if the feeling is right."

The difference between a good and a bad performance —whether in dancing, public speaking, singing, or whatever— is not of technique but of feeling. Nicolaides provides this wonderful example:

> *The actor who overacts makes his mistake, not because of lack of technique, but because he has not had sufficient practice in truly feeling his part. In fact, his desire for technique has thwarted his natural power to feel correctly, or -and most likely- he has had poor direction in the beginning. By poor direction, I mean that his training emphasized technique of presentation instead of sending him to life with an eagerness to see nature through his ability to feel.[10]*

Anything done without feeling has something wrong with it. Anything produced, said, or written without feeling is bound to appear false and artificial. For something to be real, for something to be authentic, the medium must be entered, must be inhabited. Only then can it take on meaning. Only then can it come alive.

The fact that the artistic value of a sculpture depends on the feelings that were present during its making and not the techniques applied is so obvious that writing about it touches on what I can tolerate in terms of sounding corny. But it is precisely because it is so obvious that it is so often forgotten. After all, most of the available literature on how to sculpt focuses on technique alone and does not even mention that feeling is the most important ingredient for making a sculpture.

But not only is the literature on sculpture deserted of this most vital aspect, but so is all of Western culture. Our capacity to feel is often rendered inferior to our capacity to think, and our education system teaches us to ignore our feeling sense in favor of our mind's analysis. This ecocide of our feeling dimension is also reflected in our fat-fingerdness when it comes to the words we have at our disposal to describe the subtleties involved in feeling. And because the limits of our language mean the limits of our worlds, as Wittgenstein phrased it, we remain largely ignorant and uneducated about the feeling dimensions inherent to the world.

I assume that our feeling, as opposed to our thinking, is so commonly repressed because feeling cannot be controlled from the outside. Feeling is always personal: we must do it ourselves. Thinking, on the other hand, is mostly impersonal. Most thoughts originate from somewhere outside ourselves, and we are used by them for their propagation. E.E. Cummings once summarized this point nicely:

> *Almost anybody can learn to think or believe or know, but not a single human being can be taught to feel. Why? Because whenever you think or you believe or you know, you're a lot of other people but the moment you feel, you're nobody-but-yourself.*[11]

Most people aren't connected to their feeling sense, and when asked what *they* feel, they often respond with what they *think* they feel or were told to feel, but not with what they actually feel. I, for example, found that hardly anyone I ask what they feel about my sculptures actually looks inwards for a response. Instead, people begin relating them to some sculpture they have seen before or tie them to some other knowledge they possess (or are possessed by). But hardly anyone really looks, not to speak about feels, what kind of effect, if any, they have on them.

Sadly, this is true not only for the masses but also for many art enthusiasts. Because they *know* so much about art, their ability to feel is often blocked or distorted. In fact, people with a lot of knowledge about art often utter the most uninspiring comments about my sculptures, whereas the child drawing on the concrete, the guy taking away the trash, or the drug addict living nearby often share the most wonderful considerations. I am not saying this because the drug addict is flattering in his assertions and the art critic is not. No. The addict never holds back saying "It looks shit!" whereas the knowledgeable art critic always dabbles up some nonsense instead of simply uttering what they feel.

Also, I find it irritating when people try to say *the right thing* when they look at my sculptures. Only when people actively express what they feel are they contributing. What they say is irrelevant, but it has to be connected with their feeling sense; it needs to be connected to the Now.

Anyway, let's partake in the ecological restoration of our feeling world, as Stephen Buhner put it, by looking at some ways in which feeling plays a part in the process of making a sculpture.

Kinesthetic Feeling

Our most familiar mode of feeling is the physical feeling done with our senses, all of which are a form of touch: Whether it is sound waves *touching* our eardrums, particles *touching* our olfactory and gustatory stations, or light impulses *touching* our retina cells, all physical feeling depends upon us coming in contact with our environment. And because the incorporation of these senses is so fundamental to the craft, it is worth looking at them one by one:

On Touch

Feeling the material with one's hands is the bread and butter of every craftsman. And one of its greatest joys. The tactile sense goes well beyond the ability to feel the surface of things, however. Hands are also extraordinary instruments for feeling space and form. Their ability to spot whether a curve needs some rounding, or a surface straightening, often exceeds the eyes' ability to sense such nuances.

Hands further possess the surprising ability to sense the fluidity of form: When I walk my hands across a sculpture, they can quickly discover where the form interrupts or turns in the wrong direction. At some point, my hands might want to go down, for example, but are held back from doing so because of a surface coming up against them.

A sculpture cannot appear harmonious and, in that sense, be finished if it doesn't also feel good when explored with one's hands. So as long as there is something wrong when I move my hands over it, there will be something off about its appearance. Everything perceivable through one sense is reflected in all the others. And sometimes, a different sense has to be consulted to find out what is not yet right. So, if I cannot figure out what is wrong by looking, I feel the stone with my hands instead. Perhaps they will provide me with a clue about what I must do?

Hands, and fingers in particular, have an intelligence of their own that can solve problems not unlike our minds' can. I cannot describe how to do this, but when I touch the stone with both hands, my fingers immediately start calculating the form. They, all on their own, move to where the form interrupts or where the stone turns wrongly. Goethe writes about his approach to studying the natural world:

> My thinking is not separate from objects; the elements of the object, the perceptions of the object, flow into my thinking and are fully permeated by it; my perception itself is a thinking, and my thinking a perception.[12]

The same also goes for the use of tools: Each tool possesses an intelligence of its own and wants to do specific things. When I put a file against the stone, for example, it might, as if guided by some alien force, begin to file downwards, even though I haven't perceived the surface as insufficiently rounded. The longer I have known a particular tool, the more I allow it to figure out the form for me.

On Hearing

The hearing sense, whose usefulness might appear less obvious, is no less illuminating. It is inwardly directed, receptive and soft in quality. It is a gateway to getting a sense of what is happening inside the stone: Every time a stone is hit, a resonance is created, which can reveal weak spots running through it.

Also, because every stone has a form and a body, it functions not unlike an instrument. And just like each instrument can be tuned differently and played with different materials, the form, the tools, and one's way of working can equally be adjusted in one's quest to make the best use of the material. I, for example, remember a sandstone that sounded terrible when I filed it but emitted a gentle beat when I used the flat-headed chisel. So, I knew that *this* stone did not want to be filed but wanted to be worked with the flat-headed chisel. It is really that easy. . .

Besides this obvious form of hearing, there also exists a more fundamental kind of hearing that focuses on what lies beneath the surface of sound. It is a kind of hearing that rests on the silences and rhythms, not the tones themselves. It is the same with writing. There, the quality of a text also does not just depend on the words but also on the background rhythm established through punctuation. Its effects might be subtle, but it influences the reading experience as much —if not more— than the words lying on the surface. And in precisely this way, the sculpture takes on an *inward clang* when attention to the rhythm of the beatings is given. The rhythm is somehow absorbed and stored in the sculpture's feel.

On Smelling and Tasting

Our sense of smell, and its related sense of taste, are perhaps our oldest and most intimate senses. Even though Western culture likes to refer to them using derogatory terms like *primitive* or *animalistic*, they are amongst the most elaborate senses we have at our disposal. The fact that convention describes them to be of lower status should, in fact, be enough to signal that the mind finds it difficult to gain control over them.

Like each wood, each stone has a scent (and taste) of its own, and it is by getting to know the stone through these senses that a close relationship is established. I, for example, smell each stone as well as eat a small piece of it, even though I have to admit that I do not know what the immediate benefits of these actions are. But still, putting some vein-cutting stone into my body, or inhaling some silicosis-inducing stone dust, helps me to develop an intimacy that I could otherwise not achieve. After all, we also do not get intimate with our partners just by looking at them.

On Seeing

Our visual perception is the *alpha* of our senses, and its capabilities are spectacular. However, its behavior is similar to the mind, whose serving hand it is. Like the mind, the eyes tend to laser in on individual aspects rather than allowing us to focus on the stone's overall appearance. Seeing also tends to overpower the other, more inwardly directed senses, which is why it is the only sense that needs to be curbed at times. "The eyes are hammers," Kandinsky once accordingly remarked.

In light of the exercises provided by Aldous Huxley's *The Art of* Seeing, I let my eyes move freely across the sculpture and do not allow them to be trapped by cracks, broken bits, or other such aspects they like to linger on. I keep my gaze moving from side to side and from top to bottom and apply it like my sense of touch. Since when I touch, I feel an object's body just as much as I feel its surface.

Besides standing back, another way to restrain the eye's dominion is to work in low-light conditions. Because when I work at dusk or in candlelight, I automatically have to give the other, more uncertain senses a greater role to play. And these other inwardly directed senses introduce the personal and the erotic into the work. The eyes are great tools for the surface, yes, but the perception and shaping of the depth dimensions are done by the other, more intimate senses.

Despite our eyes being our most developed sense, they are also the easiest to be fooled. Most have experienced how it is practically impossible to see past optical illusions, even when we are told that the two lines whose lengths we ought to compare are the same length. And because similar fallacies like to make themselves known in sculpture, it makes a good habit to double-check the eyes' observation against some other sense.

Nicolaides writes about this approach of utilizing all the senses:

The first function of an art student is to observe, to study nature. The artist's job in the beginning is not unlike the job of a writer. He must first reach out for raw material. He must spend much time making contact with actual objects. Learning to draw is really a matter of learning to see - to see correctly - and that means a good deal more than merely looking with the eye. The sort of "seeing" I mean is an observation that utilizes as many of the five senses as can reach through the eye at one time. Although you use your eyes, you do not close up the other senses - rather, the reverse, because all the senses have a part in the sort of observation you are to make. For example, you know sandpaper by the way it feels when you touch it. You know a skunk more by odour than by appearance, an orange by the way it tastes. You recognize the difference between a piano and a violin when you hear them over the radio without seeing them at all . . .

Actually, we see through the eyes rather than with them. It is necessary to test everything you see with what you can discover through the other senses - hearing, taste, smell, and touch - and their accumulated experience. If you attempt to rely on the eyes alone, they can sometimes actually mislead you.[13]

The visual sense is, by default, *active*. It is always switched on and tends to impose rather than to listen. The other senses are *passive* by default, are switched off and tend to reside in the background. When I sculpt, I seek to reverse these respective qualities. I seek to make the passive ones come active, and the active ones go passive. Because active listening has a beauty to it, just as looking passively has.

Non-kinesthetic Feeling

Besides our bodily senses, we also possess a non-physical sense of touch. Even though this sense is often condemned as esoteric and henceforth rendered inexistent, it is still the most reliable ally in making a sculpture.

Stephen Buhner wrote extensively about this sense. Building on the works of Goethe, Thoreau, William Gass and others, he refers to it as a *non-kinesthetic form of touch* with which we can feel the meanings inherent to objects and spaces. Every object, word, or space, he elaborates, possesses a *secret kinesis*, a hidden feeling dimension that can be accessed, perceived and, ultimately, be altered by this sense. Perhaps Kandinsky was guided by a similar intuition when he wrote: "Everything has a secret soul, which is silent more often than it speaks."[14]

In his book *Ensouling Language*, he invites us to experience this for ourselves. He wants us to look at an object in the room and, once we have observed it minutely, ask ourselves: *How does it feel?* In the moment of asking, he asserts, a unique feeling tone, an intimation of mood, a *kinesis*, will emerge out of the thing observed. This perception, he insists, cannot be explained in mere physical terms, nor is it the result of mere pattern recognition. Instead, it occurs because something from within us entered the object and conversed with its meaning.

In writing, the reality of this sense gets particularly clear. After all, the *feeling* a text evokes cannot be explained in mere physical terms: You cannot feel the physical sensation of light impulses bouncing off your retina. And even if you could, they would be as meaningful as a book filled with binary code. No, what you are perceiving are the meanings that are somehow baked into the words. Somehow, when you read, you get *inside* the words and can feel what was placed there. So what you are feeling for cannot be found on the outside but resides on the inside. Or, as Gustav Mahler put it in the context of music: "What is best in music cannot be found within the notes."

We constantly feel into objects, spaces and beings in this way; we might just not always be aware of it. Consider the following example you might be familiar with:

> *Something in the room does not feel right anymore. You cannot say what it is, but something about the couch in that corner seems wrong. It makes the room feel studenty. And because you just graduated, a studenty room does not reflect you anymore. So, a new place for the couch has to be found.*

You start by moving the couch to the opposite side of the room. Once it has arrived there, you feel into the room again. The room has acquired a different feel, but the feeling persists. Something about the arrangement feels off: the couch feels clunky. You keep moving it, this time by 180 degrees to the left. Then you feel again. You feel whether the room reflects your identity as a post-graduate, whether the room's arrangement is congruent with your initial impulse. Not quite, you conclude, so you keep adjusting until the couch has found its place.

Or not.

Then you must do something different. Perhaps the couch is not going in that room after all but will have its place upstairs? Or maybe it is time to throw out the thing for good and get a new one? Or who needs a couch anyway, and why not replace it with a table instead?

Can you feel the sense I am trying to evoke here? It is this sense with which we constantly reach into our environments to feel whether something is *right*, whether something is as it *ought to* be, whether something is at its *right place*. And whenever something is not, we immediately feel uneasy and will want to readjust, even if we do not always know why.

As long as the thing is not in its right place, there is an internal *"no, that's not it!"* that occurs. There is an inner negation, a certain restlessness, perhaps even shallow breathing. Whereas once the thing has found its place, there is an internal confirmation, a relaxation, a sort of *"yes, that's it!"* that occurs. The internal tension relaxes at the same time the thing has found its place.

Whenever this internal relaxation occurs, our inner experience and the physical reality have become congruent. The outside has become an extension of ourselves, and we will feel comfortable inhabiting it.

When I work with stone, there might be a surface that feels *funny* or *off*, even though there is no apparent reason for why this is so. We all have met a person that fits any of these ascriptions and it is the same with stone. I trust such clues more than anything; they are always right! So if I have a hole that doesn't evoke a displeasing sensation, I don't smooth it out. But if I have a smooth surface that causes an unsettling *feeling*, I keep working over it. When in doubt, I always listen to the feeling sense, never to the mind.

What makes something feel *off* differs from person to person and changes from day to day. After all, our living rooms do not all look the same and do not remain static over time. Our sense of what feels right develops with us, so whatever arrangement feels congruent today can already feel *off* tomorrow. And because that is so, sculpting will never exhaust itself because even if we finish a sculpture today, something will want to be adjusted tomorrow already.

Feeling for Life

Perhaps the most mysterious form of feeling is our capacity to feel whether an organism is alive. When I first witnessed an animal in its last moments before crossing over, I could sense the exact moment the life force left its body. In the moment of death, there was a qualitative shift, a decisive break, in which the life force —which moments ago organized the body into a whole, gave a sparkle to the eyes and a rhythm to the pulsation of the skin— was no more.

Scientifically, we can describe this moment only in terms of its secondary effects —the end of brain activity, the stop of the heartbeat, the cessation of breathing— but experimentally, we can perceive the moment of the living force leaving the body directly.

In sculpture, secondary effects such as pulse or brain activity are not present, so science can never confirm whether a sculpture has come "alive." We must trust our own capacity to feel for that.

Remarkably, assertions regarding the liveliness of any of my sculptures do not seem to lie entirely in the subjective, however. Attentive visitors to the studio often utter the *exact* same assessment I maintain for the status of any of my sculptures. This must either mean they are telepathically picking up on my feelings about a particular stone or perceiving the life force themselves. I do not know which conclusion is less preposterous metaphysically speaking, but it has to be one of them.

Due to the eyebrow-raising implications of this statement, I want to add that assertions regarding whether a sculpture is perceived as "alive" does not seem to have anything to do with its form or degree of refinement. To this day, I have been unable to make out a relationship between the clarity of form, the degree to which a stone is refined or any other objective yardstick one might propose to explain whether a sculpture is perceived as alive.

So, whether a sculpture is alive doesn't seem to have anything to do with what it looks like but with something else. What that is, as well as how one can perceive it, I do not know. Maybe its perceiving works through some kind of resonance by which one can sense the presence of the force that makes *oneself* alive within something else? Since when I am deeply absorbed in perceiving something alive, it is almost as if there is a reckoning of myself within the object observed. In fact, there were moments in which I got the sense that something was looking back, perhaps even raising the suspicion that it was I myself whom I just saw looking back out of the thing observed.[15]

Chapter 4

The voyage of the best ship is a zigzag line of a hundred tacks.
—RALPH WALDO EMERSON | Essays and Poems, 158

Counter to conventional thought, the quest of the sculptor does not lie in forcing the stone into what they believe it should become but in following the stone wherever it wants them to go. And it is by this kind of following, by doing one thing after the other, that a stone is gradually turned into a sculpture, is turned alive. "True … artists" Stephen Buhner writes, "are servants of the process, not its masters."[16]

On this journey, the stone only always shows the next step one must take. But that is also all one needs. Because to make a sculpture, one does not need to see what lies behind, nor does one need to see what still lies ahead. All one needs to see is the next step one must take. And that the stone will always provide one with.

So, one does not need to know how to make a sculpture to manifest one, just like one does not need to know how to hike a mountain in order to reach the top. All one needs to know is how to take one step after the other in the right direction. And doing so continuously will bring one there all on its own.

Thus, whenever I come to the studio, I approach the stone as if it were a total stranger. I stand back and sense for the next step I must take. I feel for what is off and search for a way to resolve it into the form. No matter what stone I put up, something will always call for my attention. And once I attended to that, something else will reveal itself that wants to be adjusted.

In this process, I seek to be clear and deliberate in my actions, for the more clear and deliberate I am, the more obvious the next step I must take will get. The next step is always an expression, yes, a logical consequence of the one preceding it, and the more thoroughly I took the preceding step, the more obvious the next step will demand itself. That is why, if I decide to make a surface straight, I make it straight, regardless of whether I will make it round again thereafter. Or if the stone wants to be polished, I do so thoroughly, even if I suspect I will have to rough it up again.

Whenever I take one of these "steps," I do not care at all about the impact of my actions on the overall sculpture but only focus on resolving *that* bit. And once I attended to that, I focus on resolving the next aspect. That is why I do not need an idea or plan to make a sculpture: I just do one thing after another until the job is done.

This book came into being in the same way. I didn't start with an idea, nor did I have a conception of its structure or thematic interrelationships. All I had was an urge, an inner necessity, to explore certain thoughts and experiences in text. And once I wrote them down, more thoughts, more experiences, wanted to be explored. And just by itself, what started out as seemingly unrelated investigations gradually revealed an overarching gestalt. A gestalt that was to become this book. I did not control where my writing was going but simply followed whatever caught my attention at any moment: When I felt like writing, I wrote. When I felt like editing, I edited. When I felt like researching, I researched. When I felt like going for a run, I ran.

Whenever I didn't work in this way, whenever I did tell the writing where to go, whenever I didn't allow the text to organize itself from the bottom up, my writing immediately got paralyzed: When I sat down to fill chapters I had predefined with a title, I immediately experienced writer's block. So it really did seem as if the book, almost violently, disagreed with any kind of structure I sought to impose on it.

I had a similar experience when carving the Platonic Solids: Once I decided to make them, acquired some fitting stones and studied how to best carve them out of a block of stone, I suddenly found myself without the company of my inner pigeon. And not only did sculpting suddenly become arduous, but my doings also didn't amount to much any longer. My beatings didn't have the same fragrance as those that occur when I take one step at a time. After all, I was operating from a different climate of mind: No longer was I exploring, eager to find the next step I must take, but stupidly working towards a predefined line; no longer was I listening to the material, but trying to force it into a predefined corset.

As long as I follow whatever catches my attention, on the other hand, the work always remains exciting. As long as I work where the stone is most pulsating, where it is most alive, I never spend time with things I am not enjoying. I remain at the cutting edge, doing what I consider most essential. And yes, days do come when I feel like fixing the workbench, writing a cover letter, or whatever work I might usually dread. But I wait for these days to arrive. I wait until fixing the workbench or writing a cover letter becomes the next step I must take. Because then these things will be a joy, and the result will reflect that.

The mind always tries to calculate ahead and anticipate what a certain intervention will do. A snipped of such calculating might be transcribed as follows:

> *"If I take this edge off, then this side will come forward, which would mean that I have to change that side and —no. That does not work." Next: "If I make this surface go in, then this edge will come out, so I would have to sand that edge to make it less aggressive, but then I would also have to change that side because otherwise it would not work together with this side and —no, let's not go there." Next: "If I make this line straighter, then this surface will appear more pronounced, which I actually do not want because it takes away some power of the surface I crafted yesterday —so no."*

And on and on the mind goes.

But all this forecasting is of no use because, when working with stone, almost nothing turns out the way I expect it to. Calculating ahead does not only not work because I might fail to execute what I have planned but because I cannot change one bit without simultaneously changing the whole. A sculpture is an ecosystem in which every part is connected to every other part, and a change on one level can have unforeseeable consequences on any other.

More than once, I wanted to straighten a line by a fraction of a degree, but doing so made the entire sculpture look and feel different, even when looked at from the opposite side, where I could not even see the change I undertook. Somehow, the straightening of the line shifted the sculpture's feel, which made the *entire* sculpture look different. Consequently, sides I thought to be finished, or parts I previously declared resolved, suddenly asked for my attention again.

I experienced the same in writing: When I moved just a single word, the *entire* sentence immediately got a different feel to it. So not only does the inclusion of a quote, of a specific concept, of a single word alter the feeling of the sentence they are in, but their effects ripple forwards and backward throughout the entire text. That is why, when writing a book, each sentence, each word, yes, each comma has to be considered; for each sentence, each word, each comma has an influence on all the others.

Everything influences the sculpture's feel: Just like each word carries certain metaphysical, societal and historical connotations, each element in the sculpture also conveys certain associations into the work. Everything — the tools used, the forms carved, the base chosen— influences the feel of the work.

What is more, all these elements can convey a different meaning depending on where and when they occur: A wooden base might work for one sculpture but not another. A claw chisel might work in the morning but not in the evening. A form might feel right when carved in Amsterdam but not in Basel. So just like it was concluded that "No word ever has the same meaning twice," no element in sculpture ever has the same meaning twice either.[17] Both are co-shaped by the material and by time and space itself. What elements go together, how they appear in space, what associations they evoke is constantly re-negotiated: A twist that didn't work on Tuesday might suddenly appear unshakable; a base thought indispensable might come to appear superfluous.

These connotations often do not correspond to the qualities conventionally ascribed to them: A cubic stone can well feel organic, whereas an egg-shaped sculpture is a long way from being guaranteed to be perceived as such.

In practice, I often cannot name or define the precise associations I am perceiving. Yes, sometimes I might be able to assess that a base makes the sculpture feel too *Brancusi-esque* or that the composition feels "right" because it adheres to the golden ratio. But most of the time, the reason I perceive something in a certain way remains elusive even to myself.

However, this is where the jump into the unknown comes in: Since these meanings and associations that arise are often homeopathic, their implications not languageable or in some other way beyond my conscious reach, I, as a sculptor, must, by necessity, commit a leap of faith into trusting my own perceiving.

So again, I do not need to know how to make a sculpture. All I need to trust is that my feeling sense knows the most recent data from the form market, knows the mercurial meanings shifting in a curve. Wallace Stegner put it most wonderfully for the realm of writing:

> *Words used poetically are a medium as fluid as watercolors, and some of the best effects may seem accidental even to the man who creates them. He [the writer] does not have to know, with his conscious mind, exactly what he is doing. He is fishing in obscure depths, he is a dealer in mysteries, a witch doctor not always easy with the forces he evokes but acutely aware of them while they are present.* [18]

What is more, these perceptions are continually metamorphosing into other associations: In one instance, I might feel as if I am carving a flatscreen TV; in the next, like I am revisiting the place Rothko drew from; then, I might come in contact with the number 0 before discovering a form that somehow resembles solipsism... Goethe could have spoken about developing a sculpture when he wrote:

> *When something has arrived at a form, it immediately metamorphoses into a new one. If we wish to arrive at some living perception of Nature we ourselves must remain as quick and flexible as Nature and follow the example she gives.* [19]

So when I feel like I am sculpting a shark, I keep refining my sculpture towards acquiring a shark-like quality. And, just on its own, there will come a moment in which the shark-like quality will transform into something else. Perhaps into that of a spear? And if I follow *that*, it will continue to transform again. Into a line? Into a thought?

In this process, I try not to value any perception over any other or neglect certain emotional responses because I cannot identify with them, regard them as improper, or as not sufficiently "deep" or "meaningful" enough. So if I feel like engraving a symbol into my sculpture, I do not refrain from doing so because I once proclaimed an "I want my sculpture to speak for itself" doctrine. Instead, I simply carve in the symbol and feel whether it is congruent with my initial impulse.

On Following a Thread

As long as I take one step at a time, I am following something akin to a golden thread. We are most familiar with the concept of a golden thread in writing. There, we know when the writing is "on the line" and when it diverges from it. As long as the writing is on the line, the words flow easily and writing and reading on it becomes almost effortless. Every sentence, then, contributes towards the continuation and manifestation of the thread. *Like this one.*

As long as I am following such a thread, the making of a sculpture supports itself with ease, and I can do almost anything without disturbing the sculpture, just like I can write almost anything as long as I am not departing from the thread behind this text.

The thread is nothing that can be grasped, though: the more one tries to grab it, the more it will disappear in Heisenbergian fashion. But despite its thin ontology, it is still our most reliable guide for making a sculpture. William Stafford writes about the nature of this thread:

> *Just as the swimmer does not have a succession of handholds*
> *hidden in the water, but instead simply sweeps that yielding*
> *medium and finds it hurrying him along, so the writer passes*
> *his attention through what is at hand, and is propelled by a*
> *medium too thin and all-pervasive for the perceptions of*

The more I can trust this thread, the more of an independent being the sculpture becomes. And the more of an individual the sculpture becomes, the more power it radiates. So again, it is in acting as a steward that greatness is achieved in sculpture, not in being able to dictate an outcome. "Only the golden string knows where it is going, and the role for a writer or reader is one of following, not imposing," William Stafford writes.[21] Stephen Buhner, whose work about writing can be seen as instructive for any creative process, adds: "True writers follow; . . . They follow the thread where it leads and write down what they find on the journey. They are, in a sense, transcribers, and good writers know it."[22]

The thread never leaves me toward a sculpture in a straight line, though. It always has me zigzag and keeps throwing all kinds of tests to see whether I truly trust it. It had, for example, made me do sculptures with nothing but right angles, even —or maybe because— I grew up in an environment that was influenced by the "no right angles" doctrine that some anthroposophists maintain. At other times, it had me oscillate between having a surface roughed or polished. Whenever I polished it, the stone wanted me to rough it up again and vice versa.

The thread is made up of elements that mean something to me. And whenever I encounter something that is part of it, a particular feeling arises, as if an internal chord is struck. Like when I am grabbed by a sudden excitement because I see the next step I must take: The lying sculpture wants to become a standing one.[23]

Goethe described it in the following way:

> *I was, indeed, then in the dark, and struggled on, unconscious of what I was seeking so earnestly; but I had a feeling of the right, a divining road, that showed me where gold was to be found.*[24]

These spontaneous bursts of excitement, that *feeling of the right* that occurs whenever I discover the next step I must take, are not confined to appearing on the workbench. They can occur at any time or place. I have experienced them when finding a specific book, going to a specific place, or meeting a specific person. But the feeling remains the same: Whenever I experience them, it feels as if I have found something that touched me on some fundamental level, is part of who I am.

So, whenever I perceive these exhilarating bursts, I follow them. Whatever lies behind them has a meaning, a purpose; I just don't know what it is yet. "A good rule is—don't respond unless you have to," William Stafford writes. "But when you find you do have a response—trust it. It has a meaning."[25]

Because the thread isn't some random fluke, some artificial invention, something that exists without reason. No, the thread *does have* agency. It wants something. And what is more, something on the other side is pulling it. Something that wants to manifest and something that I want too.

So, there is always a reason stone wants me to sculpt *that* stone and not another. Why it wants me to go *round* and not *straight*. Why it wants me to take off *that* bit and not another. Because with time, the different elements that make up my thread —the decisions I took, the books I read, the people I met— continue to coalesce into each other and reveal an overarching gestalt. They, all of their own, begin to move into each other and become an indispensable subunit of the enigma that is my sculpture.

Chapter 5

I spent all morning putting out a comma, and all afternoon putting it back in.

—attributed to OSCAR WILDE

When I begin working on a stone, nothing relates to anything else; nothing helps the stone carry its weight; nothing complements each other; nothing is connected. But then I begin. I begin to resolve one aspect after the other, one slow feeling step at a time. I make flat what needs to be flat and round what needs to be round. I keep standing back, I keep circling the stone, I keep feeling for what is *off*.

John Berger once remarked that making art is the pursuit of constantly correcting for errors.[26] And indeed, it can be said that, from the moment I begin working on a stone until I decide to stop, I am constantly correcting for what is still wrong. "Is this edge still standing out too far?"— "Is that line straight enough?" I ask myself and, guided by my feeling sense, I keep adjusting.

If I have followed the thread diligently, I will, after some time, have arrived at something akin to a first draft. The sculpture is still ambiguous at this stage, but something between the material will have started to shine. At first barely noticeable, like music playing in the far distance. But soon more rhythmically clear so I can hear some of the notes that make up the song, the instruments that play the music. But the sound is not yet crisp. There is still a lot of noise overlaying these notes. And *that* I begin to attend for now.

The method remains the same, though: I continue to stand back, I keep circling the stone, and, going back to each surface, I ask:

"What is *that* side doing?"

"It's still pushing out too much," my eyes respond. So, I walk back to the stone, double-check my eyes' observations against my hands and, indeed, the surface pushes back against them. I commit to taking off a fine layer with the flat-headed chisel before standing back again. This time I ask:

"How does it feel?"

I touch the stone with my eyes, with my non-kinesthetic form of touch; I sense the atmosphere, the mood inherent to the stone. I feel something is still a bit stiff, so I keep chiseling. This time in a different direction so that the marks point somewhere else. Then I stand back again.

"The stone feels different now. It has gotten more loose," I conclude. But something about *that* side is still not right. This time I cannot find a word to describe what is off, but I can indicate it with a gesture. But before I remove any more material, I pick up some charcoal and draw some lines across the area to express the underlying movement. Then I suddenly see what I must do: The area wants to be filed! And once I have done *that,* I stand back again and . . . ah, there! The surface sits right. It is integrated.

But how does it transition into *that* surface, the stone immediately asks? And on I go. . .

The longer I have refined the stone this way, the more times I have worked over each surface, the more condensed and orderly the stone tends to get. The complexity of the sculpture begins to move *inwards,* and the composition on the outside tends to become more simple. Some sides converge into others, balance each other out, or fall off the stone entirely. Others hold each other even, complement, or synergize in Hegelian fashion. Everything begins to take on a function until each part is an integral component of the overall form.

The further I already ventured, the more subtle my interventions tend to get. Consequently, I have to fine-tune my tools and my senses to perceive even the most subtle aspects that are still somehow off. But if I keep refining *them* also, if I follow the thread to *its* end, the sculpture becomes more and more clear, more and more refined, more and more inhabited.

With each iteration I work over a stone, my understanding of what each part is doing increases. I begin to comprehend how each element contributes towards the whole, how each side moves into the other, how each form is connected to its neighboring one. With that, the stone moves inside me, is absorbed by me, until I can remember each detail minutely. At this depth, I have unresolved aspects following me throughout the day, and I carry a holographic image of the form inside, which I can see behind closed eyelids at all times.

But even though the sculpture might continue to appear more simple on the outside, its true complexity continually increases. Because with every iteration I work over the stone, the stone continues to confront me with aspects I previously did not notice but which now also want to be integrated into the form. And while I integrate them, they continue fractalizing into even more subtle aspects. Ad infinitum. "The further in you go, the bigger it gets," Terence McKenna often said when characterizing the psychedelic experience, and it is no different with stone.[27]

But then I keep going still. I keep refining until I understand what each part of the sculpture is doing. Because as long as there still is some aspect I do not understand, some two sides coming together in a way that doesn't make sense to me, there will be something that doesn't feel right. And it is only when I have confronted these aspects also, worked over them, understood and resolved them into the form that I am fully inhabiting my sculpture.

Eventually, there should be no angle, point, or distance from which the stone does not appear wholesome. A finished sculpture is one in which all integrates, no matter how, where and under what circumstances it is looked at. So as long as my sculpture depends upon being looked at from a certain distance, angle, or a certain lighting condition, the work is not finished, and I am invited to keep going.

At this stage, I also mix in more specialized runs: Just like one can re-read a text for feel, grammatical accuracy, rhythm, sound patterning, movement cycles and so forth, I now work over the sculpture by focusing on different layers. In one iteration, I focus on the proportions, then on the expression of the surfaces, then on the transitions... All these layers support and depend on each other: A text free of spelling errors lubricates the reading experience; expressed edges accentuate the form of a surface; a background rhythm introduced through punctuation enhances the meaning of a text, etc.

As a result of this search, the surface qualities of stone —its hardness, solidity and weight— begin to move into the background, and the deeper aspects —its movement, meaning and character— begin to come into the foreground. It is like when the text is good and the perception of the words fades into the background, and all you are left with is the living dream they are meant to trigger.

I have worked over stones more than a hundred times in this way. And so with this book: I went over what I thought to be a finished manuscript well over two dozen times. But even in late runs, when I thought I would only add a comma here or there, I found myself restructuring entire sections a few pages in. So the form and size might still change drastically at this stage. What starts as filing off a few millimeters can, at any time, turn into blowing coin-sized pieces a few moments later.

I continue working over the sculpture in this way until each part leads to every other part, until each side is my favorite side, until each angle is my preferred angle. Resolving one transition ultimately means resolving the entire sculpture, so I continue until I understand each part to be both beginning and end, both condition and cause of the overall form. "To me a work is finished," the painter Hans Hofmann once remarked, "when all parts involved communicate themselves, that they don't need me."[28]

∞

What I am also doing at this stage is condensing the form. Boiling it down to the essential. By substantiating each element, I am removing the sculpture's fat. I am ridding it of its superfluous verbs, of unnecessary ornamentation and of repeating elements. In this pursuit, I revisit each aspect individually, test for its necessity, feel for its congruency.

"*This* part is going in like this. *That* part is coming out like that," I confirm internally while I have my hands glide over the sculpture — and whatever does not survive this scrutiny, whatever isn't essential for the sculpture to be itself, whatever still stands out awkwardly, is now leaving the stone.

The more I have condensed the sculpture in this way, the further I have reduced it to the bare essential, the closer my internal experience of the form and its actual form start to approximate each other. Until eventually, the gesture the stone evokes is one with its actual form. Until my experience of the form reflects its actual appearance. Until "form and essence begin to echo each other," as Stephen Buhner put it.[29] Because it is then, when inside and outside, I and the stone, have become mirrors to each other, that I have substantiated a sculpture. And it is then that I am inhabiting it. "A work of art is finished," Hans Hofmann comments, "when feeling and perception have resulted in a spiritual synthesis."[30]

∞

But let's rewind: I begin by meeting the material, by standing back, by taking one step at a time. I then authenticate one element after the other until I have substantiated how each section, each transition, each surface contributes towards the whole. Once a draft has revealed itself out of this process, I begin condensing it. I boil down the form until the sculpture is at home with itself. Until my experience of the form, as well as the actual form, has become congruent. Has become one.

"And the life force, when does it slip in?"

Answer: "Precisely when I am not looking!"

The life force finds its way into the work in sideways fashion; it slips in as a result of this continuous search. When or how a sculpture "comes alive" will thus always remain elusive even to myself. All I will be able to remember is having adjusted one thing after another until the whole thing suddenly came online.

In fact, as long as I try to make a sculpture "come alive," it will never do so. But if I keep searching for aspects that do not yet sit right, the life force might slip into the work in sideways fashion. At some moment, when I am not looking, not trying, not aspiring, but simply adjusting for congruency, some qualitative shift might occur all of its own.

So it is the *search* that makes the craft become art. It is the search that invites the life force to slip in. And yes, it is a commitment to keep searching that every artist must put down as collateral for this to continue to occur. Any kind of final form, any kind of answer, the footnote of the creative contract reads, marks the end of it. Artists are in a similar condition as swimmers in that way: those who do not strive endlessly, will go under.

I also could have written this book in a few months if I didn't care for its composition, its thread, its music. But had I released it after a few months already, it would have been all surface without any depth: After a few months, this book was an accumulation of hundreds of paragraphs — but there was no music. The individual thoughts scattered across the manuscript were like notes waiting to be composed. I could sense they were somehow connected, but I didn't yet see how. But then, guided by my feeling sense, I began picking up paragraph after paragraph, word after word, and started moving them around, sensing for their underlying connection, for the thread, for their place within this text. I ruthlessly discarded what did not belong to it and dedicatedly adjusted what *did* belong to it. Over the following two years, I hardly added any more content but spent my time weaving each thought, each paragraph, and each word into every other until the whole thing came together. As one.

And just like the quality of a book is not (solely) dependent upon the quality of its underlying thoughts, the defining aspect for the artistic power of sculpture is also not to be found in its form, but in whether each transition, each surface, each relationship has been connected to all the others, thereby creating a background-rhythm that makes the whole thing work. The elements of form are only one aspect —they are like the naked words in a text— but it is how they are arranged and related to each other that makes all the difference.

So the size, form, style, or any of these aspects are, in themselves, of no importance for whether a sculpture possesses artistic power. What *is* decisive is whether a sculpture was substantiated. Substantiated not by reason, but by feel. And to the degree *this* was done, the sculpture will possess the quality this book is trying to point towards, will possess life. For when a sculptor has felt and understood every element that makes up their work, has experienced each transition and grasped its meaning, has taken in every relationship between its individual parts and itself, has seen and not merely looked, has listened and not merely spoken, then they is inhabiting that sculpture and *thereby* makes it come alive.

So when each side was substantiated, when every side cooperates with every other side, when each aspect is understood as an indispensable subunit of something larger than itself, when all points are co-tangent, when every part leads to every other part, when form moves endlessly, when the stone's basic qualities —weight, size, type— are overtrumped by movement, form and essence, *then* the stone has crossed a threshold of self-organization: A sculpture has occurred.

These qualitative shifts often occur in a spontaneous and non-linear fashion. Taking off just a tiny bit can mean the difference between standing before a rock and standing before a sculpture. When these phase changes occur cannot be anticipated. They just happen. You might know the feel of such moments from balancing stones:

> *You pick up a stone, and you start balancing it. Immediately it falls in one direction, then onto the other. Since it doesn't stand still, you briefly lift it to investigate its bottom before putting it back down.*
>
> *Then again, you begin turning it in large movements: half a rotation to the left, a quarter rotation back and, suddenly, you feel that the stone has briefly locked. But it was just a fleeting sense, a hunch. The stone is still a long way from standing still. It would still immediately fall over if you took your hands off it. But because you sensed that it stood still even for a millisecond, you no longer turn it from side to side, but you have committed.*
>
> *But first, you stretch your back, readjust your positioning and take a few deep breaths. Then you go back in. This time you only make small movements: a tiny bit to the left, a tiny bit to the right, a little upward, and —the stone stands still: Balancing has occurred.*

Experiencing these qualitative shifts has something sacred to it: Within stone, it can be sensed in that the material suddenly appears weightless; within the environment, it can be sensed in that space itself becomes poignantly concentrated around the sculpture, like iron filings pointing towards a magnetic source; and internally, it can be sensed in the form of a feeling that can only be evoked by juxtaposing opposites: For whenever this qualitative shift occurs, I realize myself both indispensable and irrelevant, both the doer and the non-doer, both the initiator and the spectator of the unfolding event. I realize that I gave rise to something that is both from me but, at the same time, has nothing to do with me; that even though I made it, it remains a gift that cannot be called forth on demand.

In short, I realize that life was given. Life that, from now on, will live free of its maker, free of its material.

Kandinsky writes:

> *The true work of art rises 'from out of the artist.' Once released from him, it assumes its own independent life, takes on a personality, and becomes a self-sufficient, spiritually breathing subject that also leads a real material life: it is a being.*[31]

This life-force that sometimes visits a sculpture behaves much like it does in flowers: it always wants to be carried on. Once a flower has bloomed, the life force has already moved into its seeds, where it is eager to bloom again next season. Only plastic flowers bloom forever; real flowers immediately start to wilt. Yes, I can hang the flower upside-down and preserve its form, just like I can put a sculpture on a base and put it in my living room. But this flavor, this vibration, this pulsing force will always be at the cutting edge. It will always be in the Now. Making a sculpture is, therefore, an endless chase that I will never definitively reach: Once I arrive at it —once the flower blooms, once the sculpture has found its balancing point— it will take but a shift in light until it wants to be carried on.

In other words, a sculpture cannot be preserved in time. A sculpture only exists in-between time. So if photographed, all the picture will show is husk. And if explained, all that will be formulated is an idea. But the real thing will always escape: A sculpture will never be found in time.

Interlude II

Apprenticeship is everywhere an enquiry into the smallest, most hidden things in good and evil. Then suddenly one begins to see one's way and the specific direction one must take.
—PAUL KLEE | *The Thinking Eye, 22*

All processes aimed at developing something —i.e. that are artistic— are underlaid by similar principles. This can be used to our advantage because we can have our own understanding guiding us throughout the process. I already provided some examples by which I translated part of the process through actions you might be familiar with, such as by liking it to hiking, moving furniture, or solving a Rubik's cube. But this can be done with anything. You can extract patterns you have come to understand from learning an instrument, sports, or whatever else and have them guide you throughout the development of form. Here is another example:

A mathematician might conceive of a stone as a heap of unsorted data and make it their quest to "solve" the form. Like when solving an equation, they'll start by identifying the variables they know —which is to say: aspects about the stone they already have a sense for— and variables they don't know: aspects whose contributing function towards the form they do not yet understand.

Once they familiarized themselves with the data, they begin by reformulating the equation so that all unknown variables are grouped together. In sculpture, this can be done by leaving one side as an offshoot, into which all other sides culminate. While they sort the rest of the sculpture, they do not care what happens at this offshoot side, at x, but allow it to do whatever it wants. All they focus on is setting all other variables in place.

Once they condensed the equation to its most elegant expression, sorted for x, and factored out what can be factored out, they can start grappling with how to best solve for the unknown variables. In sculpture, as in mathematics, most problems can be solved in various ways, some of which are more elegant —i.e., are quick, make good use of the stone and are fun to execute— and some of which are clumsier and more laborious.

Usually, solving for *x* requires more than one step, so they might have to work over the entire stone multiple times until they arrive at a form that moves continuously. They might have to move the *x* from one side to the other, or they might even have to introduce irrational elements to perform a certain step. But whatever they do, each iteration is aimed at establishing a higher degree of order and moving the stone closer towards a solution where no unknown parts remain.

It goes without saying that the experience of the mathematician, of the sculptor, is crucial for their ability to find solutions to problems they are confronted with. The more they know, the more ways they have taken before, the better they will be at sensing what operations might work. However, the novice has the benefit of being less inclined to be operationally blind. So even though the experienced mathematician, the experienced sculptor, knows more, has seen more, has done more, they are also less likely to come up with novel solutions for unique problems they are facing. Therefore, each stage in one's artistic development is as good as any other because these opposing forces —experience and innocence— will always hold each other even.

The mathematician also understands that knowing specific ways of achieving a certain outcome doesn't make a great mathematician. They understands that the time spent learning a solution by heart is wasted, for they would be lost if the problem were formulated differently. So, the sculptor who looks at the process through the lens of mathematics knows from experience that knowing and understanding are two different things.

An infinitude of such examples can be made to characterize the process. The key is to find a language you are versed in —knitting, cooking, teaching, acting, carpeting, gardening, plumbing, nursing, engineering, driving, accounting, or whatever— and translate the process through that. Because then it will be *your* understanding that guides you throughout the process. And once you have that, you have come a long way, for what is an artist but someone who has their own understanding guiding them throughout their work?

Chapter 6

"All that is straight lies," murmured the dwarf contemptuously. "All truth is crooked, time itself is a circle."
—FRIEDRICH NIETZSCHE | Thus Spoke Zarathustra, 128

The thread is delicate, and we must pay attention not to pull too hard. In the beginning, I certainly did: I was too purposeful, tried too hard, didn't let the flatworm *ooze and crawl of its own will onto the knife's blade* but tried to pick it up directly and, in doing so, turned it into a slimy goo. Only with time did I learn to find the trust and patience to allow the sculpture to crawl into the work in sideways fashion.

There are countless ways in which I continue to lose the thread. I still spend hours, days, sometimes weeks, during which I don't contribute anything towards the becoming of a sculpture. I still find myself setting collision points, removing wobbles, or polishing surfaces instead of engaging with the form; I still find myself using the bush hammer or the file to do what should be done with hammer and chisel; I find myself trying to steer the stone towards a certain direction instead of allowing the form to arise by itself. . .

What unifies all these aberrations is an underlying lack of trust. Whenever I think to know better, whenever I seek to move the sculpture in a certain direction, I lose the thread. It is difficult to pin down what gets different when I am no longer following, but usually, just like in this sentence, there appears a mechanistic feeling, a sense of different parts not working together properly, a note of detachment, and a sense of rigidness gets apparent in the way different sides relate to each other. What comes out of the thread, on the other hand, automatically takes on a certain fluidity reminiscent of the forms found in nature. As *this* sentence does, for example.

The mind always wants to "grab" the sculpture and is impatient and skeptical about its own arising. So if there is a hole somewhere, it doesn't trust that it will resolve as a result of the continuous exploration of form and would thus prefer to take matters into its own hands.

I still waste huge amounts of time and stone doing such things, not least because no matter how long I already corrected for whatever irregularity I am trying to smooth out, some imperfection will always remain. And even if I occasionally do get a surface close to what my mind regards as sufficiently perfect, I have to discover that this "perfect" side has detached itself from the rest of the sculpture. It is no longer integrated but stands out as an alien, lifeless surface.

If, however, I can relax and just do one thing after the other, the sculpture tends to find this quality that nature always hits all of its own. That is because perfection is not what the mind thinks it is. A perfect sculpture does not result from an agglomeration of perfectly smoothed surfaces or straight lines but from the interplay of imperfect forms and shapes. True perfection is the perfection found in nature. Because when nature composes its forms, it doesn't utilize perfectly smooth surfaces or straight lines, but elements of form that are always distinguished by some degree of imperfection from their respective Euclidean ideals. And it is from these imperfections that the next form arises. And whatever results out of such interlocking forms *is* perfect.

Similar cases can be made for wanting to make a sculpture appear powerful, organic, sensual, or whatever ideal sculptors like to proclaim. Because when someone aims for such ideals, their result is destined to be less powerful than the ideal they held in mind or, at worst, will break the stone entirely. Those following such pursuits are, by the nature of their approach, forever preventing themselves from exploring something *beyond* themselves. They remain chasing an ideal which they can never reach, not to speak of transcending it. . .

Another moment in which the thread is often lost is at the end: After the tedious journey of taking one step after the other, I often look forward to giving my sculpture its final sparkle by polishing it or by putting some oil on it. But when I conceptualize the finishing of a sculpture as a separate event from the process of making it, I am one step away from disaster. For when I polish, engrave, make the sculpture stand on a base, or whatever else I might fantasize about doing, I am trying to close the process instead of searching for the next step I must take. And the more I try to bring the process to a close, the more the stone rebels against that. Such is the rule of this craft.

Also, when I do any of these things, I am trying to *enhance* the sculpture. And all efforts aimed at enhancing a sculpture always have the opposite effect than intended. With one sculpture I worked with, for instance, I fantasized about making it stand up on a pin upon completion. And indeed, when I first positioned it upright, it appeared striking. But only at first sight. Because what happened as a result of it standing up was that much of its mystique was lost. Somehow, it appeared blunt when it stood up. So for some familiar, although enigmatic reason, the sculpture appeared stronger when lying on the ground where the onlooker had to fill in the missing gaps themselves.

A related classic in which the thread is often lost occurs when a sculpture is treated after the process has finished. But how does one know whether a sculpture is finished?

As long as I am in the process, I feel intimately bound to my sculpture and carry it around with the same confidence a mother monkey carries around her newborn. Jackson Pollock once shared an impression of what this confidence feels like:

> When I am **in** my painting, I'm not aware of what I'm doing. It is only after a sort of 'get acquainted period' that I see what I have been about. I have no fears about making changes, destroying the image etc., because the painting has a life of its own. I try to let it come through. It is only when I lose contact with the painting that the result is a mess. Otherwise there is pure harmony, an easy give and take, and the painting comes out well.[32]

Equally, as long as I am in the process, I am *in* my sculpture and have no fears about making changes or destroying it. There is *pure harmony, an easy give and take* and trust that the sculpture will *come out well*. But once the process is over, the sculpture suddenly becomes an alien thing. Carrying it around then feels closer to when I first had to carry a newborn as a teenager: I feel stuck to the ground, and all I am concerned with is not dropping it.

Such a process can have any length, be interrupted, or be comprised of a set of sculptures. But once it has come to a close, I learned to resist every temptation to continue working on it.

I remember one sculpture I took back to the studio that had already left me in this way. I thought my skills had improved and I would thus be able to make the sculpture "better." I don't have to tell how that turned out. When I imposed my newfound knowledge on her, the sculpture soon appeared deformed, then violated and finally broke apart. Once I had ruined the sculpture for good, I could only assess that I was an idiot and offer my apologies to the broken pieces I had lying at my feet.

A more subtle way of breaking the thread can occur when certain invisible lines are overstepped. In writing, this can occur when a metaphysical assumption, an underlying idea, or an inherent worldview upon which the entire book depends, is made explicit.

As an example, let's assess the impact of the following quote on the rest of this book. The quote is an excerpt from a discourse given by Osho in 1978.

> *The creative person is one who brings something from the unknown into the world of the known, who brings something from God into the world, who helps God to utter something; who becomes a hollow bamboo and allows God to flow through him. How can you become a hollow bamboo? If you are too full of the mind, you cannot become a hollow bamboo. And creativity is from the creator, creativity is not of you or from you. You disappear, then creativity is - when the creator takes possession of you.*[33]

Now, do you notice how this quote oversteps the thread behind this text? It is not just another quote that contributes toward the sculpture I seek to build behind these words. No, it crosses a certain line I haven't previously crossed.

In a way, the excerpt summarizes this entire book in a few lines, but in doing so, it is not strengthening its cause, but weakens it. Somehow it exposes me, not unlike a magician is exposed when somebody explains the audience the mechanics behind a trick. Because once the audience knows that the rabbit is hidden in the table underneath, the stuff that fueled the sense of wonder when the magician pulled the rabbit will have disappeared. The situation was demystified, the artistic flavor lost.

Whether it was a good decision to include this example, I am not sure about. But something that was present throughout this book was disrupted by the inclusion of this quote. Whether my effort of making this a controlled break makes it any less damaging, I am equally not sure about since an atomic bomb dropped on Bikini Atoll is an atomic bomb dropped. Whether it was worth breaking the thread just to demonstrate this example, I also do not know, but it comes to show just how delicate such threads are.

In sculpture, such an overstepping can occur when a sculpture is given a name or when the (perceived) meaning of a sculpture is made explicit in some other way. Because if the name or some other means acts as a demystifying force upon the sculpture, it catapults it out of the unknown and strips it of its artistic power.

Interlude III

Simplicity is not an end in art, but one arrives at simplicity in spite of oneself, in approaching the real sense of things. Simplicity is at bottom complexity and one must be nourished on its essence to understand its significance.
—CONSTANTIN BRANCUSI | *The Brummer Gallery: Brancusi, 3*

"'How else should it be done then?' was always the immediate question. The answer is simple: 'Exactly the opposite way it is done today.'"[34]–I love this quote attributed to Viktor Schauberger. Because if you follow its gist as a sculptor, you will automatically do many things as proposed by this book. Convention is surprisingly consistent in getting things upside-down, so if you take any general standpoint and turn it on its head, you have usually found a good starting point to work from. And yes, it does make a good practice to start a sculpture by polishing it and working backwards from there.

I have already given a few examples by which this book's approach runs counter to conventional thought, such as that techniques or stone types aren't of primary importance; that I spent most of the time, not working on the stone, but standing back from it; that I draw on the stone as a means to express the stone's movement and not for marking the outlines of an aspired figure, etc.

Here is another one:

Convention is profoundly confused about the notion of *complexity*. Because one yardstick by which the public —which is another way of saying: the mind— assesses whether a sculpture is *complex*, is by counting the number of sides it has. The more sides a sculpture has, the mind calculates, the more complex it is. And the more complex a sculpture is, the more difficult it is to make. Convention holds a similar view of writing. Because what people were impressed by when inquiring about my writing wasn't so much the content as it was the number of pages I had already written.

Accordingly, the eight-sided octahedron is perceived as a moderately complex sculpture. Because to free an octahedron out of a block of stone, a three-step process must be applied: First, a block of stone must be carved into a cube, then into a stellated octahedron (which gives the outer edges of the octahedron) before the octahedron beneath it can be revealed. Hence, the public considers an octahedron a moderately complex sculpture (it is eight-sided) that is somewhat difficult to make (it takes a three-step process to arrive at its form).

A sculpture born of this book's approach resembling a disk, on the other hand, the mind might categorize as *simple* because it only has two sides. And since a disk-shaped form can be carved directly out of a block of stone without any intermediary steps, it is considered *easy to make*.

But if we take a closer look at this conception, we shall soon see how foolish it is. Because when this approach leads to a sculpture whose form resembles a disk, it didn't occur because the sculptor executed a one-step process but because they followed innumerable steps that led them towards this form. Starting from a rough block, they began relating aspect after aspect until a disk-shaped form appeared from the bottom up. I like to think of such forms like the forms that reveal themselves from the visualization of chaotic processes in mathematics. They, too, sometimes resemble forms that appear simple on the surface but are underlaid by a tremendous complexity.

So, if a disk-shaped sculpture arises from such a process, it really isn't to be understood as a two-sided sculpture that took one step to make but as a thousand-sided one that arose from thousands of interrelated steps. And *that* is its true complexity.

It goes without saying that bringing thousands of sides into a harmonious form cannot be achieved by following a schema. Balancing a thousand (or a million) interrelated surfaces into an overarching form cannot be done even by the best of minds since their relationships are, on top of being infinite in number, entangled in a non-linear and spontaneous fashion.

Our bodies, however, have no problem shaping this kind of complexity: the linear mind can only always do one thing. Or have you ever thought two thoughts at the same time? But our bodies can easily digest food, decode DNA, regulate the acidity in our stomach and do a million other things, all while reading this sentence. So why not allow this intelligence to extend outwards and also have it take care of the development of form?

Because as soon as the body is allowed to navigate the form, the true complexity of the sculpture begins to increase. The resulting sculpture might look simple on the outside, might be perceived to be comprised of only two surfaces, but it will develop an *inward complexity*. In fact, it might become so simple that, at some point, it will no longer be identifiable as a human-made object but appear as an artifact of nature itself.

For example, looking at some of Nirman's work from thirty years ago, I have no difficulty identifying them as typical stone sculptures. They, more or less, fit the image for "abstract stone sculptures inspired by plants." But to label his more recent work as *stone sculptures* doesn't seem to quite fit anymore. If you insist on me having to label them, I would perhaps hit closest by calling them *mountains*, *planets*, or simply: *an expression of empty space itself.*

I remember a woman who responded: "It's nothing!" when Nirman asked her to describe what she was seeing while looking at one of his sculptures. She immediately regretted her spontaneous utterance because characterizing a stone that was sculpted over months as "nothing" didn't quite sit right with her culturally programmed mind. But her comment was most wonderful. For once a sculpture truly resembles nothing, which is to say: once a sculpture has freed itself from every kind of image, it truly has become an artifact of nature itself.

So be prepared that if you work in light of this book's approach, some people might not even recognize your sculptures as such, not to speak of granting you their admiration. Once, for instance, a passer-by asked me whether I was enjoying my first day of working with stone. What she was looking at when she raised that question was the result of two months of work in my second year of continuous sculpting. This is the kind of feedback you can expect from the common person.

And the further in you go, the further away you'll move from society and its programming of what makes a good sculpture. Because to the common person, the most extraordinary things —mountains, planets, empty space— are not worthy of much consideration, whereas alien objects, like octahedrons, are.

More than once, people ran over some of our sculptures because they didn't see them. And if I had to run some statistics, I would guess that about one in every ten persons who walk by even glances at our work, about one in twenty stops for a moment, and about one in fifty takes the time to engage with us, or the sculptures.

However, when I sculpted the octahedron, these numbers shifted dramatically. Suddenly, people who would have walked over a sculpture I would have characterized as a sentient being manifested in stone, were interested and amazed by what I was doing. They applauded my technical skills —something I had hardly heard before— and wanted to acquire them —something I had also hardly heard before. But it makes sense, for who would give any attention to, or money for, mountains, planets, or empty space?

Since the outside tends to get more simple with increasing understanding, it might appear as if one is going backward in one's artistic development. But if we look at the oeuvre of artists like Hilma af Klint, Mondrian, Pollock, Miro, Kandinsky and many others, we might equally assess that they developed "backward" in terms of the apparent sophistication that was required to produce some of their later works. But when we consider their lifelong oeuvres, we can see how their later works encompass and transcend all they have done before, even if they appear more simple on the outside: their complexity has moved inwards.

Let's consider part of the artistic development of Kazimir Malevich in that regard: Because Malevich did not start out painting all-white canvasses, nor did he paint *Black Square* because he had grown too lazy to sit down and paint a still life. Rather, his search for the essential in painting led him to produce a painting that contained nothing but a black square.

Consequently, art critics began interpreting the significance of his "zero paintings"' and discussed whether they should be understood as the simplest or the most complex paintings ever made? After all, a uniform canvas can be said to contain *no* painting as much as it can be said to contain *every* painting. For if every painting were painted onto a single canvas, it would inevitably portray a black image. Or a white one. So what Malevich showed is that simplicity and complexity are two sides of the same coin. The white canvas is the most simple painting but also the most complex one: Zero (*Black Square)* the same as infinity (*White on White*).

However, Malevich didn't arrive at this conception through mental acrobatics, as I just did. Rather, he kept discarding whatever he thought to be inessential until he suddenly found himself in front of an empty canvas. So Malevich didn't conceptualize his black square but suddenly found himself *in* it. He arrived at it through *his* artistic process. In that way, *Black Square* wasn't an assault on the art world, nor did it mark the end of painting. No, it was a natural progression, yes, a logical consequence of *his* artistic process.

That is why, rather than letting my mind loose on such conceptual thinking, I try to stay with the stone and take one step at a time. Because if I state: "I am going to make the most simple sculptures," and begin exhibiting invisible sculptures into which everyone has to condense their own forms, or if I stagnate at exhibiting white canvasses that contain "all of painting," then I have missed the point totally. Because then, I have turned simplicity into a concept, and few things would be more obstructive for my development as an artist.

Chapter 7

The deeper he [the artist] looks, the more readily he can extend his view from the present to the past, the more deeply he is impressed by the one essential image of creation itself, as Genesis, rather than by the image of nature, the finished product. Then he permits himself the thought that the process of creation can today hardly be complete and he sees the act of world creating stretching from the past to the future. Genesis eternal!
—PAUL KLEE | *On Modern Art*, 45

Like a painter, who weaves together lines and colors; like a cook, who mixes tastes and textures; like a composer, who orchestrates sounds and rhythms; I, as a sculptor, compose elements of form. The possibilities in which I can do this are endless: I can create softness by having sides drop into the background, contrast by the use of different tools, drama by having form concentrate around a particular point. I can make different sides act as counterpoint to each other, make surfaces break or support each other, the top conjoin the bottom, the front mirror the back, etc. But the key to whether my sculpture will possess artistic radiancy does not lie in how I arranged these elements but in the sincerity of the underlying search that led to their expression. So the value of an artwork does not lie within its form but within the development that led to its production. Paul Klee writes:

> *Form is never to be considered as something settled as a result, as an end, but rather as genesis, as becoming, as essence. What is good is form as movement, as action, as active form. What is bad is form as immobility, as an end, as something suffered through and achieved. What is good is forming. What is bad is form. Form is the end, is death. Forming is movement, is action. Forming is life.*[35]

Once, a child pushed over a sculpture I had been working on for months. But when I found the broken pieces the next morning, I realized I was hardly affected. I immediately grasped that its value didn't lie within the form, but within the journey that led to its expression. And no one could have ever taken that away from me, not to speak about breaking in.

This, however, does not mean that I wouldn't have done everything to prevent the sculpture from breaking. Another time, one of my sculptures started tumbling on the workbench, and without a moment of hesitation, I jumped over and placed my foot under the impact zone. I yelled in pain when the sculpture landed on my foot, but I had no doubt that sacrificing a black foot was worth saving it from more serious damage.

Thus, if my sculpture ends up in an art collection, that's beautiful. If it is being pushed over and broken into pieces, that's also beautiful. Their true value remains the same. "In production it is the way that is important;" Paul Klee summons, "development counts for more than does completion."[36]

∞

On this path of development, there are many days on which the stone doesn't speak. Days on which, no matter what I do, how much material I remove, or how many times I circle the stone, the sculpture won't develop. Days on which the stone is vast asleep, not speaking to me, not exciting me, not showing me the next step I must take.

Whenever one of these days arrives, I usually begin by deploying an arsenal of resurrection strategies to reinvoke my interest: I change the sculpture's resting side, the height of the workbench, the distance from which I circle the stone; I draw on the stone, wash it, sculpt at different times of the day, try out other tools or some different way of working.

When none of these work, I resort to asking myself: "If I were to exhibit the sculpture tonight, what would I still want to change about it?" And if that doesn't do it, there is always the: "If I died tonight, would I want *this* to be my legacy?" that I can deploy. Desperate, I know. But it often works.

Once I tired all such efforts, I usually attend to household work: Maybe the workbench needs some fixing, or the tools need some sharpening? And once I exhausted these also, there is always the work of other artists I can turn toward:

It takes time and courage to discover what artists, or what works of art, truly move me. At first, I had some external authority decide for me what art I like. But I soon realized that proclaiming that I like a certain artist because they are in vogue has little value for keeping me afloat once I hit the wall: Only what *truly* moves me, regardless of its societal perception, can act as food for my inner pigeon.

By works that "move me," I don't mean works that can astound but refer to a more mysterious feeling whose quality I struggle to explain even to myself. Works that evoke such a response can be simple; they do not need to be of some Renaissance master or enjoy a high conventional standing. In fact, many works of textbook significance tend to intimidate me. They make me feel inferior and, in doing so, do not kindle my inner pigeon. Nirman's sculptures, my brothers juggling, or some of Alberto Giacometti's sketches, on the other hand, I never perceive as threatening in this way: If anything, I perceive them as a safe space, as an open ground, as an invitation to come in and start exploring the material myself.

So what I am looking for are works that I can come in resonance with, works that can draw me in. Whatever can evoke this response comes from a similar orientation of mind, from similar mental software.

But even if the works of other artists do not reinvoke my interest, I do not worry still. Restful and quiet periods are also essential because they allow something to ripe within.

Whenever I try to overcome these restful periods by force, such as by drinking two cups of coffee or by messing around the stone by doing things I was not instructed with, I might remove a lot of material but don't actually contribute towards the becoming of the form. I am engaged in more activity but committing less action.

The same applies to finding solutions to problems I am stuck with. I experience days, sometimes months, in which I don't see how to progress. But here, too, I am learning to relax and wait for the sculpture to reveal itself. Goethe writes about this in relation to his work:

> *If some phenomenon appears in my research, and I can find no source for it, I let it stand as a problem. This approach has proven quite advantageous over the years. When I found I could not solve the riddle of the origin and context of some*

problem, I had to let it lie for a long time; but at some moment,
years later, enlightenment came in the most wonderful way.[37]

If I grew impatient and forced myself onto the stone, I might have ground away the entire stone before a solution could have found me: "Nothing can be rushed." Paul Klee writes, "It must grow, it should grow of itself, and if the time ever comes for that work - then so much the better!"[38]

Often, it is only once I give up that I see what I must do. Only once I surrender totally and admit that I truly do not know how to proceed, the stone shows me the next step I must take. Usually, I then realize that I was looking in the wrong place or overlooking the obvious in some other way. But only when I stopped searching could I discover where *gold is to be found*.

So, whenever I am stuck, I let the problem rest, perhaps even take the sculpture home or continue with some other work. Months later, when I've all but forgotten about it, enlightenment might come in the most wonderful way.

This cannot be cheated or be turned into a method, however. If I put my sculpture back inside or take it home because I hope that doing so will show me the next step I must take, I will be disappointed. Only when I accept that I truly do not know how to proceed, the next step might reveal itself. I do not know why this has to be so, but it never ceases to amaze me that it *always* works like that.

Usually, I work on several sculptures at the same time as well as write something. And whenever I am stuck with one, I tarzan to another and continue from there. There is always a loose end somewhere, and another loose end will reveal itself once I attended to that. This, of course, does not have to be confined to the workbench but can also be a language course I never started, a twitched muscle I haven't stretched out, or a bike that awaits repair… But as long as I keep following whatever calls for my attention, the thread will continue to show me how to proceed. And if I am lucky, it will lead me back to my sculpture and reveal the next step I must take.

∞

Often, for a very long time, little seems to develop. No matter what I do or how much material I remove, the stone doesn't seem to progress, doesn't seem to organize itself, doesn't seem to turn into a sculpture.

But sculptures, like flowers, often reveal themselves spontaneously and abruptly. I remember a stone that barely changed for months until, in a single session, I found the sculpture I had been looking for. So whenever things do not immediately fall into place, I appreciate how slowly nature goes about doing its thing and see it as reaffirming when my sculpture develops at the same speed as a plant. "Nature doesn't hurry, yet everything is accomplished," Lao Tzu is often quoted.

Most people assume that, with time, I would get faster in making sculptures because they believe that the speed with which I can make a sculpture is a function of how fast I can remove access material. But that is, of course, nonsense. If anything, it is the other way around: The more delicate and fine-tuned my perceptions become, the more nuances I perceive, so the more I have to attend to. That is why, with each sculpture I make, I tend to get slower in progressing inwards, not faster. *The further in you go, the bigger it gets.*

But just because I sometimes spend months refining subtle aspects shall not mean that a sculpture must take a long time to finish. The mind likes to believe that something meaningful must have taken a long time or sprung out of a struggling process. But those are just ideas, not actualities: I've made a sculpture in a single session that lacks nothing compared to sculptures I have worked on for over half a year.

Whenever I finish a sculpture, there often sets in an emptiness, a kind of postpartum depression. It feels as if something has left me, perhaps even died off. The idea of making another one often dreads me and, at no time, was I able to transfer my enthusiasm from one sculpture to the next. Each sculpture, I learned, demands for its own process, and I am asked to start from zero each time again.

When I am back in front of a rough stone, I often feel as if I have forgotten everything in the meantime, and I wonder how I was ever able to make a sculpture? This is why I keep my previous work around me because, in such moments, they provide me with the necessary trust that, in some way or another, I must have done it before.

At the same time, however, I try to carry as little from one sculpture into the next, for the more independent they are, the more powerful they tend to become. That is why sculpting, or writing a book or whatever, never gets any easier, for the starting condition should always be the same, namely that of not knowing.

In fact, it is common that one's first sculpture will turn out fantastic because one is least in the way of it becoming what it wants to be. Once somebody has made a sculpture, they already have something to compare it against, which bears the temptation that they will introduce something into the work that has nothing to do with it.

All understanding is integrated into one's persona, so there is no reason to be explicit about any of it. I can also not recite a single passage from a book I read five years ago, but its content is still somehow present within me. It was integrated into my persona and has since informed, and put into perspective, everything I did thereafter. So everything I know is mirrored in *all* I do, and it shines strongest when synthesized into a new form of expression.

This shall not mean that I cannot express the same form a second or a twentieth time, however. If I explore the same form twenty times attentively, I can develop no less than if I explored twenty different forms in the meantime. Many great sculptors —think Brancusi, Giacometti, or some of the Cycladic masters— explored the same form over and over. Sometimes for a lifetime, they kept returning to the same form, approximating the essence behind it, interpreting it in varying ways. I conceive of them not as copies but as variations, like a musician interpreting the same composition over and over: This time a little faster; this time with more focus on the highs; this time with more pedal... The underlying piece remains the same, but the interpretation, as well as the experience thereof, varies each time.

Developing a sense of form is much like developing a sense of rhythm. It is nothing that can be learned by studying a textbook but something that has to be done by feel. And the harder one tries to understand it with the mind, the further away one will get from knowing it.

Sometimes, when people who claim to have no sense of rhythm are intoxicated or extremely tired, their bodies start to sync with the rhythm all of their own. But as soon as one makes them notice that they are now moving with the rhythm, they often fall back out of it because they are trying to catch their body's movement with their minds. But when mind is not, the fusion between the music and their bodies happens naturally. And the same is true for understanding form.

An understanding of form is also nothing that exists for itself. It is nothing that can be isolated from the material or can be distilled into words. A deep understanding of form might leave footprints —such as the degree to which a form rests within itself, the number of connections that can be drawn from one point to any other point, or the amount of tension present within a curve — but for none of these aspects a theory could be formulated.

Nicolaides writes about coming to an understanding of anatomy in life drawing:

> *Developing the consciousness of the form is a slow, sensitive process. It is not something that can be comprehended instantly, no matter how intelligent you are. The parts of the figure are welded together in a perfectly logical and functional manner. No one can teach you their truth, but by a certain manner of approach you can bit by bit come to know these forms and their relationship to one another. No diagrams, no explanations, will suffice, because the form speaks to you only as it does things.[39]*

No diagrams, no explanations, will suffice, because the form speaks to you only as it does things. —Exactly! So, as opposed to knowing, understanding is impossible to write about because it has no existence of its own. About all one can do is characterize its fragrance:

One characteristic of a deep understanding is a certain spaciousness that makes itself known in the work. A spaciousness that remembers of the wild, or of the void even. It is this sense that led me to characterize Nirman's sculptures as mountains or planets: They contain a vastness that makes them feel many times larger than their physical reality. I sense a similar kind of vastness in Stephen Buhner's writings. I can sense the territory, both explored and unexplored, that lies beneath the surface of each line. Alberto Giacometti's sketches also evoke that sense: Even though they are often small —some are no larger than an envelope— there is still a depth and an immensity to them.[40]

This spaciousness, which I have also perceived in Fazil Say playing the piano or in my brother's juggling, results from a deep understanding of the matter at hand. Because what I *cannot* see when my brother juggles a particular 6-ball pattern, for instance, are the hundreds of other patterns he also knows to juggle. But I can feel them *co-present* in that particular 6-ball pattern. And that is what gives it this immensity. Similarly, when I listen to Fazil Say playing his spiel on the *Turkish March*, I cannot hear the hundreds of other pieces he knows to play, but I can hear them *implied* in his improvisation.

To be sure, if somebody spent a considerable time learning the "Fazil Say version of the *Turkish March*" or this particular 6-ball pattern by mechanically moving their hands in the same sequence, the result would not possess this fragrance I am trying to get at here. The difference is that my brother can, at any time, deconstruct the pattern, show me how it builds on previous patterns, how it relates to the same pattern with four balls, how to do it "reverse," "asynchronous," "Mills Mess" or with "penguin" catches and so forth. The person who mechanically learned the pattern wouldn't be able to do that. And that difference will be reflected in the feel of the juggling. Both will be juggling the same pattern, but one will have a richness, an immensity, that the other one does not. The same goes for Fazil Say's interpretations, Giacometti's sketches, Nirman's sculptures.

∞

Sometimes, when working on a new sculpture, it feels as if I have to revisit some of my previous sculptures before I am allowed to discover a new form. Like a fetus, which also appears to go through all of evolution before it turns into the human form, I often meet elements of previous sculptures on my journey toward a new form. A form that not only encapsulates all I made before but transcends it in a new direction.

When I shared this conception with Nirman, he replied that, although he liked it, he prefers it upside down: For him, it is not about discovering a form that *transcends* all the others but about moving backward through his previous work towards the source from which all springs.

Accordingly, with time I began to sense that things, once again, started to turn on their head. In more concrete terms, I began to suspect that maybe it was only when I *broke* the thread that I was actually being creative, not when I was following one. That is because it was only in such moments that I was no longer in a fixed schema, namely that of following a thread, but truly spontaneous and in the moment.

Or else, I began to understand that standing back isn't so much a technique to create sculptures distinguished by certain qualities like fluidity of form but a technique that *induces* a state of consciousness out of which one automatically creates forms distinguished by such qualities. In that way, the technique of standing back isn't so much a sculptural technique as it is a kind of meditation, *out of which* these qualities automatically arise. So with time, I no longer continuously roped the sculpture in as previously described because I began to understand that it is about the *whirling*, not the distance from which it is done.

So you can take any notion inherent to this book and perform a kickflip on it, just like I performed a kickflip on any conventional notion about sculpture to arrive at this elevated level of sculptural understanding. This, of course, would also have to apply to this very notion of there being something like octaves of sculptural understanding, so I let your mind do whatever gymnastics it has to so that both premises are met.

However, I could only begin to sense this after I had learned to find, feel and follow a thread in sculpture, as well as to trust the technique of standing back. Had I tried to leapfrog into this kind of working where there may be no thread any longer or ignored the technique of standing back as I described it, I would have been like someone trying to juggle seven balls but who hasn't learned to juggle three.

Ultimately, all divisions into "higher" and "lower" sculptural understanding are artificial because, as Goethe said:

> *In the human spirit, as in the universe, nothing is higher or lower; everything has equal rights to a common center which manifests its hidden existence precisely through this harmonic relationship between every part and itself.*[41]

The lower is always a limited conception of the whole, and the higher is a less limited conception of the whole. That is why the higher sculptural understanding can always be found nested inside the lower. And as long as one keeps taking one step at a time, the door to a higher understanding will open once the necessary understanding has been acquired.

For example, in *Chapter 2* of this section, I wrote that I always attend to the quality first, the form second, and the surface third. But when I wrote this, I didn't yet understand why. This only became clear to me much later: The stone's surface corresponds to the mind. That is why most people find it easiest to engage with the stone's color, the contrast introduced through the use of different tools, the thoroughness with which a surface was polished, etc.

But below the surface lies the dimension of form which corresponds to the feeling sense. The form cannot be understood intellectually, but it has to be felt.

And underlying the form lies the dimension of Being, which makes itself known as a fragrance that lies even beyond the feeling sense.

When I wrote *Chapter 2*, I had already sensed that quality is more powerful than form, form more powerful than surface, but I didn't yet understand why. This I only understood much later. But this understanding can already be found *nested* inside my earlier understanding. It just wasn't yet crystallized. Later, it became clear to me that this book is about my journey from thinking (surface) to feeling (form) to Being (quality). From head to heart to belly. And this enterprise is reflected in the prioritization I give to the respective dimensions in stone.

As an example of how such a deepening of understanding can show itself in the sculpture, I remember one stone that contained a flat surface with another flat surface integrated into it, like a glass sitting in a frame. Some years later, I returned to the same impulse in another sculpture when, suddenly, the thread led me to make the window tilt inwards, thereby creating an extra dimension within the same form. This extra dimension which revealed itself was already nested in the sculpture I had made before, but it was only expressed in the later one.

When Nirman, who likes to spend more than a year with a single composition, engages with my sculptures, I am often astounded by the nuances he perceives: Subtle high- and low points, unexpressed lines, movements I barely notice, a lack of tension in a curve, all is immediately obvious to him. But all these are already inside my sculptures; I just cannot perceive or comprehend them yet.

Again, this is why I did not try to write about Nirman's understanding of sculpture because the limits of my understanding are the limits of my world. I have to remain with what I can comprehend, with what I can understand myself. But the feeling never left me that Nirman's understanding of sculpture is something I can only sense for, much like I can only sense the ocean's depth when snorkeling around its surface.

Looking across the work I have already done, I can see how a theme touched upon in one sculpture later turned out to be the main theme in another, how certain patterns re-occurred, were re-interpreted or resolved in different ways. Jean Arp characterized the development of his sculptural forms similarly:

> *A small fragment of one of my plastic works presenting a curve or a contrast that moves me, is often the germ of a new work. I intensify the curve or the contrast, and this determines new forms. Among the new forms two grow with special intensity... One work often requires months, years. I work until enough of my life has flowed into its body. Each of these bodies has a spiritual content, but only on completion of the work do I interpret this content and give it a name.*[42]

All this needs not to unfold linearly, however. In sculpture, time can well flow reverse: A stone I sculpted in 2023 can be the predecessor of a stone I sculpted three years before. That's why I learned to treat each of my sculptures equally, for I might only much later understand their role in my lifelong oeuvre.[43]

And overarching these impressions is the ever-present sense that all my works are connected, that each work is connected to, and influenced by, all others that precede and follow it. "I think the idea of a 'finished' picture is a fiction." Barnett Newman writes, "I think a man spends his whole lifetime painting one picture or working on one piece of sculpture."[44] Whether you view *all* art as a single work depends on your metaphysics, but my stone appeared strong when I asked it whether all of art is one.

Exercises

God sells all things at the price of labour.
—attributed to LEONARDO DA VINCI

The following exercises stand in the same relation to the rest of this book as meditation practices stand to Zen: As long as one follows a meditation practice, one is still putting in an effort and, in doing so, remains bound to the very thing one seeks to transcend. To Zen, which seeks to cut through all of mind directly, meditational efforts can thus be seen as obstructive, for only once one lets go of all effort, Zen maintains, can one begin to see clearly. But meditation practices are promoted even in Zen because they can bring one to a state of rest from where the jump into the unknown — into Zen— can happen.

So, do not clinch to any of the proposed exercises; perhaps not even do them. But if you do decide to follow them, regard them as instruments that can help you find ground from where to take the jump.

Exercise 1: Finishing a Sculpture

As an exercise to appreciate that it is all about the process and not the end result, continue working on a stone until nothing remains, until it is truly finished. Because when you keep exploring the form until nothing but chips and dust remains, you leave your mind nothing but chips and dust to cling onto. And since there is no final sculpture to look forward to, you are inclined to focus on each step of the way rather than some end result.

However, do not begin turning all stones into dust or intentionally destroying all your sculptures upon completion. Because then you would be following just another concept and evading being confronted with the unknown, which, in that case, would be the act of finishing a sculpture.

Exercise 2: Sculpting Basic Forms

To exercise your technique and senses, carve a basic form such as a sphere, a cube, or a triangle out of a block of stone. Approximate the ideal behind these forms without the help of a ruler, geometry triangle, marking pen, pointing machine or whatever else. Rely on your senses alone and continue working as long as you maintain interest. Doing any of these can keep you busy for a lifetime because no matter how long you have already worked towards such a form, some imperfection will always remain.

Doing these can school your eyes and serve as a reminder that all sculptural understanding can be contained even within the most basic forms. They can also have you experience the difference between a form *searched* within the whole versus a form *defined* from the outside:

One way to characterize this difference is that in the former, you are not really taking away from the stone but roping it in. Think of a sphere discovered in this way like a neutron star that has condensed its mass inwardly rather than lost it to its environment. This, of course, is a metaphor, so you probably will not feel that you are holding a collapsed core of a supergiant star in your hands once you discover a sphere within a stone. But still, see and feel for yourself whether there is a difference between a sphere searched for and a sphere defined by a stonemason's approach. And if there is, what that difference is?

Exercise 3: Sculpting Pebble Stones

Another way to further your sculptural understanding is to make miniature sculptures out of pebble stones. So find a rounded pebble, no matter the type, color, or size, and continue the work the water has already started. Because if you watch yourself doing these Bonsai-sculptures, you will find that you automatically do many things as proposed throughout this book:

A coin-sized pebble in your hand will appear roughly the same size as a chicken-sized stone from the opposite end of a parking area, thereby mimicking the desired effect of standing back. Due to its small size, you will naturally be inclined to focus on expressing its overall form instead of attending to minor aspects, such as a tiny crack here or there. While filing them, you will also continually turn and move the pebble in your hand and, in doing so, mimic the effect of walking around. Instinctively, you will also develop all sides at the same speed, and you won't hold back from grinding away half of the stone or from trying anything bold. For in case of failure, you simply pick up another pebble and start again.

This exercise can make you aware that it is *only because a stone is large* that the mind suddenly insists that one needs to have an idea, that the process needs to be structured, the outlines marked, or whatever unnatural behavior it might be identified with. They are artificial constructions of the mind that tend to grow proportionally with the size of the stone, not attributes that nature interlinked with working with stone.

To this day, I maintain that some of my best works are no bigger than a few centimeters in diameter. And indeed, some pebbles I made are miles ahead in terms of their development when compared to some of my larger works, for my mind had less of a chance to coat them with its ideas of what makes a good sculpture.

And if I had to formulate one goal I maintain, it would be that one day, I will be able to treat a large stone no different from how water treats a pebble.

Exercise 4: Practicing Synesthesia

Every block of stone, just like every person, has a core, an essence. This essence is not a thing, not a form and nothing that can be grasped, but something that can only be sensed. It's like the end of a rainbow: Once you try to catch it, it won't be there anymore. But if you just appreciate its existence without trying to claim it, its reality is clear and unambiguous.

To practice your ability to sense the essence inherent to things, translate an artwork from one medium into another. Since when you translate a work of art —or any object or idea— you have to carry over its defining characteristic, its essence. You already do this when you dance differently to different music or when you use different mouth noises to describe two paintings. Because what is going on in the background is that you are extracting the essence of whatever you are perceiving and giving it a new form of expression.

Ultimately, all forms of expression are a form of this synesthetic process, but by making it intentional and by developing it in new directions —such as by painting a song or by putting an object into a melody— you can deepen your ability to sense the essence inside things.

Ludwig Wittgenstein once said: "Remember the impression one gets from good architecture, that it expresses a thought. It makes one want to respond with a gesture."[45] Like so many of his, this statement is as profound as it is beautiful. Because what Wittgenstein is saying is that a good building expresses a thought in three-dimensional space, thereby implying that a thought has a form that can be realized in the physical. The same also goes the other way around, of course: Every physical structure can be represented as a thought. But Wittgenstein takes it further. Not only does he include the thought, the building, but also his body. He writes: *It makes one want to respond with a gesture.* A thought becomes a building; becomes a gesture. The circle is completed.

I, for example, sometimes perceive my writing to be overlaid with an architectural gestalt that occurs in some kind of fourth-dimensional plane. Consequently, I can *see* what my writing looks like. I can see whether the writing is skewed, bumped, holed, or whatever, and I can then adjust it using text, just like I can adjust the form of a stone using hammer and chisel. I never learned to do this, but it has always been there.

That is why I am so sensitive about other people editing my writing. Because when somebody edits my text without being aware of its architectural gestalt, they might unintentionally clear out some of its carrying pillars. They might make the language more correct according to a certain standard, but something more essential might be lost.

So, if you perceive your sculpture as a piece of music or a mathematical equation, be cautious about others putting it on a base or even putting it up in a particular place. Such actions have the potential to disrupt this invisible gestalt. But it *is* this gestalt that makes your sculpture art. Remember, though: It is nothing that can be pointed towards, nothing that can be photographed, but something that can only be felt. So practice sensing it.

Exercise 5: Drawing

Drawing as much as possible is probably the greatest favor you can yourself for your development as . Some of its benefits are obvious —it develops your understanding of form, line, perspective, etc.— and some are subtle —it loosens you up, clears out accumulated rubbish, or helps you understand how your arm operates in space.

As indicated in the *Overture*, the art of sculpture is sometimes framed as being more difficult than drawing because it operates in three dimensions.[46] I, however, found that a form in sculpture is somewhat easier to comprehend than the same form appearing on a piece of paper. This is because a form in three-dimensional space is more intuitively accessible than the same form translated into the two-dimensionality of a canvas. In my experience, drawing is, therefore, not the infantile child of sculpture but, if anything, its mother.

Not only has drawing, as an artform, been explored to a much greater extent, but it is also more direct and confronting. I, however, won't write much about it, partly because there is nothing I could add to Kimon Nicolaides' timeless masterpiece *The Natural Way to Draw*, a book I cannot recommend studying enough, but mainly because I can't: Drawing has always escaped my attempts of linguistic characterization. But it is precisely because it is so enigmatic that I cannot practice it enough.

One exercise I would like to share is to take a piece of paper and scribble down whatever you see when walking around your sculpture. Don't look at the paper while walking around, but simply have your arm move in accordance with what you are perceiving. Be exact in this exercise but not in the conventional way: What you should follow exactly is not the appearance of the stone but the feeling it evokes. The resulting scribbles do not need to resemble the appearance of the stone, but they can give you a sense for whether a stone is whirling or restful, dominated by the straight or the round, the top or the bottom.

Part III
Inhabiting Stone

Chapter 1

To believe your own thought, to believe that what is true for you in your private heart is true for all men, —that is genius.
—RALPH WALDO EMERSON | The Complete Essays and Other Writings, 145

If you want to get to know me, you can either meet me in person, see one of my sculptures, or read this book. They are (an expression of) the same thing.

Because at the time of this writing, there is nothing I know, nothing I would like to say or share that I haven't somehow worked into this book. There is no thought, no feeling, no experience that I didn't allow to reflect itself within these lines. In writing this book, I didn't hide or omit, nor did I keep any aces up my sleeves. No, this book contains *all* of myself. It is total and coming from my center. So . . . this is it! This is all I know. This is where I am at.

The fact that this book is a linguistic doppelgänger of who I am is what makes it so vulnerable. But it is also what gives it its power. For it is not the amount of knowledge, skill, or experience that is decisive for whether a book possesses artistic value, but whether the author has had the courage to be authentic to where they was at in the moment of its production.

The mind is generally reluctant to do that. It fears that, if it shows itself in its entirety, it would expose itself and be left with nothing to work with. It thus prefers to hold back and postpone. It prefers to keep the aces up its sleeves. But unsurprisingly, draining itself totally is precisely what it must do for an artwork to come alive. And it is also what it must do so that the space for another work is created to find its way into the artist.

It took me a while to understand that the power inherent to Nirman's sculptures stems from his quest to be authentic to where he is at. Because when Nirman sculpts, he doesn't introduce anything into his sculptures he does not understand, nor does he recycle anything he came to understand in the past. Instead, he continuously seeks to substantiate his current understanding in the present.

Looking back, he once said that it took him decades to move from doing sculptures defined by straight lines to making fully rounded ones. Not because he did not have the technical skills to make fully rounded sculptures but because he felt that he had not understood the significance, the meaning, inherent to round forms until at a later stage of his life. And because he didn't fully understand them, they didn't appear in his sculptures.

In early 2022, his frontier was to have form flow fluidly without it being dependent upon a particular point. This might sound like a triviality, but had you met him at the time of this writing, you would have seen the significance of this statement reflected in his sculpture. And had you met him in person, you would have seen the significance of this statement reflected in his persona.

So when Nirman sculpts, he doesn't seek to demonstrate his ability, knowledge of form, or whatever else, but he aims to be true to his current understanding. His sculptures do not say: "Look what I can do!" but rather speak: "Look, here is where I am at."

To give an example of what is meant here, consider Anne Frank's *Diary of a Young Girl*: What makes this book a worthwhile read (and a work of art) is not the story, her insights into the human condition, the unfolding events of her time or any other aspects that are often proposed as reasons for the book's success. For if you want to know about any of these, other sources will provide you with a much more thorough overview. No, what makes the book powerful, what makes it art, is that Anne Frank, as a thirteen-year-old girl, simply wrote down where she was at. In her writing, she did not try to reach into the future to make herself seem more developed than she was, nor did she reach into the past by recycling aspects she had already understood. Instead, she simply wrote down where she was at each time she opened her diary, regardless of whether it contradicted what she had written a few days before. And by doing that continuously, she produced a work with a depth and a flavor that much literature lacks.[1]

That is why *Das Glasperlenspiel* by Hermann Hesse is not a *better* book than Anne Frank's diary. Both are true. It just so happened that Anne Frank was true to where she was at as a thirteen-year-old girl hiding away from the Nazis, and Hermann Hesse was true to where *he* was at after a lifelong search for resolving his internal conflict of being part of society and enduring its profanity versus secluding himself into the spiritual with its piety.

So whether an artwork is "authentic," "true," or "alive" are different ways of saying the same thing. Because when an artwork reflects where you are at, reflects your understanding, it will be all of these things. It will be authentic, true and alive. Whether it is pigeons on the concrete floor or *The School of Athens* in the Apostolic Palace does not matter then.

With every sculpture I work with, there usually comes a point at which I can sense that I have reached the limits of my understanding, the limits of what I can do. I might sense that the sculpture is not yet fully resolved, but I know I do not yet possess the necessary understanding to resolve it further.

The same is true for this book. At the time of its publication, I could *feel* there were still plenty of aspects I overlooked, unconscious baggage that had introduced itself into the writing, words that I actually do not inhabit, etc. But that is irrelevant, for what I *do* know is that I wrote this book to the best of my abilities. I do know that, at the moment of its publication, I couldn't have done any better; my understanding didn't allow for more. Later in my life, I might discover some of these aspects, might develop the understanding to clear some of that unconscious baggage, might detect some of the spelling errors that remained unnoticed. But the point is that doing so would not increase the *artistic value* of this book. Because what counts for a book's *artistic value* is not whether it is free of unconscious baggage but whether it reflects where the author was at the moment of its production.

And so with my sculptures: The forms that carry my later sculptures might be distinguished by greater interdependence, clarity and order. But they are not necessarily more artistic. So it is not that my later works are automatically charged with more artistic power than my earlier works just because I deepened my understanding of form.

Art, we can thus maintain, knows no hierarchy, no better or worse. It is a participatory process in which all draw from the same source. And whatever comes from this source is infused with a certain vibration, with a certain radiance: it is infused with life. "In all things living there is a rhythm," I once heard in a song, "and all things living carry out its tune."

And this source? —is right inside us; it is our center! That is why, to reveal a work of art, we must put ourselves at the center and have it contain all of ourselves. It must reflect where *we* are at, no matter where that is.

That's why I work uncompromisingly, trust myself and only do what I want to do. That's why I treat every sculpture as if it were my last one and sculpt toward my ideals, towards divine beauty, and do not waste any time with anything that is not truly mine.

Few artists do that. Instead, they waste their time with trivialities, with aberrations they were once convinced are of importance. They waste their time with conceptual bullshit or with cynical work. They do so because they believe they are not yet good enough, don't yet know enough. Or they do so because they believe that what they think or feel has no value unless it is embedded within the voice of some authority. Or they do so because they fear they could make a fool of themselves, could be discredited, be labeled idealistic, naïve, or preposterous. Or they do so because they are afraid of the intimacy such works demand, the sacrifices that must be made. So they go on postponing: They read another book, they do another course, they wait, they hold back.

"... but God will not have his work made manifest by cowards," Emerson cuts in.

So here I say it: I am perfect as I am; I have intelligence, yes, genius inside me. There is something only I can do, something I cannot learn from anyone because I am the only one who can do it. "That which each can do best," Emerson said, "none but his maker can teach him."[2] And what is more, whatever this might be is not just of tremendous value for myself but also for the world. There is a reason I exist. There is something I ought to bring into this world. And if I don't allow it to express itself, it will eat me up from the inside. Jesus said: "If you bring forth what is within you, what you bring forth will save you. If you do not bring forth what is within you, what you do not bring forth will destroy you."[3]

So by exploring myself by expressing myself, not only will I be saving myself, but perhaps also the world. In Joseph Campbell's words:

> *People have the notion of saving the world by shifting things around, changing the rules, and who's on top, and so forth. No, no! Any world is a valid world if it's alive. The thing to do is to bring life to it, and the only way to do that is to find in your own case where the life is and become alive yourself.*[4]

"I don't know what to do," the mind immediately responds to such a proposition. But that is precisely the point!— I am not supposed to know: Once I know, I have had it! It's only when I don't know that I am living up to this quest.

That is why, instead of spending much time trying to figure out what I ought to do, I take one step at a time and see where it takes me. Later, I can look back and conclude that writing this book or sculpting that stone was my life's purpose. But while I was doing it, I was, guided by the dim light of the flashlight on my head, stumbling from one word to the next.

So, when I get the urge to do something bold, I go for it; the universe might depend on it. Or if I have an itch to try something, I do it. And I do so straight away. A moment later, the opportunity might be lost. Constantin Brancusi told Isamu Noguchi the same when he assisted him in his studio in Paris: "Never do anything as preparation for something later for you will never do anything better than what you do now."[5]

People constantly advise me to do things differently. They advise me to use machine tools, engrave patterns, make smaller or bigger sculptures, use different materials, etc. But after some consideration, I have come to conclude that all, and I mean *all*, advice when it comes to art are to be viewed as traps. I only trust that which I am convinced of and nothing else. I do what I want to do, what I like, what I believe, and I am willing to sacrifice to this end, no matter whether this means that my sculptures won't be liked, won't be recognized, or won't be exhibited.

In fact, one way to define artists is to characterize them as a group of people who don't make their work reliant on feedback. Because in contrast to producers, who are constantly engaged in a dialogue with the outside, artists must put themselves at the center and do what feels right to them, regardless of what anybody, including themselves, thinks about their works. That's why making art will always remain a courageous and insecure act because artists have to rely on *their* senses to assess whether the work is right.

So, if everyone says a sculpture is finished, but I still want to keep working on it —I do. If everyone says a sculpture is not yet finished, but I don't want to continue working on it —I don't. And most importantly, I aim to be honest with myself: I don't say a sculpture is finished just because I am afraid of confronting a certain issue, and I don't continue working on a sculpture just because I am afraid of finishing it. And even if a sculpture breaks into pieces in such a pursuit, the result is still less damaging than an unfinished sculpture in which I didn't follow through.

Also, the moment my motivations are led by external factors, such as marketability or pleasing someone else's expectations, I get out of touch with my creativity. Since when I tweak and twist my art toward the forces that dictate the marketplace, I inevitably tweak and twist myself toward these forces. The inner pigeon? Gone.

It is always tempting to make something that sells, something that gets complimented, something that gets acknowledged by some gatekeeping authority. But the more I trust myself and my process, the more my art comes to radiate this confidence. And *thereby* my art becomes valuable. And eventually, others might come to see that too. My audience might remain small —John Krenov once remarked that the quality of an artist's work stands in an inverse relationship to the size of the audience it attracts— but who cares?[6] Any day I prefer having a drug addict at the studio who truly *sees* my work over a crowd of self-proclaimed art enthusiasts who do not really look. So economic success can come as a side effect, but it cannot be the driving motivation.[7]

Also, the deeper my understanding of sculpture becomes, the larger the carrot society is willing to offer for me not to continue listening to stone tends to get.

Accordingly, a stranger once asked me how much I would sell him my sculpture for. I responded that the sculpture was not for sale, whereupon he countered:

"I can see that. That's why I want it!"

That is why I stay authentic and do not allow myself to become a producer who can be commissioned for a certain kind of work. Yes, you could ask me to make a gravestone, but you could not ask me for a specific design or form. You will have to trust that a fitting form for the deceased person will arise on its own. Or if you asked me to make a sphere, I would have to answer that I don't know how to make a sphere, even if I just made one. "There are things some of us simply cannot do, even if our life depends upon it," the cabinetmaker John Krenov writes, "Give me a piece of clay, put a pistol to my head, and say, 'Make a rabbit!' and I'll have to say, 'Shoot and be damned!'"[8]

You see, when I sculpt, I don't know what the result will be. Because as soon as I did, I would no longer be creating but executing. I would no longer be searching but defining. I would no longer be listening but speaking. I would no longer be receptive but aggressive.

But not only can the marketplace usurp the process of searching for the authentic in stone. Most of all, it can be the voice in our heads. Thoughts like "I could become an established sculptor!" might arise after you have carved a few sculptures. They certainly did in mine. But turning an artform into a profession is a bucket with a million snakes inside. Because when one has commissions to fulfill, one is constantly tempted to take the familiar way out. So those who succumb to speeding up in this way are actually slowing down. Since when one rushes towards producing a sculpture one hasn't substantiated, nothing internal is developed. And nothing that is not a result of an internal development can take on artistic value. Soon then, one will have become a producer who makes decorative pieces, not art.

So not only can the quest to turn sculpture into a profession bring one out of touch with one's creativity due to the forces that dictate the marketplace, but also because the mind can slip in and hijack the creative process. The mind is perfectly prepared to have us turn our journey of finding form in stone into our profession just to come back into control.

Since it knows that it will have a bigger role to play once we *have to* make money from making sculptures.

One could, in fact, declare my decision to write this book as such a trap I had fallen into. After all, my mind must have known that it could use this book to get back into control; it must have known that it could have me research technique, art history, the mechanics of the creative process and so forth: the very things that would illuminate the unknown I was thrown into. If true, then my mind did so by clothing itself in the language of the esoteric —such as by proposing that I felt an *urge* to write this book— and thereby hid itself amidst my psyche like an octopus that sits unseen at the center of a rock.

The mind does not shy to go any length to get back into the driver's seat. From the viewpoint of the mind, becoming a professional sculptor, or writing a book that requires years of work, is nothing in terms of courage needed when compared to surrendering into not knowing what the fuck is going on.

Another data point that adds evidence that this book was, at least in part, coopted by my mind occurred when I read somewhere that only those write books that seek to impose their knowledge on other people. Reading this made me, at least in part, feel exposed. Because those who are truly free don't write books, and even less so about how to make a sculpture come "alive." Maybe you can also feel why this hit a nerve, even if you cannot pinpoint where this becomes evident? One clue might be that this book possesses a slight undertone in which I am trying to convince the reader of something. But as long as someone is trying to convince, we intuitively understand that this person hasn't sufficiently realized what they are trying to convince the reader of themselves. It is just like we know that those who write at the beginning of their books that they were not concerned with anything outside the words that make up its text, were not free of external motivations at all. The very mentioning proves it. It's very subtle, but we all know that it is so.

However, instead of not writing a book at all, my effort of being open about these issues, by working *through* them in these lines, is the way of transcending them. And paradoxically, it is by admitting that I am not free, that my writing is not entirely pure, that it gets more authentic. However, because my mind knows this is so, it can use this knowledge to write this paragraph, thereby burring the lie even deeper. And perhaps, by calling this book a form of diary, whereby I suggested that this book is really targeted at myself rather than the reader, I buried the lie even deeper still? So maybe it is mind all the way down and there is no way out? Who knows?

To check whether I am authentic, I like to imagine myself on a lonely planet of which I am its only inhabitant. Because whatever I would create in such a condition is more likely to be genuine. After all, it would be absurd to make something externally motivated when nobody is around. Jean Dubuffet, the founder of the *Art Brut* movement, writes:

> *The creation of art, to have its full measure of interest, necessitates a concentration and a solitude that are hardly compatible with the social life of our professional artists. It's when a man is alone, when he is seriously bored, when he cannot count on any kind of distraction or enjoyment coming from outside, no kinds of celebration, that the conditions are best fulfilled for the need to arise in him to contrive for himself by his own means, all alone and according to his own idiom, a theatre of celebrations and enchantments.*[9]

So the impulses I have in moments of boredom, solitude, or daydreaming are the ones I follow. My mind might view them as childish, simple, or kitschy and thus regard them as unworthy to be given physical form. But there is power inherent to such outbursts, regardless of whether they seem trivial at the moment of their conception.

In fact, it is precisely this unhinged way of working behind so-called *Outsider Art* that gives it its power. *Outsider Art*, formally known as *Art Brut*, is art made by children, people from mental institutions or otherwise disabled people, art made during altered states of consciousness, by accident, or art made by animals. Traditionally, what unifies these works is that none of their makers had any affiliation with, or knowledge of, the traditional art apparatus, which is implied to be *the inside* of the art world.[10] Their makers just act out whatever they want to. Or have to.

Jean Dubuffet characterizes these works:

> *We understand by this works made by people free from all artistic culture, on whom imitation, contrary to what happens with intellectuals, plays little or no part, so that their makers draw everything (subjects, choice of materials, means of transposition, rhythms, ways of writing, etc) from their own accounts and don't borrow from the schemas of either classical or fashionable art. Here we witness the artistic process quite pure, raw, reinvented by its author in the entirety of its stages, starting off with only his own impulses.*[11]

Most propose that one should expose oneself to some external stimuli to get inspiration for one's work. Read a book, go to a museum, visit an exotic place, they say. I, however, move in the opposite direction. Instead of looking for inspiration outwards, I look inwards. Often, there is a mile of junk clothing up what lies there, so I might have to wait a little until something surfaces. It's a well-known maxim among writers that every writer has a million words of bullshit to get through, so I, too, often have to work through thousands of beats with the chisel until a sculpture begins to reveal itself.

But even when following such propositions, it can, in practice, be difficult to discern what is authentic and what is bullshit. With this book, for example, I repeatedly thought, "It's all bullshit!" and wanted to delete everything. But once I worked through these feelings and allowed them to flow into the work, they always dissolved and led to something that felt *true enough*, as Wittgenstein put it. So, after months of writing, something behind the text began to crystalize, which I felt was genuine. Or at least: genuine enough.

So the *authentic* cannot be found in any word or line that makes up this book (for the authentic —i.e. the truth— is nothing that can be grasped or named in and of itself) but lives somewhere inside the work; It is not to be found on the surface but somehow submerged below.

∞

There are infinite ways in which authenticity can be lost when making art, and most can be hidden from the public: Sculptures can be made to appear more "advanced" by the use of power tools, screws, glue, or by copying or imitating other artists. Books can be made to sound more elaborate by the inclusion of quotes or through the use of artificial writing assistants, etc.

Auguste Rodin, sometimes characterized as the father of modern sculpture, writes:

> *Whatever is false, whatever is artificial, whatever seeks to be pretty rather than expressive, whatever is capricious and affected, whatever smiles without motive, bends or struts without a cause, is mannered without reason; all that is without soul and without truth; all that is only a parade of beauty and graces; all, in short, that lies, is ugliness in art.*
>
> *When an artist, intending to improve upon nature, adds green to the springtime, rose to the sunrise, carmine to your lips, he creates ugliness because he lies.*[12]

Again, this does not mean that sculptors cannot use machine tools, screws, or glue —or quotes in the case of writing— as part of their arsenal. The lie only occurs when these are used to make something to cover up the lack of understanding that would have been necessary to produce the same without such help. When I see a sculpture that appears as if it was made of a single block, I feel betrayed when I find that the artist glued it together to make it appear so. But not only has the artist betrayed the spectator but also themselves. They lied.

To illustrate this point, let's consider the Italian painter Salvatore Garau. In 2021, he exhibited an invisible, immaterial sculpture titled *I AM*, which was auctioned for about $18,000. He described the meaning of the sculpture as follows:

> *When I decide to 'exhibit' an immaterial sculpture in a given space, that space will concentrate a certain amount and*

density of thoughts at a precise point, creating a sculpture that, from my title, will only take the most varied forms... After all, don't we shape a God we've never seen?[13]

So, if Salvatore Garau truly discovered that it is not the form and not even the material that is essential but that which is condensed into its space, then his creation of a vacuum that holds all possible sculptures is a stroke of artistic genius, the result of a profound insight into the nature of reality, or the outcome of an immense spiritual insight, which are three ways of saying the same thing. However, if he took a shortcut and clothed his lack of understanding in spiritual truisms he borrowed from some other place or from physics concepts he does not understand, then his act of selling an invisible sculpture is ugly. Then he lied by using profane truths he did not understand for his personal interest.

I leave you from this chapter with a quote from Dostoevsky's *The Brothers Karamazov*. I let you feel for yourself whether I found it when I engaged with his works or whether I discovered it in the quotes sections of some internet page.

Above all, don't lie to yourself. The man who lies to himself and listens to his own lies comes to a point that he cannot distinguish the truth within him, or around him, and so loses all respect for himself and for others. And having no respect he ceases to love, and in order to occupy and distract himself without love he gives way to passions and coarse pleasures, and sinks into bestiality in his vices, all from continual lying to other men and to himself.[14]

Chapter 2

Why do you send fools to judge my work?
—attributed to MICHELANGELO

True art exposes. It allows others to see *into* the artist. My sculptures, for example, do not reveal forms that I conceive as *pretty* or *interesting,* but they approximate my most private and intimate ideals. Most people are intuitively aware of this and thus extra careful when criticizing somebody else's art.

I assume that part of the reason Nirman hardly comments upon the form of my sculptures is that he understands that they are, in some very important way, private. That they are intimate and only available for revision once consent is given. In fact, when we speak about the forms of our sculptures, we always do so with our clothes on. Because the expression of form itself, we both intuitively understand, forever remains a highly private affair.

Whatever lies at our core cannot become any better, improve, or grow through criticism. All it can do is develop. And much like a tree, which also doesn't get any better when criticized, it tends to grow strongest when left to itself: any kind of interference is generally worse than no interference at all.

What is more, especially in the beginning, it is somewhat unfair to let the critical voice —which has developed over several decades and might even hold a Ph.D.— criticize a child who just learned to walk.

That is why you should treat your first chisel beats as if they were made by a four-year-old. Because they were. And much like you celebrate the developmental stages of children, celebrate the beginning stages in which you frequently messed something up. Because even if your first doings don't look like much, they still signify where you are at in this moment. And that moment is as significant as the moment you will finish your *Magnus Opus.* Someone like Bernini wouldn't have been able to sculpt *Apollo and Daphne* if he had not started making holes in stone many years before. "If people knew how hard I had to work to gain my mastery," Michelangelo supposedly once said, "they would not call it genius."

Also, there is no speeding up or bypassing certain stages, nor is there such a thing as starting where another artist left off. Everyone has to start where everyone else started: At the beginning. With making holes in stone.

In the beginning, it thus makes a good habit to secure your sculptures from your parents or anyone else who thinks to know anything about sculpture. Because consciously or not, they will judge your work as if it was made by *you* rather than a four-year-old. Which it was.

But it is not just other people's critiques that you should be cautious about. The harshest critique will often come from your own mind. In fact, since art originates from *beyond* the mind, the mind usually wants to claim or neglect what was produced through the body it inhabits. And because both tendencies have the potential to disrupt the creative process, it is worth looking at them one by one:

Claiming one's Work

The first tendency, namely that the mind likes to claim what was gifted from the inner pigeon, became most obvious to me after I made a coal drawing with my eyes closed. Because once I opened my eyes, I very much liked the outcome and thoughts like "This could be the beginning of a series and be worth thousands in the future!" appeared in my head. So, I quickly went on to sign the paper with my everyday signature to ensure its place within my future catalog raisonné. But before I had finished setting the mark, it already dawned upon me what I had done: I had claimed something that had nothing to do with me. The *I* that signed the drawing and assigned it potential monetary value was not involved in its production. It felt worse than stealing; it felt more like I had betrayed something sacred.

Claiming an artwork as one's own is like locking the inner pigeon into a cage. It is one of the worst forms of violence against oneself. It happens everywhere: When people are desperate to claim a patent for an innovation that came to them, when mathematicians fight for the recognition of a theorem that was offered to them in silence, when chess players explain why they made a certain move even though the move came to them, rather than the other way around, etc. It also happened to me, such as when I collected plaudits for insights that were revealed to me while writing this book. And not only does it feel like betrayal, but it also closes the door to where these gifts are received from.

I soon realized that I was not alone with this trouble. John Krenov wrote in *The Fine Art of Cabinetmaking* that his customers basically forced him to make a signature on his cabinets. J.S. Bach signed all his works with S.D.G.– Glory to God Alone. Michelangelo only signed his *Pieta* and nothing after that. And after I checked through Nirman's arsenal of sculptures and drawings, I wasn't surprised that none of them were signed either. Jean Arp also wrote about this:

> *We do not want to copy nature. We do not want to reproduce, we want to produce. We want to produce like a plant that produces a fruit and not to reproduce. We want to produce directly and not through tricks. As there is not the slightest trace of abstraction in this art we call it concrete art. Concrete art should never be signed by its makers. These paintings, these sculptures—these objects—should remain anonymous in nature's enormous studio, like clouds, mountains, seas, animals, people.[15]*

Would a chicken put its signature on its egg? Obviously not. After all, the chicken does not *make* an egg, but an egg just pops out of the chicken on its own. That's just what a healthy chicken does. A chicken also does not say: "Look at that perfect shape; please praise me for my sculptural mastery." No, a perfectly shaped object, which also happens to be alive, just pops out of the chicken all on its own. Of course, laying an egg might, at times, be painful and cause some degree of suffering, which is why we don't want to discredit the effort of the hen. But that doesn't change anything about the fact that the egg, the sculpture, wasn't made by the hen, the artist, but that it just occurred naturally.

And what is more, an egg does not need to be signed by the hen because it carries the signature within itself. The hen's DNA is within every cell of the egg, so adding a name on the surface would be tautological at best.

The text that makes up this book is equally infused with my persona: the way I arranged the words, the rhythm I introduced through punctuation; all are a reflection of who I am. And those who know me will *feel* that this is so. Perhaps they will even use my voice in their heads to read this book to themselves. And even though it is impossible to define what makes this writing undoubtedly mine, it is still easy for anyone to sense it. "A writing does not need to be autobiographical to explore the nature of identity," Stephen Buhner writes in *Ensouling Language*.[16]

And in that way, each sculpture, too, reflects the person working on it, just like a dog often reflects its master. Sometimes, when I approach Nirman's sculptures, it feels as if I am approaching Nirman himself. Or when somebody starts to touch my work, it also often feels like they are touching a part of my body.

Every authentic work carries its signature within itself. It is trivial to recognize the difference between a Bach and a Mozart, between a da Vinci and a Raphael, without having to check the label of the respective work. One does not even have to see or hear an entire piece of them, but one recognizes them even within a fragment of their work. Rodin also spoke about this:

> *And the mind of the great artist is so active, so profound, that it shows itself in any subject. It does not even need a whole figure to express it. Take any fragment of a masterpiece, you will recognize the character of the creator in it. Compare, if you will, the hands painted in two portraits by Titian and Rembrandt. The hands by Titian will be masterful; those by Rembrandt will be modest and courageous. In these limited bits of painting all the ideals of these masters are contained.[17]*

Ultimately, the pursuit underlying this approach to sculpture could be distilled as the quest for coming to an understanding of form. But not any form, or form as a geometrical discipline, but of *our* form. And everyone has their own form, both physical and as an expressive force. So just as everyone uses distinct tones and words to express themselves, everyone will use distinct elements of form to express themselves in stone.

Like everyone, I have an intuitive sense of how tight a curve should be, what elements of form function together, what makes a good line, or how sorted a composition must be. But I do not know what these are for themselves. I just *know* it when I see them. And it is these unconscious preferences that influence every decision I take that gradually give my sculptures my unique touch. My unique signature.

The same can also be formulated the other way around: With any sculpture that is not mine, there are aspects that I do not understand, that I do not want to inhabit, that I cannot inhabit. This might be because some line turns wrong, the surface is not stretched enough, the composition too stuffed, or whatever else. There is something about other people's works that always makes it evident that it is not mine.

Also, when I began to sculpt, I was afraid that I, contrary to other artists, do not have an individual mark that distinguishes my works as being unambiguously mine. But, as I went along, I found that I also possess a certain handwriting that runs through all my work. This handwriting only I possess, and even though it is expressed in all my works, I cannot say what it is in and of itself.

Since how I shape stone reflects my preferences and impulses present during its making, nobody will experience or express form as I do. This is why, as long as I am true to expressing my feelings, I must not be afraid that my sculptures will resemble anybody else's. Plagiarism will never be an issue.

Neglecting One's Work

The opposite reaction, namely that the mind does not want to be identified with what was brought into existence through the hands it inhabits, equally befell me:

The only condition Nirman set for working at his studio was that I "do not give shit" to my sculptures. And this is easier said than done because the mind often "gives shit" in very subtle ways:

Every day for a few months, Nirman encouraged me to draw a portrait of myself without looking at the paper. After I had followed this exercise for some time, Nirman asked me whether I would show him some of the drawings I had made. I agreed, whereupon he asked me to sort the best ones out. That was easy because I already knew which ones I wanted to keep and show to others and which ones were destined for the bin. But once I sorted the ones I liked from the ones I considered failures, he countered that he had little interest in seeing the first stack: He wanted to see those destined for the bin. Among them was a drawing in which I circled a pen to make it work; one in which I started to draw a portrait but aborted mid-way by violently wiping out what I had already drawn; one in which it looked like I had drawn the devil; one in which I had moved some soil carelessly across the paper, so that, not even with the wildest imagination, a portrait could be discerned. . . These were the drawings he wanted to see. He wanted to see them, and not the ones I liked, because they were furthest away from my mind —which is full of ideas about what a good portrait looks like, what I look like— and thus closer to what we are trying to express.

"But doesn't this mean I cannot throw away anything, even a piece of paper I was *just trying to get a pen to work?*" I asked in response. But while I asked this question, the answer already dawned upon me: The very distinction between "this is a work of art" and "this is just scribbles" is a distinction made by the mind. And the distinction between "now I am doing art," and "now I am trying to get a pen to work," is too.

You see, this approach to sculpture is total. It takes in every moment of waking life. "I am always working!" Nirman once mumbled when I asked him when he would be back at the studio. And when he offered his full attention to the scribbles that resulted from my efforts to get a pen to work, I felt as if I had gotten a glimpse of what he meant.

Another subtle way I "gave shit" to some of my sculptures was by hiding some of my works I did not like: In the first months, when somebody asked me to present them with my work, I would only show them the sculptures I liked. But hiding some sculptures I perceived as less fortunate made me feel like someone hiding their crippled children in the basement. Once I became aware of this tendency, I always put everything out when somebody wanted to see my work, including the misfits, the bastards, the freaks and the weak. And surprisingly, most people could not see a difference between what I regarded as my best work and what I considered failures.

The critical voice can occur in many faces and knows to camouflage itself in the most elaborate ways. Sometimes it is subtle and difficult to spot, as when I disregarded some of my self-portraits. At other times, it is in plain sight: On some days, I wanted to break my sculptures or throw them into the sea. Sometimes I even placed them at dangerous places, hoping they would fall over and break. I hated my sculptures at times, just like I hated this book at times. And I mean really hated. With my sculptures, I hated how I frequently did things I knew were not going to work but, for some masochistic reason or another, still went on doing it; I hated how I often hit an edge one more time, even though I knew that doing so was going to break it; I hated how I sometimes lost patience and violently banged the stone, ruining what I had delicately carved before...

I remember one sculpture that looked worse every time I hit it until, after only God knows how many hours, the damn thing finally broke apart. I hated pretty much everything about that stone: the way it looked, the way it sounded when I hit it, the way it didn't lie still in the sandbag I rested it in, just everything. This sculpture also had me swearing out loud, and more than once a hammer was seen flying through the studio.

But when I returned to my senses, I always learned that these associations had nothing to do with the stone but everything to do with me. After all, all the stone does is respond to my doings.

Later, it turned out to be *this* stone that made me realize that it is not big things, such as taking off a whole side, that have the greatest effect on the appearance of a sculpture, but small things, such as undertaking tiny adjustments here and there. Because once I offered the half-butchered stone my undivided attention and set a few chisel beats here and there, the sculpture soon began to take form. So what turned that stone into a sculpture were not big amendments but small interventions. This stone made me understand that small things are actually big things because the understanding required to see that small things can make a big difference *is a big thing*. So big jumps in understanding often result from small changes in stone and vice versa.

∞

After a while, I noticed that the opinion of most strangers doesn't mean anything to me because I could sense that they *don't get it*. Besides wanting me to concretize on all kinds of figurative associations, people usually suggest something like taking an edge off, engraving a saying, or carving in a pattern. In general, I could not care less for such suggestions, for they seem so far removed from what I think my sculptures are about. But Nirman once made me realize that it is only a small jump from understanding that the stranger who wants me to engrave *"Live, Laugh, Love"* into my sculpture does not *get it*, to understanding that *I*, as the artist, also do not *get it*. Because as long as I *think* to understand what my work is about, I am still in the way of allowing the sculpture to become what it wants to be. Since when I truly submit to the process and focus on taking one step at a time, such contemplation becomes irrelevant. I just execute what I am told and do not interfere with my ideas. Arnold Schoenberg writes:

> *The artist's creative activity is instinctive. Consciousness has little influence on it. He feels as if what he does were dictated to him. As if he did only according to the will of some power or other within him, whose laws he does not know. He is merely the instrument of a will hidden from him, of instinct, of his unconscious. Whether it is new or old, good or bad, beautiful or ugly, he does not know. He feels only the instinctual compulsion, which he must obey … Right or wrong, new or old, beautiful or ugly – how does one know who only senses the instinctual urge?* [18]

Exactly. Right or wrong, male or female, abstract or figurative –who knows? That's not important. Later, other people, and perhaps even myself, will look at my sculpture and talk about such things. But during the creating, none of these are of any relevance.

So when I sculpt, it does not matter whether I *like* what I am making or what I, or anybody else, think of my doings. As a sculptor, I am in service of something else. I am simply an arm, an instrument, for someone, or something, to work through me. And in that process, I must refrain from judging.

∞

The inner pigeon is tremendously delicate and does not like to be exposed. A single cynical comment can make it fly out for weeks. So we must be careful when speaking about our work, and we might, in fact, be better off not speaking about it at all. I discovered three reasons, all of which are interlinked, why speaking about one's work-in-progress is hardly a good idea:

First, our societal contract demands a certain cynicism in which we are asked to put ourselves down, minimize our work, or be overly modest about our aspirations. This tendency, which, I believe, has evolved historically, serves as a safeguard against megalomanic or egomaniac tendencies that could threaten the social fabric.[19] But if we speak cynically or overly modestly about our art —"*I am just making holes into a piece of stone!*"— we betray our inner pigeon. The inner pigeon is grandiose, idealistic and, like a child, full of dreams and aspirations. Putting it down or insulting it will have it retreat inwards, perhaps so far that we won't be able to find it again.

Second, by speaking about our art, we are apt to intellectualize or rationalize our work. And cold comments, whether coming from our or anybody else's mind, equally tend to make the pigeon leave the nest. Perhaps Henry Moore was onto something similar when he shared:

> *It is a mistake for a sculptor or a painter to speak or write very often about his job. It releases tension needed for his work. By trying to express his aims with rounded-off logical exactness, he can easily become a theorist whose actual work is only a caged-in exposition of conceptions evolved in terms of logic and words.*[20]

Multiple times, I experienced how expressing my work with *rounded-off logical exactness* made me lose the thread. Suddenly, after having languaged what I was after, I no longer perceived the subtle meanings shifting in a curve or how a transition was reflective of my lover's touch. Instead, I found myself banging on an inert block of stone. Empty, hard and without meaning.

Any content aimed at disenchanting the creative process, no matter the medium, can have such a paralyzing effect. In that way, the deeper we investigate into what creativity is, the further we tend to move from knowing it. Because once we are provided with an intellectual explanation of what is "really" going on when we believe to be "creative," no longer will we see, not to speak about feel, the deeper dimensions inherent to stone. In doing so, we will have become too self-conscious and gotten out of touch with our feeling sense.

And third, the artist inside does not distinguish between manifesting something in stone, manifesting something on paper, or putting something in words. It only does everything once and won't do it again. So, if we explain to someone the contents of our book, we cannot write down the same thoughts later on. They won't feel and *be* true anymore because, as we maintained, repeated truth becomes a lie. So, whenever we work on a piece whose underlying drive we already put into words or given it any other form of expression, we are working on a dead copy. Whatever we do, then, will be no better than the dozens of copies of Michelangelo's *David*. They will be replicas with no artistic value.

Everyone will inevitably hurt or insult their inner pigeon. But this does not matter as long as we keep returning to it. And when we keep fostering this delicate relationship, not only does the inner pigeon grow more confident, but we also learn how to speak about our work without insulting it. It is a kind of relationship we are cultivating that, like all relationships, takes time and effort to maintain. But every step taken is worth it. The resulting works prove it.

Every artist, I believe, has to learn the hard way that it is not really them who make the art; that it is not *them* who can perceive the feeling a stone evokes or any of the other invisibles they are shaping. And every artist has, by necessity, to learn to care for their inner pigeon.

It is an old doctrine that the degree to which nature reveals itself depends upon the integrity of the observer.[21] The more someone lies, is not true to themselves, is not trusting their feeling sense, the less Nature, of which the stones we are shaping are a part, will be revealed to the artist working with it. I, for example, have found my inner pigeon tremendously sensitive to lying, not just in relation to sculpture but to any kind of lying. My ability to sense the next step I must take seems to be directly linked to my level of honesty.

Why? Because Nature does not lie. Nature cannot lie. So, whenever *we* lie, we move away from Nature. We alienate until we see nothing but surface. Stephen Buhner arrived at a similar conclusion when he wrote: "The more we lie, are out of accord with the truth that is found in Nature, the less we are able to perceive of the depth dimension of nature."[22]

That is why this work is not something that can be done at a certain time or day. When we are insensitive to a pet or eating low-quality food, the more subtle dimensions inherent to stone will no longer be perceptible to us when we are back in front of the workbench. Sculpting depends upon our entire being and takes in everything we are.

Chapter 3

Stones are mute teachers; they silence the observer, and their most valuable lessons cannot be put into words.
—GOETHE | Maximen und Reflexionen, 460, auth. transl

As indicated, repeatedly emphasizes that the stone does the teaching, not him. So, how does stone teach? And what are some of its principal lessons?

Most of all, stone wants me to be present. To help you understand why, imagine that you are the stone and someone is undertaking surgery on you. Now, if you, the stone, suddenly realized that the physician is not properly engaged anymore, you would be horrified and make every effort to make the physician aware of their slipping attention. And this is precisely what the stone does too: Every time I lose my attentiveness, the stone appears deformed, or an edge breaks off, which are stone's way of telling me to bring back my attention or to take a break.

Stone teaches in this corrective way with every quality: Whenever I force myself on stone, the stone forces itself on me, making sure that I cannot sculpt like this for long; whenever I am overly cautious, the sculpture continues to appear boring until I am willing to take some risks; whenever I am impatient, the sculpture takes forever to develop; whenever I am overly hard-working, the sculpture doesn't develop until I relax...

Or whenever I think I no longer need to stand back, the stone also starts to deform. That is because stone does not care for what I think, believe, or know, but only about whether I am receptive to its speaking. And when I do not stand back or do something else to get out of my mind, the stone continues to take on unsettling forms.

In this interplay, I cannot win over the stone, and I can't cheat it. Stone will always break my body first before I have broken all of stone; stone will always outlive my impatience, so it is in no rush in teaching me serenity; stone knows an infinite array of weird forms it can take until I am ready to reengage, to listen.

In all this, stone always only responds to what I am doing. No more, no less. That is what makes stone both gentle and merciless as a teacher.

146

Gentle, because it is honest, reliable, and never crossing any lines: Stone never makes me suffer more than I directly ask for. Merciless, because stone does not even wave me a single uncaring blow.

Stone is a bit like cold water in that regard. Because no matter who you are or how many times you already went into it, cold water will continue to be cold. It is totally reliable in doing that because that is just what cold water does. And in the same way, stone will continue to make your doings visible because that is just what stone does.

Stone is flawless and mirror-like in this behavior: Not once did something break where I wasn't dead sure I was the one responsible for it. Not once did I have the impression that stone was lying, inconsistent, untransparent, or not overflowing with love and compassion. Not once has the stone made a mistake, done something stupid, uncalculated, irrational, or evil.[23] Whenever something happened, I could always trace it back to me. Yes, stone does split, break, fall off the sculpting table, or dissolve into dust, but it always does so only within the boundaries I am directly responsible for.

Over and over, I have to discover that I am responsible for messing something up and no one else. That it is *my* fault, and not the stone's or anybody else's, that something turns out the way it does. Stone shows that it is *always* me who is responsible. And this is, at times, hard to take in.

Of course, I often curse the stone into the ground and talk myself into believing that all of this is bullshit. But this does not change anything about the fact that the stone is right when it exposes me as uncaring, for example. And I know it.

Even with a sculpture that got pushed over by a child, I knew I was responsible for its breaking. After all, it was *me* who did not secure it properly after my workday. As a matter of fact, when I found the broken pieces the next morning, the stone had me look into some dark corner of my psyche where some destructive thing resides that may have deliberately left the sculpture standing in the hope it would fall over and break. "Are you satisfied now?" I heard the stone speaking within me when I found the pieces lying at my feet. This sent a shiver down my spine because I could sense that the stone truly does have knowledge of, and access to, every last corner of my psyche.

The mind always likes to blame the stone, or something else on the outside, when confronted with an issue that would question its supremacy. To give an example of how the mind likes to construct a narrative to blame something on the outside, consider the following example:

As I already mentioned, I ran into an unpleasant sculpting experience when I sculpted the Platonic Solids. Usually, sculpting grounds me and is among the most joyous activities I know. But this was not my experience when I carved the Platonic Solids: The stone resisted, the work was hard, and the clock moved slowly. Obviously, my mind had an explanation for why this was so. Its reasoning might be transcribed as follows:

> *When I sculpted the Platonic Solids, I felt as if I ventured into a mapped landscape. A landscape, deserted of spirit, where thousands have struggled before in their pursuit to live up to a certain standard. When I carved them, I didn't feel like an explorer who ventured into the realm of form, like a child running up and down a coastline, but as someone who wandered in the same street that houses conformism, institutionalism, elitism and other isms of this sort. Although beautiful, the Platonic Solids seemed to have absorbed some kind of morphogenetic field that burdens everyone with the anxiety that others have accumulated around them.*

Now, when I first wrote this paragraph, it didn't stand out to me because it camouflages itself in similar language that the rest of this book frequently draws upon. It does indeed read as if it were coming from *me*. But then, I noticed a decisive difference: Its implications are not in line with the metaphysical background of this book, for it blames something on the outside —in this case, the form— for my negative experience working on it.[24] And it was only this subtle difference that made me, upon revision, realize that there must have been something unresolved going on in the background. My mind must have felt stepped on and, to avoid being confronted with this unresolved issue, must have created this story in its defense.

Once I sat with this for a while, I had to acknowledge that I made the Platonic Solids because I sought confirmation from the outside. And because my mind knew that the public is easily impressed by geometric forms, it had me sculpt them. In that way, they did not grow out of me the same way *this* sentence did, for example, but were driven by some hidden desire to be recognized. And because stone does not like such hidden motifs, it generated an unpleasing sculpting experience, which my mind, in its defense, interpreted as being the forms' fault instead of confronting itself with its unresolved issue of not feeling sufficiently worthy.

Another such example occurred when I spoke to an artist about the issue of signing one's art. Because after I shared him my shtick about why I do not sign my works, he responded that he conceives of it differently: Instead of viewing the signing of his artworks as an act of claiming them, he considers it part of the work itself. He, not unlike a Zen disciple who draws an Ensō every day, simply finishes off his works by putting the same mark on it which others happen to identify as his signature. And indeed, when I spoke to him, I got the impression that he did not relate to his signature in the same way I did: Somehow, he seemed to have lifted it out of its cemented meaning by repeating it onto his artworks, not unlike a word can be divorced from its meaning when repeated vocally.

Once such associations, like the relationship between the unpleasing sculpting experience while making the Platonic Solids, or the unpleasing experience of putting a mark on a piece of paper, are brought into one's awareness, they can be overcome. Consequently, the same action then often presents itself free of its emotional undertone. Sculpting the Platonic Solids or signing one's artworks then suddenly poses no problem anymore because the underlying conflict has been resolved.

Such leaps are, of course, delicate, for the mind is an expert in hiding itself. After all, it is easy for the mind to claim that it has detached itself from one's signature or that it is free from the desire to be recognized, just so that it can have one continue doing these things.

But stone will always reach one level deeper than the mind can. Stone *is* ground zero and will always remain out of the mind's reach, so I can always go back to it and check whether I have truly overcome my internal conflict or whether I am still entangled in some game.

And the yardstick by which I assess which one applies is by paying attention to how the sculpting *feels*: As long as it comes easy, makes time fluid and makes me stand up straight, I know I am exploring. Whenever my back starts aching, time starts dragging, and my posture starts hunching, I know I must be evading.

∞

Stone does not teach by giving but by taking away. Stone doesn't provide knowledge or beliefs but frees from knowledge and beliefs. And it is through this kind of shedding that stone guides toward sculptural understanding, which is almost the same as saying: towards knowing thyself.

As part of this process, the stone continually asks me to give something. This can be an attachment, a belief, some knowledge I maintain to be true, or whatever else. And only when I find the courage to surrender it does the stone allow me to progress. Translated into the language of sculpture, this can be formulated as follows: Whenever I find the courage to give up a side I regard as my best (such as a particular edge), give up on insisting that a sculpture must contain a specific form (such as a hyperbolic paraboloid), or let go of a beheld truism (such as that two convex surfaces must never touch), *then* I experience true progress in sculpture. Because then I gave something I superimposed upon reality. And *thereby* my art progresses.

Accordingly, I remember a sculpture that had a side I liked very much. I didn't want to change anything about it because I was afraid that, if I did so, some of its power might be lost. But the side interrupted the overall form and prevented the rest of the sculpture from being lucid. So it was *me* who was in the way of the form moving continuously. The stone asked: "Please, can I go round here?" And I responded: "No, I would like you to remain straight!"

Later, when I found the courage to go round, not only did the form get more lucid, but the part I was initially reluctant to change appeared even more powerful. So, as always with such barriers, my worries were not just unfounded but in the way of me progressing.

Unfortunately, this does not get any easier, for the stone continues to find aspects I am reluctant to surrender, and my mind keeps finding more subtle and eloquent ways to conceal its unwillingness to let go. And the more elaborate its conception, the more courage it takes to remind myself that it is this conception, however eloquent, that is in the way of me progressing.

I remember the day vividly —it was around one year after I began sculpting— when Nirman made me aware that the technique of standing back, which I formerly understood as a method I could always fall back on, can be the most hindering of all. That is because by continuously standing back, one is inclined to discover a form distinguished by a certain perfection, by a certain balance, perhaps symmetry. But such attributes linked to beauty are the hidden nemesis of creativity. Because, as the child drawing on the concrete floor or the dog peeing on my sculpture has confirmed, they are ideals beheld by the mind, not attributes of nature itself. So if I really want to progress, I must eventually let go of these also.

Stone can also be approached actively and be consulted like an oracle. And since I came to understand some of its language, I found that it holds the answer for resolving any kind of inner conflict. The answer it provides is rarely the answer I want to hear, but it always gives the answer I know is right.

For instance, I repeatedly wrote a chapter of this book and went back to the studio to check whether it held true when working with stone. Or when I wasn't sure about a decision I had to take in any other life circumstance, I also excused myself because I had to "go ask the stone."

Remarkably, stone can also guide beyond the duality of language: As many have noticed, all of language is such that every concept uttered automatically contains its opposite, i.e. its antichrist.[25] And the more courageous a statement, the more outrageous the opposing implication simultaneously raised. Consider a person proclaiming to be God as an example: Did this person achieve the supreme realization that they is infinitely entangled with the cosmos, creating reality in every instant and thus is right in calling themselves God, *or* has this person just put the final mark on their medical certificate to be shipped off into the psych ward for they have made the most delusional claim possible?

In that way, every attempt at grandeur is immediately punished by its linguistic opposite: Every group devoted to a cause simultaneously rendered a cult, every stroke of artistic genius understood as an act of madness, every authentic statement taken as a testimony of one's inflated ego.

Or applied to this book: When a schooled mind (which operates on the basis of language) reads my chapter in which I write about the fallacy of technique, it might object that I am an arrogant dilatant who is too lazy to do the hard work of learning sculptural techniques. It might further claim that I am only advocating non-figurative sculpture because I do not have the skills to make something of the respective other. It might also call out my chapter on criticism as a lousy attempt to a priori discredit any kind of criticism coming towards this book. In the grand scheme of things, it might even render this book as a Trojan Horse in which I am trying to indoctrinate the reader with my spiritual convictions by clothing them up in a book on sculpture.

In that way, every statement or concept uttered immediately creates an evil double, an antichrist, which turns its inherent implication on its head. In fact, even the statement this book rests upon —repeated truth becomes a lie— can be said to entail its opposite. For doesn't a repeated lie also become the truth?

Not quite; it becomes its antichrist, a mirror image of sorts. A "Pollock" created by someone who seeks to mock the art world by carelessly throwing paint on a canvas might produce a painting indistinguishable on the surface, but their inherent value could not be further apart.

But because language cannot decode the difference, one has to rely on something *beyond* language to assess whether one is in a cult or part of a group devoted to a cause; whether one is crazy or on the road to artistic genius; whether one is venturing on the path towards truth or deceiving oneself; whether one is reading a book on sculpture or whether one is spiritually indoctrinated. Ethics alone cannot do that. One cannot reason themselves out of such juxtapositions. To find answers to these sorts of questions, one must go beyond the confines of language —of mind— which gave rise to these conflicts in the first place. And such a place can be found in stone.

Stone is, by no means, the only place there is. It is simply *a* place that, at times, has worked for me. So it does not matter whether one picks up juggling balls, knitting needles, an instrument, or whatever else, because it is not the medium that matters but something else entirely.

The reason I stuck with stone is that it is non-human and that it is gentle. By gentle, I mean that it doesn't pose the physical or psychological risk as taking LSD or free diving does, for example. And by non-human, I mean that it cannot be contaminated by a hidden agenda, for if one is working with stone, one is working with the substance of the Earth directly. And even if there is a hidden agenda embedded within it, one is following the agenda of the Earth and not that of a human institution.

What sets sculpture apart from writing in that respect is that the latter is more likely to be co-opted due to the close relationship between the words and the very thing we seek to get rid of in the process. The author(s) of various (religious) scriptures claim that their minds were totally absent in their writing process, and all they did was put to paper what their *inner voice* —which they might identify as the voice of God, Jesus, or whoever— dictated to them. Whether such works truly represent the unaltered word of God or whether such reasoning has been used to justify certain means is for everyone to decide in private. But one can see how difficult it is to spot a lie with approaches that are so closely linked to the mind.

The beauty of working with stone is that there is no intermediary medium present, such as with the anonymous letters that make up a text through which a message must be translated. In sculpture, the result *is* the message: language becomes seeable; the word is made flesh. So the understanding, the authenticity, can be sensed directly.

"The stone is one; the words are many," an attentive visitor to the studio once mumbled while looking at one of Nirman's sculptures. Whether he was guided by a similar intuition when he uttered that statement, I do not know. But I felt it came from, and pierced into, a similar feeling as I tried to work into this chapter.

Chapter 4

Man, as a form, bears within him the eternal principle of being, and by economic movement along his endless path his form is also transformed, just as everything that lives in nature was transformed in him.
—*KAZIMIR MALEVICH | Essays on Art, 165*

Making art exposes. That is why I was so afraid to engage in it during my knowledge-ridden adolescent years. My mind could sense that art exposes and makes visible like few other things do.

When I began working on my first sculpture, it soon appeared scattered with holes and lines as if a mouse had gorged over it. After a few sessions, I even assessed that I made the stone look worse than when I first started working on it. But not only that: On top of concluding that I had moved the stone further away from being a sculpture, I could sense that these unorganized doings reflected *me* in some ways. I, and also others I believe, could see that it was *me* who made these unrelated wobbles, lines and holes into the stone.

Guided by the voice in my head, I immediately set out to cover up my lack of sensitivity, patience, receptivity, clarity, attention and so forth that made themselves evident in my doings. But by trying to reverse and smooth out some of these doings, I made the stone look even worse, for as soon as I was trying to correct, I was entirely in my head, which is full of ideas about what a sculpture is supposed to look like, and out of touch with my feeling sense. A few moments later, not only had I made more holes and lines into the stone, but I had violated it. I had forced something on the stone that had nothing to do with it but everything to do with *me* and my ideas of what a sculpture was supposed to look like. And it is *that* which truly moved the stone further away from being a sculpture.

Sculpting is like taking one's clothes off: Without them, there is no hiding possible, but all is exposed in the open. And what one can see is not what one wants to see or wishes to see, but simply what is.

So, if you are fearful when you first step in front of a block of stone, then that is a good indication that your attitude is right. It shows you are vulnerable, open and prepared to become intimate, a necessary requisite for making art. Yes, there are ways to circumvent or cloth up this confrontation, such as by hiding behind citations when producing a text or by hiding behind follow-along guides when working with stone. But such undertakings have little to do with making art. For anything to be of artistic value, it must have grown out of the deepest, most intimate part of the self. And citations or step-by-step guides seldomly do so.

To this day, each stone I work with soon develops the quality of a portrait. Not in that the forms begin to resemble features of my face, but in that they come to reflect some essence of who I am. What the precise nature of these reflections is I can seldomly language, but there is the ever-present sense that the forms represent *me* in some way.

But there is more: Not only is the stone reflecting who I am, but there is an entanglement that occurs between me and the stone. Somehow, parts of me seem to move inside the stone, which are then reflected back at me. Consequently, not only can I investigate my psyche in the physical reality of stone, but I can also shape it into form.

In this process, the stone continually presents me with resolved —i.e. conscious— aspects, as well as with unresolved —i.e. unconscious— aspects about myself. The conscious ones make themselves known in aspects I already like and whose function towards the sculpture I already have a sense for. The unconscious ones hide in aspects I do *not* yet like or whose contributing function towards the form I do not yet understand.

This psychic infusion (of unconscious material) into the form can perhaps be understood through the lens of Jungian psychoanalysis, where unresolved aspects are understood to facade themselves behind metaphors or symbols. In sculpture, unresolved and unconscious aspects like to hide behind aspects that cause an unsettling feeling or evoke a sense of *offness*. Like a bulbous feeling that persisted marking one of my sculptures, no matter how much material I already took away.

Most of us are familiar with this kind of psychic infusion from the relationship we maintain with our bodies: Almost everyone has a body part they condemn as *off*, even though (most) others do not recognize its peculiarity. That is because part of our unconscious, or some other unresolved issue, has nested itself into that body part, which consequently evokes this negative association. What feeling a body part, an element of form, evokes is, therefore, dependent upon one's psychological makeup and not upon the body part, the form, itself.

One way I became aware of this psychological entanglement was when I discussed my sculptures with strangers: When I explained to them what aspect I was not yet happy with, they, in many cases, had no idea what I was talking about. To them, aspects I condemned as unresolved appeared no different from the rest of the sculpture. And in turn, they often highlighted aspects *they* thought as insufficiently developed, which didn't bother me at all.

So, if there is an aspect about my sculpture that causes me to experience an unsettling feeling, then this has nothing to do with the form but everything to do with *me*. Some part of my unconscious must be projecting itself into that form, which is then reflected back to me in the form of a negative feeling. Aspects about my sculptures I do not like or understand are, in that way, nothing but reflections of aspects that I do not like or understand about myself. And as long as I haven't become conscious of them or integrated them into my persona, the sense of *offness* won't subside. Its focal point might move from one place to another —after I had my cheeks lifted, I might suddenly perceive my nose to be off—but as long as the underlying conflict hasn't been resolved, the unsettling feeling will persist marking the sculpture.

With time, the boundaries between solving the form and solving internal conflicts might even get blurred: I remember a stone that brought up an issue from my past and, before I made that phone call, I wasn't shown how to proceed.

In that way, when I finally discovered what I must do to free that sculpture of its bulbous feeling, it was not because the stone had changed but because *I* had changed. Some understanding had happened, which allowed me to perceive the sculpture differently. And that was sufficient to have me see the next step I must take.

The solution for resolving an issue is often elsewhere than initially expected. You might, for example, be convinced that the stone feels *wobbly* because a side isn't flat. But sometimes, the reason a side feels wobbly has nothing to do with the flatness of its surface but with something else. Perhaps because the edges aren't expressed? Or because you have some unresolved issues with a relative? Or because you accidentally took some LSD? . . . And whenever you discover the true cause of the wobbly feeling, what you must do suddenly becomes blatantly obvious. You then know that you must express the edges, sit down with your relative, or sober up for the sculpture to become tender. "How could I have ever missed that?" you will wonder. . .

This deepened understanding can also make itself known in your speaking, in that your words take on a new clarity, a deeper meaning. Sometimes, I was most surprised about things that came out of my mouth following such breakthroughs, for I couldn't remember having heard or studied any of them. But somehow, resolving a certain issue recontextualized the entire structure of my self, giving my speaking, among other things, a clearer pronunciation.

Sculpting is, therefore, not a one-way street in which the sculptor is giving form to stone, but the stone is, just as much, giving form to the sculptor. The sculptor is not only the shaper but also the shaped. Theodore Sturgeon describes this relationship most wonderfully in his short story *Slow Sculpture*. The story centers around the art of growing Bonsai trees:

> *There is an exclusive and individual treeness to the tree because it is a living thing, and living things change, and there are definite ways in which the tree desires to change. A man sees the tree and in his mind makes certain extensions and extrapolations of what he sees, and sets about making them happen. The tree in turn will do only what a tree can do, will resist to the death any attempt to do what it cannot do, or to do it in less time than it needs. The shaping of a bonsai is therefore always a compromise and always a cooperation. A man cannot create bonsai, nor can a tree; it takes both, and they must understand each other. It takes a long time to do that. One memorizes one's bonsai, every twig, the angle of every crevice and needle, and, lying awake at night or in a pause a thousand miles away, one recalls this or that line or mass, one makes one's plans. With wire and water and light, with tilting and with the planting of water-robbing weeds or*

*heavy root-shading ground cover, one explains to the tree
what one wants, and if the explanation is well-enough made,
and there is great enough understanding, the tree will respond
and obey—almost. Always there will be its own self-respecting,
highly individual variation: Very well, I shall do what you want,
but I will do it my way. And for these variations, the tree is
always willing to present a clear and logical explanation, and
more often than not (almost smiling) it will make clear to the
man that he could have avoided it if his understanding had
been better. It is the slowest sculpture in the world, and there
is, at times, doubt as to which is being sculpted, man or tree.*[26]

… and there is, at times, doubt as to which is being sculpted, man or tree.
Yes!

So what I am effectively shaping isn't so much a piece of stone, as it is
my self: whatever I develop in stone, I simultaneously develop within
myself. Whatever breakthrough I experience in stone will, in some way or
another, be reflected in my persona; whatever understanding of fluidity,
movement, balance, rhythm, or simplicity I arrived at in sculpture will be
reflected in my being. This interlinkage between me and my art might even
find its way into my very flesh. Charles Baudelaire writes in *The Painter of
Modern Life*:

*The idea of beauty that man creates for himself affects his
whole attire, ruffles or stiffens his coat, gives curves or straight
lines to his gestures and even, in the process of time, subtly
penetrates the very features of his face.* [27]

So just as I infuse my quality into the stone, the stone infuses its quality
into me. In turn, not only do my sculptures begin to emit a *me-ness*, but I
also begin to emit a *stoniness*. There is a transaction that occurs. And when
I keep touching the stone in this way, both physically and non-
kinesthetically, there are moments in which something touches me in
return. There are moments in which I can feel some kind of response, some
kind of reckoning from inside the stone. When they occur, I can feel that I

am seen by the stone, just as I can sense that I am seen by a cat, for example. Because when I look into the eyes of a cat, I can feel something behind the cat's eyes looking back at me, touching *me* with *its* non-kinesthetic form of touch. I can sense that there is an awareness inside the cat that is non-human but interwoven into the fabric of reality. Most know this to be so: with humans, it is trivial; with animals, common sense; with plants, already less so; and with stone, an obscurity. But it is real. It does happen. And whenever it *does* happen, whenever my awareness meets the awareness of the stone, there is a meeting, a merge, in which my quality flows into the stone, and the stone's quality flows into me.

It is in such moments something invisible, something non-human, is exchanged. And as a result, some timeless, non-human quality entangles itself with me and consequently radiates off me, just as some quality of me entangles itself with the stone, which consequently radiates off its material.

Each stone I work with usually culminates in a certain topic I have to work through: This can be a specific relationship, a long-held belief, a worldview I inherited, or whatever else. When I begin working on a block of stone, I never know what this will be. Whatever comes up roots from the unconscious, from the unknown, and is, therefore, by definition, out of my conscious reach. Starting a new sculpture is, therefore, always a little like taking a psychedelic drug. Because there, I also do not know what will be stirred up from the unconscious. All I *can* be sure about is that I won't be confronted with an issue I already had in mind when I went into the experience. So if I am afraid that a certain relationship might cause me a bad trip, for example, I can be sure that *this* relationship will not be an issue during *that* trip. That is because the problems underlying *that* relationship were already on my radar and thus no longer unconscious.

Stones, like psychedelics, seem to be particularly gentle to newcomers, however. First-timers usually get to swim in the coral reef where colorful fish, iridescent shells and waving anemones are to be met. Yes, there might be a stingray or a reef shark swimming by, but they are usually friendly and concerned with other business. It's only after a while that newcomers will discover the reef's edge, where cold water from the depth comes flowing up against their chest. Where darkness looms and a certain rustling is emitted from the blackness below.

So, making a few holes into a piece of stone won't instantly confront you with your inner and outer demons. Everyone gets a few easy sessions before they are confronted with megalodons and other creatures thought to be extinct that live 3,000 meters below one's conscious awareness. However, don't be put off by this expectation because the courage needed to take the next step will always remain constant. To be allowed to progress in the coral reef might mean you have to make an uncomfortable phone call. A thousand sessions later, to get out of some pitch-black labyrinth underneath the Bering Sea, you might be asked to temporarily cut ties with whom you once considered your best friend. So the demands might grow, but the courage needed to take the next step will always remain the same.

All that *is* guaranteed when you embark on another journey is that *something* will come up. And as long as you keep going back into the waters, you will continue to stumble upon aspects you were previously blind for. Aspects you previously did not see, did not notice, did not know were a constituent part of your psychological landscape. And whenever you have arrived at them, worked through them, integrated them, the thread will lead you further, will lead you deeper, stir up more fundamental tensions, more unexamined questions, perhaps even from previous lifetimes.

On the flip side to these unresolved aspects that came flying at me are those aspects I stored away in the back of my psyche. Parts of my personality that I, or someone else, once declared as my "oddities." Parts that I learned to control, manage, or hide, not only from others but also from myself. These aspects, too, like to surface during the process; these aspects, too, want to inhabit parts of my sculpture.

Because I have repressed them for so long, many of them have grown distorted, perhaps even become insane. And indeed, initially, they made themselves known through annoying and destructive tendencies. One of them, for example, was in the driver's seat when I left the sculpture standing in the hope it would fall over and break.

At first, I dealt with them like I always have: I forced the door shut and hoped they would no longer interfere with my sculpting. But after a while, I could no longer ignore them, for they kept messing up my work whenever I was not looking. Too many times, they ruined some of my work by making me do things I knew weren't going to work. Too many times, they maneuvered me into breaking something off in moments of inattentiveness. Too many times, they slid through my unconscious and acted out their destructiveness. So, eventually, I saw no other way than to give up and let them out: I took a piece of stone and hammered it to pieces. I sent a hammer flying through the studio. I surrendered.

When I first let them out, their rawness scared me, and I wanted to put them back into the bag as quick as possible. But, after I allowed them out a couple of times, I noticed that they began to undergo their own development. Soon then, no longer did they just want to be destructive, but they also wanted to participate in the creation process.

And with time, I came to see that my oddities, which I initially regarded as unworthy, ugly, or evil, are actually noble, delicate, and, in their own way, beautiful; that they have their own preferences, their own ways of working. Ways that might be far from convention but truly underground in flavor. I came to understand that it is, in fact, *them* who know how to infuse the life force into the material.

And eventually, I allowed them to participate in the creation of all my works. And as a result, my sculptures no longer appeared as some cultivated bred, like some domesticated sausage dog, but became original, wolf-like. Because once I allowed my oddities to make themselves known in my sculptures —that is to say: once I allowed cracks, wobbles and broken bits to remain and no longer insisted on polishing everything out— the qualities of the backwoods began to enter my sculptures and really made them come alive. No longer were my sculptures mere decoration then, but they became insisting in their own right. They became of the same material as Stephen Buhner's writing:

> *I believe in writing that burns the blood, in which you feel forest wolves tensing behind you, writing filled with wilderness, writing that forces the margins, writing that challenges, that*

insists, that bleeds when it's cut, writing that uplifts the best in us and defies the worst, writing that's not afraid to breathe the same air as evil, writing that unashamedly believes in the good, that is undefended, writing that has death in it, writing with the same power that fills ancient redwoods, writing filled with darkness, writing with untamed wildness flowing through it, writing carrying an eagle's call, floating in the high cold winds of a mountain pass, writing that is not civilized, not contained, not channeled in irrigation ditches of tired grammatical form and civilized demeanor, writing that grabs readers by the neck and shakes them, writing that stirs the deepest parts of the soul, that allows the mythic to flow again into consciousness, writing that undoes, that unmakes, that touches on chaos, writing in which the old gods live, writing that touches on the deepest parts of the human and finds no definite line between us and other life forms on this planet, writing that surges, strains, demands, forces, rages, writing in language as liquid and mercurial as life itself, writing that is nonlinear, filled with luminosity, deep psyche, writing that DOES NOT SHUT THE FUCK UP.[28]

And not only did these qualities flow into my sculptures, but they also started to be reflected in my persona. I ceased to be flat and one-dimensional but began to develop a 360-degree personality that is as liquid and mercurial as life itself. For what I am doing when I integrate these abandoned oddities is rewilding myself. I am engaging in the ecological reclamation of the self by reincorporating aspects that I, or somebody else, once declared as a weed or an invasive species. As a result, I am no longer a garden, symmetrical and clear-cut, but something of a forest, of a wilderness that is self-organized according to the habits of chaos.

In that rewilding process, one absorbs a certain flavor, a certain aroma, that all wilderness possesses. Stephen Buhner describes it as a "quality, a value, that emerges from within, from the center outwards, when your individuality is entangled with that of the world."[116] It brings a certain posture, a certain depth of voice, a certain radiance. One begins to walk upright and absorbs a certain brilliance in the eyes, regardless of whether one's back is humped or one's sight is bad. But don't be fooled — these extensions do not just grow sideways, inwards, or upwards, but also downwards. For the closer one flies to the sun, the larger one's shadow becomes.

∞

I once asked a few children to help me find *the most beautiful* stones in a driveway full of pebble stones. After a few minutes, they returned to present me with their selection. But what they laid out before me were stones of the most ordinary sort. They weren't stones I would have called aesthetic by any means. In fact, most of them were broken. To be sure, I asked one of the girls whether the broken fragments were indeed the most beautiful stones she could find, whereupon she responded with a decisive "Yes!". Her glowing eyes wandering across the muddy pieces gave me no reason to doubt her.

But before I lost myself in confusion, I realized that my (or the) notion of beauty was nonsense. That is because I realized that what I regard as beautiful is somehow tied to an internal image I hold about myself. An image that I then superimpose upon my environment. For when I think of a beautiful stone, I think of a stone that is smooth, clean, whole, marked by an interesting pattern and so forth, all of which are qualities my mind holds about itself.

But because children do not yet carry an internal image of themselves (or a rucksack of unconscious baggage) that they could project onto the outside, they are free and non-judgmental when experiencing form. To them, each stone can thus be an equal source of beauty. They do not relate it to some internal image of themselves, nor do they project some unconscious material on it. They just look.

To find back to this childlike way of inhabiting stone is what this approach is ultimately after. Because once I can inhabit any stone, any form, without it causing an unsettling feeling, I have freed myself of any kind of unconscious baggage. And consequently, I am no longer projecting an illusionary image of myself upon the world but simply perceiving it as it is. And from such a perspective, the notion of one stone being *more beautiful* than any other stone would become nonsensical at best.

But if this is the end, then why even sculpt? Why even begin altering form when, as the children have confirmed, every form is as good as any other? Why spend hundreds of hours, perhaps even a lifetime, developing a language in stone when, eventually, I might realize that all of form is one?

To explore this question, let me return to the analogy I drew to introduce the section on *Exercises*, where I juxtaposed following a meditation practice against Zen:

As long as I resolve the form one step at a time, I am venturing on the same path as those venturing on the path of Vipassana meditation. I am, one step at a time, resolving an internal issue, a Sankara, until I have freed myself from any kind of baggage that can nest itself into a form.[29]

The way of Zen, of course, would be to take any stone and enter Zen from there. Such as when this woman, Nirman, and I offered a random piece of stone our undivided attention. Because then it becomes blatantly obvious why every effort to alter a stone's form towards higher beauty is like adding 1 to infinity. Can be done, yes, but it does not change anything about it. Infinity remains infinity.

So ultimately, both paths converge at the same destination. Both lead to the same final understanding. Only the way differs.

Chapter 5

Every idea, extended into infinity, becomes its own opposite.
—attributed to GEORG W. F. HEGEL

When I practice perceiving and experiencing stone through all my senses, not only does my perception develop, but the perceiving also develops me. My understanding developed in stone is not confined to my understanding of form but also informs my understanding of the other arts, the natural world, and myself. So whatever I develop in stone will not be limited to my understanding of sculpture but will be reflected in *all* I do. "Your progress is charted, not on paper," Nicolaides remarks, "but in the increased knowledge with which you look at life around you."[30]

But this kind of understanding has little to do with technical understanding or any form of knowledge that can be acquired from studying a textbook. It is not a knowing that I possess, such as when I learned the elements of the periodic table, but a knowing that manifests itself in how I interact with my environment. I cannot catch this knowing or define it. About all I can do is play with it, develop it, and have it interact with the uniqueness found in everything else.

So sculpting stone does not teach me anything I can recite, but it makes my perceptions more nuanced, delicate and sensitive. I continue to *feel* more, perceive more. Perhaps the feeling can be likened to permanently being on a small dose of LSD in that I become aware of things I always knew to be there but somehow had forgotten about. The fact that the history of an object is vibrating out of its mass, that there is a feeling tone to every space, or that there is a reckoning of myself to be found everywhere in nature were some of these realizations I made, to name but a few.

Also, my ability to understand how items, forms and materials contribute towards the feeling of a space evolve together with my understanding of how to arrange colors, textures and tastes so they function together. Today, no longer is everything around me a mess, a simple accumulation of functional stuff, but everything has a meaning and a place.

My sense for aesthetics and quality also continue to develop: Marble, wooden floors and plants have a *felt* different to their artificial surrogates; biodynamically farmed food a *felt* difference in taste and bodily effect; hand-crafted shelves a *felt* difference to ready-to-assemble ones.

This deepening of perception that stone can elicit is bottomless. No matter how long I have worked with stone, it continues to make me aware of layers inherent to reality I was previously unaware of. "There is always a bigger truth," Nicolaides writes, "undiscovered – unsaid – uncharted until you meet it."[31]

In fact, if I were to fully perceive the stone as it is, if I were to be fully aware of every nuance, every relationship within it, I would, this is my conviction, be looking at the cosmos in its entirety. For, as William Blake writes in *The Marriage of Heaven and Hell*: "If the doors of perception were cleansed everything would appear to man as it is, infinite."[32]

I deliberately chose the comparison to LSD because LSD is often proposed as the most reliable gateway to bridge us into the metaphysical background of the world. So why not just drop acid? Why sculpt stone if we could simply eat a sugar cube instead?

Perhaps the main difference between the psychopharmacological road and the one through stone is speed (no, I don't mean amphetamine but the rate at which something moves). Psychedelics tend to catapult me into the metaphysical background in minutes, sometimes even within seconds. And because of its vastness, I might, like someone falling overboard a ship in the middle of the ocean, be fully occupied with maneuvering my sanity to the other side instead of being able to learn from the profundity surrounding me.

Stone, on the other hand, is more gentle. Instead of catapulting me into the multidimensionality of Being, it takes me by the hand and has me take one step at a time. I am slowly guided inwards and given enough time to map the landscape. And I am also gifted with physical artifacts discovered on my way.

Drawing and writing also work, but I find them more difficult to submerge into. When I sit down in front of a white canvas or before an empty page, it takes me an immense effort to overcome the initial inertia to even begin. John Steinbeck once remarked about his experience as a writer: "The getting to work is a purely mechanical thing, as you well know – a conscious and self-imposed schoolroom. After that, other things happen, but the beginning is straight pushing."[33]

Stone is less confronting because it always offers something to adjust. And since I can always work with something that is already there instead of having to create something out of nothing, stone allows me to submerge slowly. That's why I hardly ever have to overcome an initial resistance towards sculpting; it simply does not have the immediacy that sitting in front of a blank page has. So the destination, the *Unio Mystica* that resides at the heart of all creation, can be reached following many roads, but the one through stone seems particularly gentle.

Sculpting further has the potential to refine one's worldview, one's metaphysics. I, for one, find materialism, atheism, rationalism and other static models of the world increasingly absurd for I experience a very different reality in sculpture: When I work with stone, I experience the world to be a conscious, self-organizing and intelligent organism instead of a dead, dumb and random accumulation of meaningless matter.

However, just because I have arrived at such conceptions shall not mean that you must entertain any of them. If you are a die-hard materialist-atheist who insists on the Earth being nothing but an agglomeration of innate matter governed by rigid laws of physics, senselessly swirling in a universe devoid of spirit and with no cause or direction, then this too is a good starting point. Simply take these convictions to the stone and see how it responds to them. Or applied to sculpture: if you disagree with any of the propositions made throughout this book, that's great: If you want to make everything explicit, define points first and develop the form second, refrain from standing back, work only with machine tools, or drink three cups of coffee before you sculpt, then this is a wonderful starting point too.

Because ultimately, it does not matter which axiom you believe in when you step in front of a block of stone because all axioms followed to their end converge into the same mystery. For if you go deep into contemplating the materialist position, for instance, you won't be disappointed in terms of mysteries to be encountered. For materialism possesses a depth, and holds a mystery at its heart, that most materialists are a long way from grasping.

Also, just like the "backward" development from complexity to simplicity cannot be leapfrogged towards, one's metaphysical assumptions cannot be leapfrogged towards certain convictions either. Nor should they be. Because if somebody proclaims stone to be intelligent without having experienced it so, they are just uttering empty words, if not lies. So again, it is about being where you are at. And if you are currently convinced that stone is dead and dumb, then so be it. And if you go into expressing that, then *that* too can be beautiful.

When working with stone, the learning can and will never stop if you continue to show interest. Even if you explore the most basic elements of form, such as the straight line or the curve with honesty, you will never stop discovering deeper qualities within them. One can easily spend a lifetime exploring the most simple elements of form without ever reaching closure in terms of their understanding.

On this journey, your attitude towards elements of form might undergo transitions: At times, you might behold that straight lines are alien forms that are to be viewed as the root cause for our culture's derailment; at other times, you might behold them as transcendental ideals, coming down to us from the subliminal realm of mathematics and thus regard them as men's obligation to manifest them in the physical. The meaning you behold for certain forms might also swap their place: For a while, you might connote the round and the curve with the feminine and the straight and the line with the masculine. But when you keep exploring these forms, roundness, at a certain point, might suddenly take on a masculine or even a transgender quality and have you reassess your hasty conclusions about gender associations to form.

Changes in perspective or shifting attitudes towards certain styles are, in that way, a natural part of one's development. So what should worry you is not when the perception of these changes but when they remain constant over time. Because when sculptors, after thirty years of working with stone, still yell that straight lines are from the devil, then chances are that they did not fully explore either the straight line or the curve because ultimately, the straight line and the curve, are one.

Because when one goes deep into exploring either of these most basic elements of form, one discovers that there is no such thing as a straight line, nor is there such a thing as a curve: Every curve, including the circle, can be shown to be comprised of nothing but straight lines when zoomed into; and every straight line can be shown to appear curved due to the Earth's gravitational field when zoomed out of. So just like the physicist, who, in their search for a perfectly straight line, has to get acquainted with the chaotic realms of curved space, so will the artist, who sought to go totally curvy, have to discover that every curve is made up of nothing but straight lines. So despising one in favor of the other would be absurd because they are inherently one.

This swapping of perspectives can occur in any aspect. I, for instance, set out by stating that I do not concern myself with technique but that I allow my sculpting to develop naturally. But the opposite approach is also possible: I also could have started by applying nothing but technique and would eventually have ended up at the same place this book is trying to point towards.

Kandinsky wrote in his essay *Concerning Form* that there are two ways through which the modern painter can enter the mystery. The first is through "great realism," which, as he correctly predicted, would become ever more indistinguishable from everyday reality. The second is through "great abstraction," by which artists move further and further away from objective representation. Both, he asserted, will eventually lead to the same destination because they are inherently one. He writes: "The poles open two paths, which both lead to *one* goal at the end."[34]

As an example, consider the dispute about whether electronic music or classical music can claim the gatekeeping authority to the divine. The former insist they win this juxtaposition because they claim that a machine can never mimic the sound coming out of an instrument. According to their ears, the electronic imitation is a soul- and lifeless insult to the instrument it is meant to represent. And rightfully so! Because as long as one forces electronic music to mimic the sound coming out of an instrument, it will always fall short of the sublimity the instrument it is meant to represent can evoke. However, in the same way, an instrument, such as a timpani, will always fall short when it tries to mimic the liberating power of a sub-woofer.

But when these respective genres are thrown back onto themselves and freed from having to mimic the respective other, both have their own laws, their own mysteries and their own sublimities.

The sound created by an instrument and that emitted by a synthesizer must, therefore, be kept independent of each other. They operate on different levels, work according to different rules, are governed by different laws. Both however, will eventually lead to one goal at the end. Both can bring about the sublime.[35]

Or take this example: When I sculpt a surface, I hold the chisel loosely. I grab it with just enough force so it doesn't fall out of my hand. I am relaxed and let the hammer do the work. And by not imposing myself on the material, I am creating a good result. But the opposite approach is also possible: I once met a stonemason who, when he sculpts, clamps the chisel into his hand so that it does not move even the slightest bit when he operates it on the stone. When he carves, his core is tight, his legs positioned, his shoulder adjusted, his wrist fixed, and his actions focused. And, because his approach is total, he also gets a good result. Diametrically opposed to mine, but just as good in quality. What does not create a good result, however, is when I tense up like the stonemason but do not hold on to the chisel properly. Or when my body is relaxed, but I fixate the chisel so it cannot move around my hand.

So, when I work loosely, I do so fully and do not introduce any half-baked notions of technique into my ways of working. Or if I decide to follow rules —be this of proportion, technique, straightness of line, or whatever— I do not allow any form of sloppiness into my work. I avoid all in-betweens, all middle grounds: Either I follow nothing but technique *or* dispense of them totally; either I go totally straight or totally wobbly; either I go to a concert hall or to an underground rave. Half-baked approaches won't get me anywhere.

But also, there is nowhere to *get to* in sculpture. Sculpture, like all the arts, like all of life, is a circle. You cannot reach a final point on a circle, for every point is simultaneously the beginning and the end. All you can do is walk on the circle until, at some point, you have come full circle. And at each point, you can either walk to the left or to the right, both of which will, if you follow through, eventually return you to the same place.

To give an example, consider some of the abstract expressionists. They started out by stating: "Enough with technique!" and began throwing buckets of paint against their canvasses. But by abandoning technique totally, they inevitably discovered a new one: Action painting. Their effort to abandon technique totally eventually returned them into the same waters they initially sought to break free from. They have, in that way, come full circle.

Or think of Jean Dubuffet's *Art Brut* movement. By exhibiting works outside the mainstream art apparatus, he sought to break free from, and overthrow the, established art apparatus. But soon after he started to exhibit works created offside the mainstream, *Art Brut* began to be subsumed by the very establishment it sought to overthrow. Today, *Art Brut's* successor *Outsider Art* has become just another movement within the established art world that some artists like to identify with.[36] Jean Dubuffet's *Art Brut* movement has, in that way, come full circle.

Or consider this circle drawn by Aniela Jaffé in *Men and His Symbols*. It is more difficult to grasp but more penetrating: Artists of the Dada movement —think Marcel Duchamp or Jean Arp— sought to break free from the preceding cause-and-effect dogma hovering above the arts by giving chance a greater role in the creation of their artworks. Arp, for example, titled one of his works *Leaves Arranged according to the Laws of Chance,* and Duchamp picked up random objects from the street and exhibited them as works of art. Painters like Jean Dubuffet or Paul Klee also began to emphasize the role of chance and credited *random* events or *mistakes* as important allies in the production of their works. But once the genie was out of the bottle and chance had become a standard ally in many artists' workshops, something began to make itself apparent: Artworks made in (semi)unconscious ways (i.e. by chance) were often distinguished by a handwriting that reminded of the handwriting found in Nature. Works produced with the inclusion of chance increasingly began to resemble organic and inorganic elements of form. They have, through the backdoor, become figurative again. C.G Jung commented on why this is so:

> *The deeper layers of the psyche lose their individual uniqueness as they retreat farther and farther into darkness. 'Lower down,' that is to say, as they approach the autonomous functional systems, they become increasingly collective until they are universalized and extinguished in the body's materiality, i.e. in chemical substances. The body's carbon is simply carbon. Hence 'at bottom' the psyche is simply 'world.'*

So what C.G. Jung is saying is that by including chance in the creation process, or by working in an unconscious way, one begins to work in accordance with the laws of nature. That is because the unconscious *is* nature. Aniela Jaffé concludes:

> *The artist is, as it were, not so free in his creative work as he may think he is. If his work is performed in a more or less unconscious way, it is controlled by laws of nature that, on the deepest level, correspond to the laws of the psyche, and vice versa.*[37]

The *Dadaists* have, in that way, come full circle.

However, it would be misguided to conclude that the artists behind *Abstract Expressionism, Art Brut,* or *Dada* failed in their aspirations just because they ended up in the same waters they sought to break free from. No, their attempts can be seen as examples of supreme genius, for they penetrated so deep into their conflict that they came all the way, came full circle, until they arrived at the same place from where they started.

But calling it full circle does not really do it justice because it does not hint at the internal development that is made. Leveling up a spiral thus serves as a better analogy because one does not just return to the baseline, but the journey is kept within.

So, it does not matter whether one develops through an academic exploration of form or through the more childlike way underlying this book, just like it doesn't matter whether one starts with studying grammar or following golden threads and alike. Because at a certain depth, one will lead to the other and vice versa. To explore grammar, one needs words and sentences that carry meaning. And to convey meaning, one needs some kind of grammatical structure. So both will lead to the respective other when explored deeply.

The reason I chose this route is that I am already fully immersed in my mind. And if you are fully immersed in the mind, it is more difficult to get beyond the mind *through* the mind than when you start from the opposite end through chaos. Equally, the reason I am drawn to non-figurative sculpture is not because I have something against figuration but because working with a fixed idea tends toward false conclusions made by the mind. Whereas if I start from chaos, I give my mind fewer opportunities to attach itself in the first place.

But ultimately, it does not matter from which side I enter because, at a certain depth, they converge into each other and become one. At a certain depth, technique becomes chaotic, and chaos becomes technical; theory becomes practical, and practice becomes theoretical. So whether I start with grammar or semantics, with chance or deliberation, with electronic or classic does not matter then, because they are two sides of the same coin, and therefore one. All that matters is that I am total in whatever path I choose.

In Hermann Hesse's *Steppenwolf,* in a chapter titled *The Treatise of the Steppenwolf,* the protagonist lays out his dualistic nature by describing himself as half wolf and half human before assigning each half various, incompatible character traits. But after he has done so in length, he realizes that the act of splitting his self into two distinct sub-personalities —the human with its affiliation with the bourgeois, and the wolf which, above all, strives for independence— is a gross oversimplification, yes, an insult vis-à-vis his identity, which, as he notices, is not comprised of two competing archetypes —the human and the wolf— but of hundreds, yes, thousands of interrelated selves. He then ponders whether it is perhaps this Faustian division itself that is responsible for his struggle and dissatisfaction with life.

And likewise, I want to conclude that the distinctions made throughout this book, such as the one between technique and feeling, between traditional tools and power tools, between the stonemason and the sculptor, between art and decoration, are themselves to be overcome as part of the journey.

Because in reality, which is to say, outside of the conceptions made by the mind, there is no clear-cut difference between any of these. After all, if I take any of them —say, technique and feeling— I cannot find where one ends and the other begins. So when looking at each distinction drawn, I find nothing but the distinction made.

Let's take mountain climbing as an example. Earlier in this book, I juxtaposed someone climbing Mount Everest as part of a commercial expedition against someone climbing it in Alpine style. But if one looks closely, one cannot define where "Alpine style" ends and "commercial expeditions" begin. Yes, one might insist that the use of supplemental oxygen disqualifies the criteria of the former. But what about the Gore-Tex shoes, the carbide ice pick, or the power gel? All our ancestors did not have, nor can any of these be found in the natural world. But resorting to arguments like "our ancestors did not have" or "do not occur in the natural world" already opens up new distinctions that would equally dissolve when looked upon closely.

So, every line drawn between the natural and the artificial, between the traditional and the conventional, between the true and the false, begins to dissolve when scrutinized. Because ultimately, all arguing for a "pure" or "right" way to sculpt, which can be taken ad infinitum, are tricks performed by the mind, which clinches itself to a concept, to an image, to an idea and thus, yet again, stands in the way of artistic creation, which is mind- and imageless.

So those who only use hand tools, not because they arrived at using hand tools due to their understanding, but because they like the image or the idea of being sculptors who only use hand tools, are, in that way, further behind than those that do not make a fuzz about such categorizations and simply use the tools they have at their disposal.

And even, or especially, the notion of mindlessness is nonsense. Because to introduce a difference between artworks that are mind-born versus creations that surfaced from beyond the mind is absurd. Since when you apply this concept to the works of someone like Hermann Hesse, for example, its foolishness becomes immediately obvious. Because to say that Hermann Hesse states and does not channel, that he speaks and does not listen, that he was guided by mind and not by feel, would be as ridiculous as proposing the opposite. No, he ventured so deep into the conflict that forms the basis of all his work —the tension between living in the *vita activa* versus committing to a life in the *vita contemplativa*— that he ended up transcending both.

Equally, to render the compositions of J.S. Bach into categories such as *mind-born* versus *developed by feel* would be an equally foolish insult directed at his work. He, not unlike Hermann Hesse in writing, ventured so deep into music that applying such dualistic notions to his compositions appears ridiculous. His compositions are, at every moment, *both and*.

So just like the notion of abstraction is meaningless because every sculpture can be understood to be both abstract and concrete, every other distinction made throughout this book is equally meaningless: Ultimately, there is no such thing as technique precisely because everything and nothing can be understood as it.

In reality, which is to say, outside the confines of the mind, it is obvious why distinctions like "now I am applying technique" and "now I am feeling the material" are meaningless. I automatically feel the material when I focus on getting the technique right. And when I get the technique right, I automatically feel the material. So, the only thing that truly is in the way of creative action is (the very distinction made by) the mind. So let's get rid of it.

Now if you, having reached this point, don't know what to do, then my writing shall have fulfilled its purpose. As a matter of fact, if I left you with any kind of instruction you know to apply—be this regarding the use of tools, the role of technique, or the process of turning a stone into a sculpture more generally— then I apologize for having left some doors unclosed. For in writing this book, I tried to leave no statement without its opposite, so for every statement made, there should be another statement that directly contradicts it. In that way, I hope to have left no method, no assertion, no technique your mind can stand on once you step in front of a block of stone.

To be sure, I have written that I transform the stone totally, but that I only accentuate its form; that I always know exactly what I am doing, but that I never know what I am making; that I do one thing after the other, but that I do everything at the same time; that the technique of standing back is a method I can always fall back on, but that it can be the most hindering technique of all; that I focus on expressing the form first and the surface second, but that I do not conceptualize the process; that I focus on the whole, but always focus on one part only; that the process can be messy, but that my sculpture always appears finished; that there is no such thing as a mistake, but that I correct for one mistake at a time; that I do not hold an image of the finished sculpture in my mind, but that I approximate the form until it is congruent with my experience thereof; that I only focus on the process, but that I finish the sculpture at every instance; that I keep on striving, but that I must give up striving to see the next step I must take; that I do not start with an idea, but that I continue exploring my impulses.

And further: that the thread *will* have me manifest a sculpture, but that I might grind away the entire stone in the process; that I do not study what others have discovered, but that I constantly look for artists that move me; that my work isn't inspired by anything, but that my sculptures reflect my innermost ideals; that I do not jump into what I do not understand, but that I must jump into the unknown to see the next step I must take; that the form organizes itself, but that I make it my quest to organize the form; that I do not introduce any meaning into the work, but that I only do what I perceive as meaningful; that I become visible in my makings, but that *I* do not introduce anything into the form; that I only do what the stone wants me to do, but that I only do what I want to do; that I take time off from sculpting, but that I am sculpting in every moment of waking life; . . .

176

So in the end, I hope to leave you with nothing in the same way that Nirman does not *teach* me anything. But even though it gets less and less clear what I should do —Should I stand back, or not? Should I focus on technique, or not? Should I study art history, or not? Should I sculpt figuratively, or not? ... — I can sense that I am continually getting freer in my way of working. I am reminded of Eugen Herrigel, who writes in *Zen in the Art of Archery:*

> *"Do you now understand," the master asked me one day after a particularly good shot, "what I mean by 'it shoots,' 'it hits'?"*

> *"I'm afraid I don't understand anything more at all," I answered, "even the simplest things have got in a muddle. Is it 'I' who draws the bow, or is it the bow that draws me into the state of highest tension? Do 'I' hit the goal, or does the goal hit me? Is 'It' spiritual when seen by the eyes of the body, and corporeal when seen by the eyes of the spirit -- or both or neither? Bow, arrow, goal and ego, all melt into one another, so that I can no longer separate them. And even the need to separate has gone. For as soon as I take the bow and shoot, everything becomes so clear and straightforward and so ridiculously simple ..."*

> *"Now at last," the Master broke in, "the bowstring has cut right through you."*[38]

Chapter 6

Whatever appears in the world must divide if it is to appear at all. What has divided seeks itself again, can return to itself and reunite. . . in the reunion of the intensified halves it will produce a third thing, something new, higher, unexpected.
—GOETHE | Scientific Studies: Polarity, 156

There is one saying almost guaranteed to occur in every article, book, or conversation about sculpture. It is the following quote attributed to Michelangelo: "Every block of stone has a statue inside it, and the role of the sculptor is to discover it." Different alterations of this quote exist but what bounds them all is the same underlying conception, namely that a finished sculpture already exists within a stone waiting to be freed by a sculptor. And what also unifies these alterations that swirl around popular media just as much as academic literature is that Michelangelo never said any of these things. At least there is no written record of it. Looking at the quote's genealogy, it rather appears as a fabrication of Western thought. As a fantasy.

However, like with every lie, the quote does have a connection with something true. After all, a lie cannot be created out of thin air but can only exist as a distorted form of truth. And with this particular quote, this residue seems to stem from a line in one of Michelangelo's poems. To be more precise, the quote seems to be inspired by Michelangelo's Sonnet 151. It reads as follows:

> *Non ha l'ottimo artista alcun concetto*
> *ch'un marmo solo in sé non circonscriva*
> *col suo superchio, e solo a quello arriva*
> *la man che ubbidisce all'intelletto.*

> *The best of artists hath no thought to show*
> *which the rough stone in its superfluous shell*
> *doth not include; to break the marble spell*

is all the hand that serves the brain can do.[39]

As with all of text, and poetry in particular, translating from one language into another creates all kinds of problems. Not only are subtle rhythms linked to sound, visual appearance and length of the words altered, but the meanings carried by certain words are not the same between any two languages. In this particular case, I find the translation by J.A. Symonds, which I chose above, of *intelletto* into *brain* debatable. But the direct translation into *intellect* also does not capture the poem's essence. A popular translation in German uses the word *Geist*, which I find more fitting. Here is another version by James Saslow that more accurately reflects the gist of the poem while altering its poetic structure:

> *Not even the best of artists has any conception*
> *that a single marble block does not contain*
> *within its excess, and that is only attained*
> *by the hand that obeys the intellect.40*

But let's go back to the popular saying that states that every block already holds a statue inside and that the role of the sculptor is to discover it. Because when we compare this saying with the actual Sonnet —which I assume to be the root of the popular quote— we notice that it is incomplete and that one side is missing:

Because if we pay close attention to the popular version of the quote, we find that it suggests that the sculptor does not actually matter. It proposes that the sculptor is merely freeing an image already present within the stone. Thereby, it suggests that *any* sculptor, or robot for that matter, could be working on a block of stone. Because all that matters is the freeing of the image already within the stone. But that's obviously nonsense. Because if one really freed the form that was already inside a stone, one would have to carve every block of stone into tiny crystals because these are the forms that most stones, on the microscopic level (if you want to stop there), are made of.[41]

What the popular version omits is the artist. It omits that the artist also matters. Michelangelo's sonnet expresses this interplay. He does not stop after the first two lines, which clearly reflect the popular saying —*The best of artists hath no thought to show which the rough stone in its superfluous shell doth not include*— but he keeps going and emphasizes that the artist must also give something —*to break the marble spell is all the hand that serves the brain can do.*

According to Michelangelo's sonnet, a sculpture is always a result of an interaction between these two. Between the material and the intellect that resides behind the hand that moves the tools. Notice how Michelangelo's sonnet actually makes sense, whereas the popular version really doesn't. Yes, one might conclude that his sonnet is trivial, but every true statement is trivial upon second looks.

I included this example because it illustrates three important aspects:

First, it shows how popular culture likes to take something it doesn't understand, chops it up and then reassembles it to create a romantic image that can be used for all kinds of abuse. I already wrote in *Part I* that many sculptors use this quote as a Trojan Horse through which they impose themselves upon a stone. They hide their violence behind the quote instead of being honest about their way of working. They claim to "simply free the image that was already within the stone," even though they impose an image upon it. That is because there is no finished image within the stone except for the one *they* introduce into it! So, every sculptor that uses the popular version of the quote to justify the image *they* imposed on it is, effectively, lying.

Second, it provides a wonderful example that art originates from a tension between two opposing poles. And third, it demonstrates that something exists between these poles which cannot be expressed directly but can only be revealed as a feeling. Because by the juxtaposition of opposites, an in-between, a middle is created, which is inaccessible to the mind but only accessible to our feeling sense.

> *The best of artists hath no thought to show*
> *which the rough stone in its superfluous shell*
> *doth not include; to break the marble spell*

is all the hand that serves the brain can do.

And it is in this in-between that art occurs. It is in the interplay between the first statement and the second —both of which are true and yet, for themselves, incomplete— that the magic resides.

Notice, however, that it is not an in-between in the conventional sense. If I, as I highlighted before, went half technique and half loose in my way of working, I wouldn't get anywhere in terms of producing art. If I sculpted a horse following an exact work plan and then decided to give it an "artistic touch" by adding some wobbles in the end, I would forever produce bungling work, like somebody who seeks to write "creatively" by throwing spelling errrors into a text. It is a different kind of in-between: An in-between that occurs between polarities. And this in-between can only be discovered if any one side is followed totally.

And if any one side is followed totally, the other side will automatically hold the scales even. So then, it is *because* Nirman does not concern himself with technique at all, that his works end up technically masterful; it is *because* Stephen Buhner does not concern himself with grammar at all, that his works end up structurally flawless. So eventually, technique and feeling, inside and outside, idea and substance, artist and stone, balance each other out and, in doing so, give rise to a third element: the artwork.

Chirico once said: "A work of art must relate to something that does not appear in its visible form," and thereby emphasized that the invisibles give art its power.[42] Oscar Wilde wrote: "It is only shallow people who do not judge by appearances. The true mystery of the world is the visible, not the invisible," and thereby reminded us that the mystery resides in plain sight.[43] Both are true, but when they stand for themselves, they are incomplete. It is only when they are put next to each other that they really come to flower. Because when I read both statements together, I feel something exists between them. Something which cannot be said but only be felt.

Kandinsky writes:

> *Form, even if it is quite abstract and geometrical, has an inward clang; it is a spiritual being with effects that coincide absolutely with that form.*[44]

The sculptor Naum Gabo writes conversely:

> *Form is not an edict from heaven, form is a product of Mankind, a means of expression. They [sculptors] choose them deliberately and change them deliberately, depending on how far one form or another responds to their emotional impulses. Every single shape made "absolute" acquires a life of its own, speaks its own language and represents one single emotional impact attached only to itself.*[45]

On the surface, these statements, too, seem to contradict and exclude each other. Kandinsky states that each form is a being that exists independently, whereas Gabo asserts that form is a product of mankind, a means of expression without an inherent agency. These, too, are solid investigations but incomplete when they stand for themselves. Only when they are put next to each other is something true revealed between them in the form of a feeling.

Again, I tried to write this book so that both sides are reflected: I wrote that art ceased to be when it is identified as such, but that the defining characteristic of a work of art is that it is immediately recognizable as such; that stone is mindless, but that stone is infinitely intelligent; that the form is irrelevant, but that it all depends on the form; that the time spent carving basic forms is wasted, but that carving basic forms is a great exercise for developing an understanding of form; that sculptures developed in light of this approach are guaranteed to be beautiful, but that the pursuit for beauty can be obstructive for the creative process; that the life-force doesn't abide by any laws, but that it will move into the work sideways when the underlying search is sincere . . .

Christoph Tobler, a contemporary of Goethe, wrote a wonderful essay titled *Nature!.* It reveals this in between most wonderfully.

> *Nature! We are surrounded and embraced by her— powerless to leave her and powerless to enter her more deeply. Unasked and without warning she sweeps us away in the*

round of her dance and dances on until we fall exhausted from her arms.

She brings forth ever new forms: what is there, never was; what was, never will return. All is new, and yet forever old.

We live within her, and are strangers to her. She speaks perpetually with us, and does not betray her secret. We work on her constantly, and yet have no power over her.

All her effort seems bent toward individuality, and she cares nothing for individuals. She builds always, destroys always, and her workshop is beyond our reach.

She lives in countless children, and the mother—where is she? She is the sole artist, creating extreme contrast out of the simplest material, the greatest perfection seemingly without effort, the most definite clarity always veiled with a touch of softness. Each of her works has its own being, each of her phenomena its separate idea, and yet all create a single whole.

She plays out a drama: we know not whether she herself sees it, and yet she plays it for us, we who stand in the corner.

There is everlasting life, growth, and movement in her and yet she does not stir from her place. She transforms herself constantly and there is never a moment's pause in her. She has no name for respite, and she has set her curse upon inactivity. She is firm. Her tread is measured, her exceptions rare, her laws immutable.

She thought and she thinks still, not as man, but as nature. She keeps to herself her own all-embracing thoughts which none may discover from her.

All men are in her and she in all. With all she plays a friendly game, and is glad as our winnings grow. With many she plays a hidden game which is ended before they know it.

Even what is most unnatural is nature. The one who does not see her everywhere sees her nowhere clearly.

She loves herself, she adores herself eternally with countless eyes and hearts. She has scattered herself to enjoy herself. She brings forth ever new enjoyers, insatiable in her need to share herself.

She delights in illusion. Whoever destroys this in himself and others she punishes as the sternest tyrant. Whoever follows her trustingly she takes to her heart like a child.

Her children are without number. From none does she withhold all gifts, but upon her favorites she lavishes much and for them she sacrifices much. She has lent her protection to greatness.

Her creatures are flung up out of nothingness with no hint of where they come from or where they are going—they are only to run; she knows the course.

She has few mainsprings to drive her, but these never wind down; they are always at work, always varied.

Her drama is ever new because she creates ever new spectators. Life is her most beautiful invention and death her scheme for having much life.

She wraps man in shadow and forever spurs him to find the light. She makes him a creature dependent upon the earth, sluggish and heavy, and then again and again she shakes him awake.

She gives us needs because she loves movement. A miracle, how little she uses to achieve all this movement. Every need is a favor. Soon satisfied, soon roused again. When she gives us another it is a source of new pleasure. But soon she comes into balance.

At every moment she prepares for the longest race and at every moment she is done with it.

She is vanity itself, but not our vanity. For us she has given herself paramount importance.

She lets every child practice his arts on her, every fool judge her; she allows thousands to pass over her dully, without seeing her. In all this she takes joy and from it she draws her profit.

We obey her laws even in resisting them; we work with her even in working against her. All she gives she makes a blessing, for she begins by making it a need. She delays so that we long for her; she hurries so that we never have our fill of her.

She has neither language nor speech, but she makes tongues and hearts with which to feel and-speak.

Her crown is love. Only through love do we come to her. She opens chasms between all beings, and each seeks to devour the other. She has set all apart to draw all together. With a few draughts from the cup of love she makes good a life full of toil.

She is all. She rewards herself and punishes herself, delights and torments herself. She is rough and gentle, charming and terrifying, impotent and all-powerful. All is eternally present in her. She knows nothing of past and future. The present is eternity for her. She is kind. I praise her with all her works. She is wise and still. We may force no explanation from her, wrest no gift from her, if she does not give it freely. She is full of tricks, but to a good end, and it is best not to take note of her ruses.

She is whole and yet always unfinished. As she does now she may do forever.

To each she appears in a unique form. She hides amid a thousand names and terms, and is always the same. She has brought me here, she will lead me away. I trust myself to her. She may do as she will with me. She will not hate her work. It is not I who has spoken of her. No, what is true and what is false, all this she has spoken. Hers is the blame, hers the glory.[46]

And now I describe you how I feel: I feel a silence that has fallen. A susurrous emitted by the empty space surrounding me, an iridescence shimmering off this page. And I remember that it is *that* feeling that is the teaching.

Part IV
Sculptural Ecology

Chapter 1

You take the blue pill… the story ends, you wake up in your bed and believe whatever you want to believe. You take the red pill… you stay in Wonderland, and I show you how deep the rabbit hole goes.
—*MORPHEUS | The Matrix*

The deeper I plunge into the artistic process, the less in control I feel. And because the mind does not like to give up control, it continues to create all sorts of stories for why I should abort the journey I have started.

On top of this internal struggle, my environment, too, isn't always reassuring:

"You have lost yourself!" some said to me after I had been sculpting for a while, for my life's purpose suddenly moved from following the evening news towards adjusting a surface that didn't yet sit quite right. And because I no longer participated in certain societal conventions, some attested that I had "gone weird" and that they were "worried about me." The fact that I began to cite stone and not statistical evidence as the basis for some of the decisions I took did not help in that regard. In effect, some said that "the pendulum has swung too far" and that they saw it as their obligation to call an intervention to "bring me back to normal."

To me, however, even though I do not know what I am doing, whom I am following, or where I am going, it does not feel like I am losing myself but, to the contrary, that I am slowly finding back to myself. I also do not feel that I am getting any less normal but that my previous lifestyle was anything but normal. Like Neo in *The Matrix* who, even though he could not quite put the finger on it, had always sensed that something about the world he previously inhabited was not quite real, not quite solid, I found a world in stone that is more real than the one I departed from. A world with different hierarchies in place, with different laws governing its structure: A world in which intelligence has nothing to do with knowledge, in which intention is more important than the result. A world in which I suddenly perceive the highest as the lowest, the smartest as the dumbest, the most morally schooled as the most psychopathic, etc.

And just like those plugged into the Matrix can sense that something about Neo is off after he swallowed the red pill, my environment, too, began to sense that something about me has changed. That I crossed some kind of bridge and that I am now walking on the other side. And consciously or not, they try to pull me back over it:

Some suggest that, instead of making non-figurative sculptures, I should spend my time making *something practical* or *useful*. And if I do insist on making sculptures, and not stonemason's work, they suggest that I should, at least, use machine tools, mass produce, copy, take on commissions, sculpt more "realistic" figures or make more "complex" forms.

Some even insist that my skills and education are wasted and that I am not repaying my debts to society because my engagement with stone *doesn't make a difference*. I, however, feel that I *am* making a difference, in fact, a bigger difference when offering a piece of stone my undivided attention, than if I gave my time to some organization I feel no connection with. Such responses are usually rendered invalid, however, and judged as a testimony of moral bypassing, laziness, or as an unwillingness to confront my responsibilities as a citizen.

Apart from those convinced that I have somehow lost myself in sculpture, are those who try to frame me so that I am still part of "the system." They do so by seeing the value of me making sculptures in its potential for economic wealth creation. Implicitly, they regard the worth of me doing sculpture to the degree it supports our economic system. So if I made a sculpture but then decided not to sell it, my time making would, in their view, still be effectively wasted.

Others who are more generous in framing my sculpting as not being completely senseless even when I am not generating economic value regard it as a valuable part of my "personal development." Such commentators say that me doing sculpture might be beneficial because it contributes towards the development of certain traits like patience, attention to detail, my ability to put my hands to work and so forth, which, once I abandoned the senseless pursuit of making sculptures, I can put to use in a *proper job* or in making something *useful*. In their view, the value of making sculpture only shows itself indirectly, namely when it leads to the development of certain traits or skills that can then positively inform whatever I do thereafter. The making of the sculptures, or the sculptures themselves, they still regard to be without intrinsic value, however.

Others again acknowledge my sculpting as a valuable public good in and of itself. They appreciate the spontaneous coming together around a sculpture and the simple joy of looking at it. In their view, the value of art lies in its ability to present them with a different view on reality, in its ability to inspire, or in offering them a moment of silence. Accordingly, they see sculptors, like museums, to be fulfilling a certain societal function and thus value art to the degree it is brought to the people. So if I sculptured alone in the desert and threw my sculpture into the sea upon completion, they would still assess the worth of my creation as zero. To them, the value of (making) a sculpture is thus still not intrinsic but only established through its societal effects.[1]

But none of these framings I am repeatedly put into fits with my felt experience. I, for instance, don't perceive my sculptures as worthy to the degree they generate economic value, nor do I see their value in their indirect contribution to my "personal development." I also do not perceive their value to be connected to the degree to which they are brought to the people. To me, the perceived value of my sculptures remains the same, regardless of whether they are seen by thousands or by nobody but myself. The same holds true for this book: I don't see its value in the economic value it creates, in the indirect effects it has on me, sculpture as an art form, or society at large. Picasso must have spoken from a similar place when he said:

> *Look, this painting, which I have just completed, is going to have a certain effect; but this effect would be exactly the same, metaphysically speaking, if I wrapped the painting up in paper and consigned it to a corner. It would be exactly the same thing as if ten thousand people had admired it.[2]*

Paul Klee held a similar point of view in that he asserted that each work of art, once manifested, becomes part of the work of all humankind and can never be erased from the world, regardless of whether it is destroyed or lost. He said:

The work of art, since quality possesses individual character, must be elaborated by the individual, but it will acquire a collective meaning; its power will be incommensurable, its active presence will never be erased from the world. The artist's work, though it proceeds according to his own rhythm, will intertwine itself with the work of all mankind.[3]

Another reason none of these framings feel congruent with my experience is that they all share a common assumption I am not sure is met, namely that I decide to sculpt in this way because I *want* to do so. That is because I am, just as much, under the sense that I *have to* sculpt in this way as much as I *want to* do so. The same can be said for this book: This book didn't (just) present itself as something I *wanted to* write but, just as much, as something I somehow had *to* write. And if I didn't, I feel that the consequences would have been much more severe than those that came with following its call (loss of income, alienation from society, etc.). In fact, by meeting Nirman, I feel as if I got entangled in a lineage, in what Stephen Buhner called a "relay race of souls," that I cannot just abandon for my own comfort or for the sake of conforming to a societal narrative.

Notice further how all these framings are underlaid by a subtle accusation of escapism, of me having to justify myself for spending my time sculpting because it is not *useful* or because it does not contribute anything towards society. And underlying *that* accusation resides another one, namely that I somehow use this way of sculpting to avoid confronting the reality of the world, i.e. the marketplace.

But I find this assumption equally topsy-turvy: Sculpting, like writing, isn't some airy-fairy undertaking but as real and confronting as anything. Stone gets everywhere and, if I do not want to go under, it continues to have me work through cut-to-the-bone aspects. Stone demands for radical self-examination and for sacrifice. Not trivial sacrifices in which I am asked to donate some money or time, but real sacrifices in which I am asked to give constituent parts of my identity. In fact, one day, it might even ask for my name. "The progress of an artist," T.S. Eliot writes, "is a continual self-sacrifice, a continual extinction of personality."[4]

The confusion about making art being some airy-fairy undertaking is a bit like the confusion surrounding doing nothing. Because if people uttering such things ever tried to meditate, which is to say, if they ever tried to do nothing, they would know that doing nothing is the most difficult thing to do. And with making art, it is similar: They might assume that to do sculpture is easy because artists do not have to bother with customers or superiors. But even though that might be true, they must deal with something else instead: their own self. And to be confronted with *that* is the nemesis, the kryptonite, the ultimate frontier. Not because the self is evil or deceitful. Not because it is oppressive or full of tricks. No . . . it is much worse than that: Because it does not exist! And to realize *that*, which all artistic quests ultimately lead towards, demands for many painful sessions. To arrive at this final understanding, many previously polished sides must be blown off again, many lines written in sweat and blood deleted.

∞

However, those who do find the courage to have themselves guided by their inner pigeon also get something in return: The inner pigeon has tremendous energy and will provide anyone with all the energy they need to accomplish whatever they have come here to do. It won't provide them with the kind of energy they get from eating food, but with a higher energy, a kind of spiritual energy, that will power them throughout the process. This energy will also support them in standing their ground vis-à-vis their environment, such as when they are accused of neglecting their responsibility as a citizen. And besides that, it can provide them with something that cannot be bought in the marketplace: a life filled with meaning, magic and purpose.

Working with stone, I have seen matter get entangled, change its state when being observed, stone communicate with other stones and other phenomena usually reserved to occur in fairy tales or the quantum realm. Working with stone has also provided me with a sense of meaning, with a sense of purpose. Before I sculpted, all I knew was an artificial kind of meaning, a meaning I was told to experience but not one that I truly felt. *That* I have only experienced since I began working with stone.

So, working with stone is not all blood, sweat and tears. It is, for the most part, fun and joyous. And that's the way it should be. Always. In fact, I can think of few things more fulfilling than coming to the studio in the early morning, when the dewdrops still hang on the grass, and my exhalation is turned into white smoke. For me, there is no greater joy than meeting a piece of stone with my bare hands, than drawing some lines across it to accentuate its underlying movement, than chipping away some material to express its underlying impulse. And, of course, there is nothing more transcendentally fulfilling than those flickering moments in which a stone finds its balancing point and comes alive. When the sculpture sits there, condensed to its essence, resting within itself.

Mark Rothko writes:

> *The unfriendliness of society to his activity is difficult for the artist to accept. Yet this very hostility can act as a lever for true liberation. Free from a false sense of security and community, the artist can abandon his plastic bank-book, just as he has abandoned other forms of security. Both the sense of community and security depend on the familiar. Free of them, transcendental experiences become possible.*[5]

Chapter 2

For a positivist, indeed, "singing [of birds]" is merely "an accident, a "by-product." But in reality it may be that singing is the principal function of a given species, the realization of its existence, the purpose pursued by nature in creating this species and that this singing is necessary, not so much to attract the females, as for some general harmony of nature which we only rarely and imperfectly see.
—*P.D. OUSPENSKY | Tertium Organum, 140*

I already indicated that I felt as if I *had to* write this book as much as I wanted to do so. There was a force operating on me that pulled me back behind the blank page until the job was done. This "inner necessity," as Kandinsky coined the experience, is no stranger to the art world and sits at the center of artistic experience. Albert Einstein, for example, wrote that "True art is characterized by an irresistible urge in the creative artist," Arnold Schoenberg said: "Every chord I put down corresponds to a necessity, to a necessity of my urge of expression," and George Orwell concluded about his experience as a writer: "Writing a book is a horrible, exhausting struggle, like a long bout with some painful illness. One would never undertake such a thing if one were not driven on by some demon whom one can neither resist nor understand."[6] [7]

So, what is this "inner necessity" that operates on me and keeps me going even when the path is excruciating? What is the nature of this force, and, perhaps more importantly, *why* do I experience it? And even though the answers to such questions might forever remain opaque, why not entertain them a little, such as by seeing the world through the eyes of a honeybee:

Soon after a honeybee emerges from its pupa, it will want to fly out. It will feel urged to join the other bees in their search for the sugary secretion inside flowering plants. It will feel pulled to do so, will experience an inner necessity to fly out and start collecting.

The bee probably doesn't realize that, by following her urge, she is about to provide an immeasurable service to the ecosystem she is embedded in. And even if one could explain to the bee that its act of picking up the sugary secretion is actually pollinating the flower —good luck explaining that concept to a bee— which leads the flower to produce a fruit that contains seeds that must be eaten by another animal to be transported to a different place, where, if the circumstances are right, the process will start over, thereby ensuring that the bee will find nectar in the following years to come, the bee will probably shake its five-eyed head in disbelief. Its environmental role is so far beyond what it can comprehend with its intellect —at least, this is my assumption— that the bee cannot grasp its role within the ecosystem it is embedded in. But that doesn't matter. All that matters is that the bee does fly out. The rest takes care of itself.

For some reason, however, mankind does not seem to consider that such a limit of understanding might equally apply to them. Men break their heads about whether their *ecological function*, if they have one at all, lies in plowing land, herding sheep, or in building rockets so that they can spread life across the universe. But with such naïve thinking, they simply apply the ecological role they observe for bees to themselves without considering that they might (also) be blind to their (full) ecological purpose.

Because even though it is only a sense, I sometimes feel that (the making of) my artworks has a wider significance for the environment they are in. A significance that lies beyond what I can comprehend by rational thought alone. One way to characterize this perceived significance is that they seem to charge their surrounding space with a psychic force, electrifying it in a particular way —too subtle to be measured with an ammeter but too vital to be discarded as a mere illusion.

Feng Shui, Zen gardening, or landscape acupuncture rest on similar metaphysics in that their proponents understand that not only do we have the ability to center ourselves through means of Yoga, Qigong, or breathing techniques but that the same can also be applied to space itself. And indeed, I sometimes perceive my artworks doing something similar to space as acupuncture needles do to a body.

So, it might just be that this "inner necessity" that drives me to go to a specific place, meet a specific person, or sculpt a specific stone is actually a force that drives me toward fulfilling my ecological purpose.[8]

In that way, each work that results from following my inner necessity has a specific function and contributes to the well-being of the ecosystem it is born into. And perhaps it is only by following this force that an equilibrium —both internally and within the ecosystem— can be maintained.

One popular representation of what is meant here was portrayed in Christopher Nolan's *Interstellar*. The movie dramas with the idea that love is a higher-dimensional force that leads us toward fulfilling our role in the universe. Love, in the understanding of the movie, operates on us like a force that nudges us in certain directions so that a greater whole, which the movie assumes to be residing behind all and everything, can unfold. By following love, the movie proposes, not only are we doing something good for ourselves but also for the world. The movie further hints that sacrificing such feelings for the mind's analysis, or simply not trusting them, can be seen as the root cause for disease, disharmony and turmoil.[9]

So just as love might be a higher dimensional force that leads us towards taking certain (irrational) decisions, the creative force, which manifests itself within the artist as the desire to create, might equally be such an invisible, incomprehensible and unknowing force that is expressed by the *Unus Mundus*. And because, as Christopher Tobler wrote,

> *She has neither language nor speech, but she makes tongues and hearts with which to feel and-speak.*

She needs *us* to manifest these works. She needs our hands, our tongues, our tools to bring forth these objects and make them real. She needs us to scoop them out of the potentiality and condense them into a piece of matter. And *therefore* plants the urge to create within us. "Form is expressed *only* to fulfill ecological purpose," Stephen Buhner summoned in *Plant Intelligence and the Imaginal Realm*.[10]

Art, in that way, is a necessity. Because just like the bee *must* fly out to collect honey for the ecosystem to remain intact, artists must follow their inner necessity to bring forth whatever they have come here to do. The dynamic equilibrium that is ecology might depend on it.

Accordingly, I feel that the purpose of me doing sculpture does not lie within the economic value my sculptures create or any other such thing. Instead, it feels like I am fulfilling my ecological purpose. What this ecological purpose is, I do not know. But I do not need to know, just like the bee does not need to know its role within the ecosystem she is embedded in. All that matters is that I do fly out.[11]

Up to this point, it might read as if this book wanted to be written, and I was the one to put it to paper; as if I was used by the book to write itself; as if the environment called forth this book, and, because I was available, it manifested itself through me.

But this view only provides half the picture. It is only half the truth. Because if I stopped there, I would be no better than those discarding the less romantic half of Michelangelo's two-sided sonnet. Because just as much as I was driven by this inner necessity to write this book, did I *want* to write this book. So, I felt as if I *had to* write this book as much as I *wanted* to do so.

So how can this two-sided conception be reconciled in the moment?

Whenever I wrote a line, it was as if the book provided me with a feedback on whether my writing was in line with what the book wanted to become. Or, to offer the opposite view of the same sentence: Whenever I re-read a line for feel, I checked whether it was congruent with what I wanted it to express.

And whenever I found a sentence that was to become part of this book, an internal confirmation occurred. And this internal confirmation seemed to come from the book itself. At the same time, this internal confirmation occurred *only* when the writing reflected what I wanted it to express. So at heart, what I wanted this book to be, and what this book wanted to become, were one and the same thing.

The same mechanics are also at play in sculpture: When I feel for the effect of a certain action, I simultaneously perceive whether my action contributes towards the sculpture becoming what it wants to be, as well as whether I moved it closer towards what I want it to become. It is *one* feeling but generated from two directions.

So the moment in which I decide to sculpt, to write, to move furniture, coincides with the moment in which the sculpture, the book, the furniture, plants the urge within me to undertake the respective change.[12]

A matching worldview would sound something like this: Whenever the environment has a need, it plants the urge to create something within me that would fulfill this need in the form of an ideal. At this moment, I experience the desire to create. I then communicate with this ideal and seek to approximate it with my doings.

I say ideal because I am often under the sense that my works are but an imperfect instantiation of some ideal that already exists in some sort of Platonic Realm. So just as every leaf seems to be a unique expression of some *ur-pflanze* which Goethe attested, each of my works also seems to be a unique expression of its underlying archetype. And just like each physical expression of the "ideal" leaf is shaped by lighting, soil quality, air pressure and so forth, each of my sculptures, too, is shaped by the environmental circumstances it is born into. And because environmental conditions are never the same, no leaf, or sculpture, will ever turn out the same either.

Let me repeat: Whenever the environment has a need, it places an order to fulfill this need into some immaterial realm. And to be made manifest, it needs some substance: It needs words, examples, analogies, or stone to appear in the material world.

In that way, what I was communicating with when I was testing whether a line was to be a part of this book was the ideal behind this book. And because of my biography, the chosen language, the year of this writing and other such factors, the book happened to take on this form. Had any of these differed, the book would have taken on a different form. But only on the surface: The essence, the heart of the work, would have been the same.

Most are, at least to some degree, connected to this realm where these archetypes reside in their pure form. In general, I found that most people have an immediate sense for the ideal behind this approach and can extrapolate its implications based on a minimum of information. As a matter of fact, I assert that you, too, already knew the ideal this book is trying to approximate? Or formulated differently: Don't we find those books good that tell us what we already know?

So maybe it is the function of artists to sense what the environment calls forth and try to approximate it with their doings? And in doing so, perhaps not only are they finding honey but also cross-pollinating the environment they are embedded in.

Chapter 3

Art in its highest manifestations is a path to cosmic consciousness.
—P.D. OUSPENSKY | Tertium Organum, 275

Most words to characterize the shift in consciousness that occurs when I am deeply involved in the search seem either awkward or inept. Some have compared the creative trance to a form of dreaming, others to a form of meditation, others again to a form of hypnosis. None of them really hit home in characterizing its quality, for it is unique and different from all these others. The writer John Gardner characterized as follows. He writes that when "the juices are flowing," . . . "an invisible wall seems to fall away" that guides the artist "from one kind of reality into another" into "an altered state, a brief sense of escape from ordinary time and space," that brings with it the attainment of a "strange magical state."[13] Others have called it "flow," "creative trance," or simply being in "the zone." But because these terms mean anything to anyone, the experience must be evoked sideways instead of being labeled with a word. So, I invite you to follow me on a journey inside stone:

Whenever I begin to sculpt, I perceive the stone like most people ordinarily do. I am on one side; the stone is on the other. There is a clear separateness between me and the material. When I give the stone my first beats with the chisel, I can feel the stone pushing back. The stone resists, feels hard, and, more often than not, I ask myself: What am I even doing? When I look at the beatings that occur at the beginning of each session, I often wonder how I was ever able to make a sculpture?

But then I keep going. I circle the stone to get to know the material. I sense the stone's quality, its form, its essence, the wilderness that resides within it, the uniqueness it contains, the personality it carries. I reach out with my hands, with my non-kinesthetic form of touch, searching for a way in.

On some days, it only takes me a few minutes to find a door. On others, it takes hours. Often, I do not submerge at all and I put the stone back inside. But sometimes, I am lucky; I strike gold and the stone allows me in.

When the door opens, my environment falls out of focus and the stone begins to take in my entire field of attention. Aspects on the surface — cracks, holes, broken bits— .start moving into the background, and the deeper aspects start coming into the foreground.

You know the difference in the state of mind from writing: When you read a text for grammatical accuracy, you are in a different state of mind than when you read the same text for feel. In the former, all you perceive is surface: you perceive the individual letters, words, sentences but not the living dream they are meant to trigger. But when you feel for the meaning inherent to a writing, you do not really perceive the words at all. Your awareness is somehow submerged below the surface of the text.

Thoughts can still be around at this stage but they are, just like the plane flying over my head, the children playing nearby, or the chatter coming from the neighboring restaurant, in the background and no longer disturbing me. They are floating around me while my focus is lasered on finding the next step I must take. At this depth, much like when driving a car, I can still listen to music or maintain a conversation, but I am acutely aware of what is happening on the workbench. Unintentional things still sometimes happen, but I am generally pretty confident in my actions.

But sometimes, it goes deeper. Often in the early mornings, the stone allows me to fully submerge. In doing so, I move into my senses and away from the thinking mind. A feeling of intimacy accompanies this intensification and an erotic component introduces itself into the work. I touch the stone on all sides —now gently, now with force; now playful, now demanding— and I also let the stone touch me. I allow the stone to move inside me, to feel me, to get to know who I am.

At this depth, I am confident in handling my tools, decisive in my actions, and continually present with the stone's overall gestalt. Chiseling now becomes more than just a clash of two materials: it becomes a form of intercourse.

The sculpture I am now forming extends well beyond its physical dimensions. I have broken into the sculpture, and the sculpture has broken free of its material. In this interplay, I communicate with the stone. I get to

know it, it gets to know me, and we whisper intimacies into each other's
ears.

Like with established dancing partners, hardly any unintentional things
happen anymore because I am acutely aware of the stone's feet. Whatever
I do now is apt to look good, feel good, and contribute towards the
becoming of the sculpture.

What characterizes this state is that everything except the work falls out
of focus. And yes, that includes the book I read last year, the place I traveled
to last month, and the thoughts I had during breakfast. That is why notions
of meaning, story, or inspiration are so absurd to me, for when I am present
with the stone, there is no room for any of these. There can be no room for
inspiration, ideas, images, or whatever because when I am in the zone, all I
perceive is the stone and nothing else. And if I did begin to concern myself
with any of these outsides, I would immediately lose touch with the
sculpture.

But on some days, it goes even deeper. On some days, I and the stone get
absorbed so deeply into each other that our perceived boundaries begin to
overlap. With that, thoughts subside totally and a silence occurs that coats
everything with the cloak of serenity. With the boundaries between me and
the stone blurred, I begin to perceive the form from the inside: No longer
can I see what I am doing *to* the stone, but I can feel what the chisel is doing
from the perspective of the stone. At this point, the tools have become like
parts of my body — I handle them with ease and with utmost precision.

I am in full control.

I know the material; the material knows me. Doubt has subsided, and I
feel *on par* with the stone. We meet at eye level. I am not above stone;
stone is not above me. We are partners now, operating on the same level,
participating in some kind of dance.

When deeply absorbed into the stone, it is as if my consciousness can
rotate along different axes of reality. I can feel what the stone looks like
from different angles simultaneously (inside, outside, above and below)
and sense its change across temporal axes: I can sense its past (what did
the stone look like) and see into the stone's possible futures (what will it

look like) together with other, indescribable features that overshadow my multisensorial perception in this tranquil state.

I usually do not notice when such shifts occur but only get aware of them when I come back out on the other side. This could be because a stranger approached me or because my body got thirsty. It is only then that I realize how deeply absorbed I was, and it is only then that the boundaries between inside and outside, between me and the stone, are re-established.

As soon as I am separated from the stone again, the stone often looks different from how it looked just moments ago. Just as your partner's face looks different when you are "hot," something seems to overlay or infuse the perceiving with an electric force. Everything glows and glitters, radiates beauty, communicates, is enchanted.

Besides such states being the secret gems of making art, they are also incredibly nourishing, if not rejuvenating. I sometimes remarked to myself that if there ever has been such a thing as "food for the soul," then being engaged with something outside myself in this intimate way must be it.

When I come out of such experiences, I also often find that I did things I could not identify as if they were done by me. Something else must have directed the work in that stone-induced ecstasy.

In fact, at times, I have had a hard time believing I made some of the sculptures that revealed themselves to me. They seem to exceed my understanding by a landslide, and I would have struggled to imagine, not to speak about render or sketch, some of their forms. Also, I am sure I could not reproduce any of them. Some of them are marked by a complexity, by a degree of interdependence and relationship that exceeds what I could have controlled. So, while I was absorbed into the stone, something, or someone else, must have worked through me that was a much more advanced sculptor than I could ever be.

Whatever originates from such experiences is automatically infused with a certain radiance, even if convention insists on labeling it as false. In fact, even if I split a stone in two, or whatever society might label immoral during such a meeting, the result is still true and pure: Everything that is revealed out of such a profound involvement is showered with a certain integrity, even if the image revealed goes against convention. It is bathed within a certain flavor that makes the sincerity of the underlying search evident.

I remember a night I was working on a sculpture in dim candlelight. The flame was small, so I could only see about half of the stone I was working on. And even though I worked in the dark, I worked furiously and without reservation. Guided by my hands, I felt like dancing with a stranger at an underground rave whose name I didn't know and whose face I did not see. But this didn't matter because both of us, me and the stone, knew we were exchanging on a deeper level. That night, I didn't care at all what the stone would look like the next morning because, in that moment, I was one with the stone, and there is no act more sacred than that, even if the sculpture lies broken the next morning.

But sculpting has taken me even further. In fact, it has taken me all the way. Because there were moments in which I was unsure whether I was the stone, or the person working on it. Moments in which I no longer knew whether I was chiseling or being chiseled on. There were moments, which were as fleeting as they were eternal, as imperceptible as they were overwhelming, in which my point of view flipped into its opposite: No longer was I looking at my hands, my stone, my environment, but I was my hands, my stone, my environment looking back at me. For a brief moment, the world and I swapped their place: I was everything but myself instead of being myself but not everything. For a timeless instance, the boundaries between me and the stone had dissolved into each other and become one.

Chapter 4

I believe in God because God is unbelievable.
—OSHO'S spin on Tertullian's "Credo quia absurdum est" | Get out of
your own way, 30

The space surrounding the studio often feels a little different, a little enhanced. Flowers seem more happy and richer in color. Stone seems strangely alien and familiar at the same time. Light likes to take on an ethereal quality in that it doesn't seem to be emitted by the sun, but as if it is emitted out of space itself. Space, too, is often distinguished by a quasi-psychedelic quality in that it doesn't seem empty but closer to the Japanese conception of negative space, known as *Ma*, in which space is understood as "an emptiness full of possibilities, like a promise to be fulfilled." Time also doesn't always operate in the same way. To say that it stands still would be too cheesy, for it does move normally. But it is as if it were freed, like how it was before humans locked it inside the clock.

On top of that, everything is infused with a sense of the archetypal and the real: "Everything is as it ought to be," I often internally remark, be this in reference to the sound the broom makes when I push away the pieces after a workday or the way starlings murmurate towards the open waters during the sunset.

All things, be these grand concepts such as time and space, or matters sometimes perceived as trivial, such as how a green beetle struggles up the ridge of a stone, are distinguished with a significance, with a meaning. And what is more, there is a silence, an underlying peace that gives the area a sense of the sacred. A sense of preciousness that must be conserved. The studio appears as one of these places that James Lovelock characterized as "reference points of health against which to contrast the illness of the present urban or rural scene."[14]

Sometimes, when I look over to the small patch of wilderness in front of the studio, when I let my gaze wander across the surrounding water, when I look up into the sky and watch the moving clouds, I find myself suspended in time, free of thoughts, free of worry, in sync with the shifting reality of my environment.

I remember a day this sense was particularly strong: On this day, the whole world suddenly quieted in a specific way. Silence took on a penetrating sound of its own, and sound became distinctly three-dimensional: The studio door bouncing against the metal, the wind blowing through the leaves of a nearby tree, the chirping of a cricket in the grass — all reverberated perfectly clear in that single moment suspended in time. Everything shimmered with an inner light, with a liquid luminescence. Everything throbbed with an aliveness, with an awareness. And in the midst of this moment in which everything had become more of itself, there stood my sculpture. To give a flavor of how it rested in space, consider the following comparison:

Once, about two hours after I had taken a dedicated dose of LSD, in moments in which everything in my visual field was moving, whirling, spinning, morphing and rotating in and out of each other, my gaze found a pair of duck eyes, which, unlike everything else, rested perfectly still in space. Even though the rest of the duck's body was blending and morphing in and out of its environment, its eyes always remained impeccably located in space. They were of a different quality than everything else surrounding me. Labeling them as black would have been a gross understatement, for they rather appeared as black holes from which nothing, not even light, could escape. The void that met me in the duck's eyes was infinitely deep, alien and mysterious, almost like death itself. They appeared as windows to a world outside of time and space, outside the rhythms of birth and decay. And on this day, I imagined perceiving a similar quality radiating off my sculpture. Not in the totality I had witnessed in the duck's eyes, but as laying on the same continuum. Just like the duck's eyes, my sculpture stood in space but, at the same time, was also somehow outside of space.

Later, I wondered whether this qualitative shift in perception was, in fact, *initiated by* my sculpture, not unlike the shift in perception under the influence of LSD was initiated by 250 gamma of lysergic acid latching onto my serotonin receptors? Because it appeared as if my sculpture did something similar to space, of which I was a part, as acupuncture needles do to a body. In a body, acupuncture needles allow *Qi* to move more freely; in space, my sculpture seemed to impregnate it with this psychedelic quality.

∞

My education has trained me to be skeptical about the realness of such experiences —actually, of all experience!— and taught me that nothing that cannot be replicated and proven in isolated experiments is to be trusted. Accordingly, a skeptic might want to conduct some experiments to verify some claims I made throughout this book. Such a person might, for instance, challenge me on the notion that a sculpture sometimes appears different when a small change is undertaken, *even when looked at from the opposite side*. Most likely, I would fail every test aimed at disproving me on this notion. Or even if this person were willing to take some LSD before looking at my sculpture, I am not sure they would perceive it to be performing acupunctural deeds on the empty space surrounding it. Most likely, all they would see is a whirling stone.

But *all* phenomena art depends upon cannot be proven. And the universe seems to hold the reservation that they do not reveal themselves to those who approach them with a skeptical mind. Trust is needed. So is faith. One has to *give* something in order to perceive them. One has to risk one's sanity, one's knowledge, yes, one's identity, to be open for the perceptions of these dimensions to occur.

So perhaps delusion and magic are two ways of characterizing the same phenomenon. And those unwilling to take the risk will miss out on both of them. So for those who are afraid of being labeled delusional, stone will never communicate with other stone; stone will never come alive and start operating on its environment. For those who shut themselves off from the possibility that such dimensions of reality exist, they won't. One must be open to the possibility of such events occurring to perceive them: One must believe in magic to encounter it.

Chapter 5

Art no longer cares to serve the state and religion, it no longer wishes to illustrate the history of manners, it wants to have nothing further to do with the object, as such, and believes that it can exist, in and for itself.
—*KAZIMIR MALEVICH | The Non-Objective World: The Manifesto of Suprematism, 74*

Since the very beginning, I have been under the sense that Nirman, and also myself, are standing on the shoulders of giants. That this approach, which I have called *Exploration of Form,* is a logical and destined part of the natural evolution of the art of sculpture.

So let me characterize this way of sculpting, as well as its implications, in some more depth:

As indicated, this approach seeks to free sculptures from any sort of outside. The theoretical implications of this "freeing of the outside" were already established in the first half of the 20th century by art movements such as *Concrete Art* or *Suprematism.*[15] The former, most prominently Max Bill, sought to free their work from any sort of outside in order to create a universal language made of "purely artistic means." These purely artistic means they found in mathematics, which is why they used geometric elements as the basis for their compositions.

Malevich, the founder of *Suprematism,* on the other hand, sought to liberate art from the constraints of representation. This quest also led him into the realm of mathematics, but contrary to Max Bill, he didn't start from it but discovered it underlying the world of feelings. But how did Malevich arrive at the conception that art should be granted the freedom to represent itself?

As part of his artistic inquiry, Malevich discovered that it is *the feeling* that gives rise to a painting that makes it "artistic" and not that which it depicts. Malevich wasn't against figuration per se, but he emphasized that figurative elements tend to conceal or distract from the true value of an artwork, namely the feeling that gave rise to it. Subsequently, he sought to reduce the content of his compositions until nothing but *pure feeling* remained.

The "pure feeling" that seeks to be expressed, he writes in his manifesto, *The Non-Objective World*, originates from the subconscious or superconscious mind. And only when *it* is directing the work something of artistic value can be revealed. So what Malevich means by "feeling" isn't so much what we like to think of as an emotion, as it is something more autonomous that seeks expression. And because the feeling exists independently of the artist, it should be granted the freedom to represent itself.

I share Malevich's conception that it is not the form *per se* that gives a sculpture its artistic value but the feeling that gave rise to it. I also share his conception that the feeling that seeks expression stems from below or above the conscious mind. And the more the artist took themselves back, the less the artist introduced into the artwork —be this by likening it to an object or an idea— the more powerful the work will be. Since when the artist has removed themselves as much as they can, the feeling that sought to express itself through the artist can show itself most clearly.

Accordingly, a sculpture revealed in light of this book's approach can be characterized as a feeling representing itself in three-dimensional space. A feeling that gave form to itself by planting an urge within the artist to make it manifest. We remember Paul Klee's words: "He [the artist] neither serves nor rules – he transmits. His position is humble. And the beauty of the crown is not his own. He is merely a channel."[16] But from the artist's point of view, it is still an active experience. The artist is expressing their feeling, but they simultaneously know that the feeling is not theirs.

Since an infinitude of feelings exist, the forms such works can take are inexhaustible. Malevich's *Suprematist* paintings are mostly comprised of geometric elements or free of form or color altogether. My sculptures appear more living, both in shape and quality. Other people's work might come out figuratively altogether. But what the work depicts is irrelevant. It is the feeling that gave rise to it which is decisive for its artistic value. This is to say: the state of consciousness the person was in during its production.

One unifying characteristic that bounds all works born out of such an orientation is a certain balance: no matter which direction, distance, angle, or environment they are looked at, they always appear balanced. Malevich sometimes hung the same painting differently depending on the exhibition, and I also frequently change the resting side of my sculptures. Feelings don't have any fixed direction in space. Nor in time.

$$\infty$$

A societal ghost surrounds the art of sculpture, namely that sculpture, as an art form, and stone sculpture in particular, has exhausted itself. That everything that can be done has been done, and that there is nowhere for the art of sculpture to develop towards. Of course, this is as nonsensical as declaring the use of words as exhausted because sculpture is a language and, in that way, forever inexhaustible. Yes, sometimes a genre might get into a bottleneck, but it is precisely at such moments that radical breaks can occur. Think of abstract painting, techno, absurdism— all were born out of fields that were previously declared exhausted. And so, too, one might, perhaps rightfully so, conclude that all externally motivated pursuits, such as those for making smaller, bigger, more grotesque, or more violent sculptures, have long overstepped their boundaries; that representational sculpture has exhausted itself; that the paradigm of stone having to serve as the carrier of a human idea has discovered its end.

But just like the eye has a blind spot at its center, this obvious way of working, whose theoretical foundations have long been established, has, to a large degree, remained elusive. I say obvious because many metaphors surrounding the creative process point in its direction. Because when people characterize an ideal type of the sculptural process, many intuitively use phrases like "It's all about the process, not the end result," "It's about listening and following," or even the corny "The sculpture is always finished." Collective thought thus seems to be intuitively aware of the approach underlying this book, but nearly nobody seems to be actually living it. Most still sculpt towards an end result, don't follow the stone but impose themselves on it, and do not finish their sculptures with every chisel beat, even though they decorate their homepages with sayings that would suggest they do. So perhaps it's time to actually do it? To have sculpture step into its center; to allow it to take the next step in its natural evolution? That is, to free sculptures from having to show "new" forms or break records of size and scope, towards sculptures having to be born out of one's inner necessity.

Or else, that the defining criteria for whether a sculpture is of artistic value is no longer made dependent upon what it depicts but on the quality of its execution. And quality can only be discovered when the focus rests on the process, not the end result.

Within such a conception —as exemplified by Japanese Zen art, for example— the possibilities of sculpture are, once again, made endless. Because in such a conception, it is no longer about how large a sculpture is, what material it is made of, or what it depicts, but about the state of consciousness the person was in during its production.

So ultimately, this approach seeks to reinstate the individual into the art of sculpture by making *their* quality of consciousness the focal point of artistic interest.

Commonly, such shifts, as well as their resulting artworks, are not immediately understood or appreciated by the general public. I already provided examples of how most people tend to be blind to works born out of this approach, not to speak about appreciating their significance as part of art history. Malevich wrote about this:

> *The public, to be sure, evaluates works of art on the basis of external characteristics which are in accord with the familiar - the approved – on the basis of subject matter, the fidelity to 'nature' of the thing depicted, etc. If, then, a picture displays new additional elements so that it is no longer possible to fit it into the framework of the familiar norm, it is rejected by the public... The public lack of understanding, however, does not alter in the slightest the actual artistic value of a picture so that when, after a certain lapse of time, the people have accustomed themselves to the unfamiliar, the picture will inevitably come into its own.[17]*

That is because that which is truly contemporary, the public has not yet developed the language, yes, the sense organs, to perceive their meaning.

To perceive a sculpture that speaks for itself, that is itself, *is* for the majority of people as overwhelming as listening to a piece by Schoenberg. To this day, for most people, his music is too mysterious, too powerful, and thereby tends to overwhelm or "floor" the person coming in contact with it. "But I just don't understand it!" the common person often says to justify why they dislike this kind of art. But one is not meant to understand! — *that* is precisely its point!

In a conversation, a sculptor once told me that he no longer insists on potential customers having to see his sculptures in person because he witnessed how overwhelmed some get by their presence. Whereas if he presents them with a photograph, they are already much better able to "handle" what they are seeing. Through photography, we agreed, the sculpture's multidimensionality is translated into a format for which people already have a faculty of mind for. People can digest a photograph but the real thing tends to overwhelm them. They thus prefer to see a photograph to assess whether they want anything to do with it. And indeed, I also sometimes had the impression that some preferred to see pictures of my sculptures instead of meeting them in person.

Susan Sontag wrote an essay titled *Against Interpretation* in which she argues that interpretation serves a similar function. She argues that the act of interpreting, much like photographing, is a way of *translating down* an artwork to make it more manageable: "By reducing the work of art to its content and then interpreting that, one tames the work of art. Interpretation makes art manageable, conformable," she writes.[18] The direct confrontation with the Mysterious, with the Unknown, with the Out-of-Control, is not bearable for the egoic mind, she argues. Therefore, we have developed a habit of concealing artworks behind stories or interpretations. "Interpretation is the revenge of the intellect upon art," she concludes her masterpiece.[19]

Those who do not possess the language to slay the sculpture with the word often fall silent when they encounter one. Unfortunately, most are uncomfortable with this silence, so they immediately seek to divert their attention elsewhere. And indeed, I found that some people, and those societally "close" to me in particular, actively *look away* when confronted with any of my sculptures. Some even act as if they are in the presence of a *Gorgon*, you know, that creature from Greek mythology that turns you into stone when you look at it, in that they avoid eye contact with my sculptures at all cost.

One reason some people seem to have such negligence towards artworks born out of this place, I believe, is because they are, in some fundamental way, perceived as threatening. Because just like the majority of people, and those societally "close" to me in particular, are not prepared or interested in hearing about, not to speak about experiencing, the mind-bending realities I witnessed under the influence of DMT, people are equally unprepared or uninterested in engaging with a sculpture born out of this place. Their minds seem to sense that they are coming from a place they have no control over. Their minds can sense that they arose from an ungoverned process, from chaos, and not from a controlling approach. And because the mind seeks, above all, control, the sculptures themselves are perceived as threatening. In that way, they possess similar ego-dissolving capabilities as psychedelic drugs. "For make no mistake," the painter Robert Motherwell confirmes, "abstract art is a form of mysticism."[20]

What is more, because it is evident in works born out of such an orientation that the artist did not care for the image but only for the material, the resulting work somehow violates the dominant *Weltanschauung*, in which matter only serves a subordinate role to the mind. And because the mind can sense that such sculptures, just like consciousness-expanding drugs, threaten its worldview, it immediately diverts its attention elsewhere. That is, it diverts its attention —such as by asking for the hammer's weight or the type of stone— at best. Because many (although only a few do it openly) actively despise them, just like they despise psychedelic drugs.

The fact that so little literature on stone sculpture exists can further be regarded as testimony that the linear mind finds it difficult to get a grip on. There is something about working with stone that makes it so blatantly obvious that nothing can be said about it that is not immediately realized as nonsensical. In fact, I, too, am convinced that if I had continued working on this book indefinitely, it would eventually have folded up on itself. That is, I am sure that had I continued working on this book, I would eventually have returned it to the empty page. The fact that I wrote most of this book at the beginning of my artistic journey in which I was still convinced that there was something to be said about it —in which I was still filled with enough nonsense— is thus perhaps the only way it could have ever come into being. Because after a few years of working with stone already, I could sense how the process pushed sentence after sentence, paragraph after paragraph, chapter after chapter into each other so that they canceled each other out.

Since these dissolving effects also operate on the psyche, I, as a sculptor, must, by necessity, maintain mental hygiene. When working with psychedelics, for example, it is common knowledge that one must take time to integrate following an experience. Because if the foot is kept on the psychedelic pedal, they will soon destabilize the psyche in unbearable ways. Unfortunately, this is not as widely accepted with making art, although it is no less applicable. So, if I want to keep going, I must keep my Qigong postures, herbal tea and my meditation cushion as my constant allies. Otherwise, my own creations have the power to drive me insane.

One's art will always be ahead of oneself. One's art will always pull one towards the source, towards "the powerhouse of all time and space" as Paul Klee put it, just like psychedelic drugs will always pull one towards the "womb of creation, where the secret key to all lies guarded."[21] So the more grandiose one's art becomes, the more centered one needs to be. Otherwise, one won't be sculpting for long. As Brancusi said: "It is not the work itself, it is to keep oneself in condition to do it, that is difficult."[22]

Those who tend to say that this is nonsense are the same people who say that psychedelics are the easy way out. Of course, such people would never explore the art of sculpture beyond a Sunday's worth of workshop, nor would they come close to a serious dose of psychedelic phantasmagoria. But not because they do not work or because they are the easy way out. No, precisely because they *do* work and truly deliver on their promise. And their minds can sense that, which is why they are condemning it in the first place. They thus rather commit to another workshop on sculptural technique or on drinking Matcha tea instead of jumping into the center of the mandala this very afternoon.

So perhaps the best comparison to working with stone really are psychedelic drugs: Both gain access to deeper dimensions of reality, both dissolve the supremacy of the linear mind, both demand for radical self-exploration, both can lead to the final understanding. . . And both are self-regulatory: The harder one pushes them, the harder they push back; and only when one keeps integrating their lessons, only when one keeps taking one step at a time, only when one keeps centering oneself, can a partnership be maintained and the journey inwards be continued.

Inevitably, those who venture into novel directions are always mavericks. Mad people who follow their inner necessity, regardless of the feedback their culture, their social environment, or even their own minds give them. They do so not just because they want to but because they must. Their authority lies with something else, with the material, with the stone, and they trust that what it asks them to do is right. Some of them find a way to cope with it and rise to glory. Many do not and fall into the abyss of psychosis or depression.

In the beginning, nobody but a few will see the significance of their work. Some might openly despise it. But with the lapse of time, often long after they are dead, the culture begins to catch up and understand, or at least appreciate, what these pioneers have done. Few today doubt the revolution that took place in 1915 when Malevich exhibited *Black Square* or when Schoenberg dispensed of tonal structures. But it took time for the general public to catch up. It took time until the sense organs, the language, to assimilate them into thought developed.[23]

So, it might take time until the significance of this approach is appreciated. This way of working is in its infancy and has, by no means, percolated into the art world, not to speak about the general public. It is but a few who have sensed that the time is ripe to move beyond all truisms that govern the realm of sculpture. That the time is ripe to allow form to appear from the inside, through chaos, through a search, and no longer from the outside in, through order, and through predefined forms.

Chapter 6

Whereof one cannot speak, thereof one must be silent.
—*LUDWIG WITTGENSTEIN | Tractatus Logico-Philosophicus: Prop. 7*

I have proposed that works of art are called forth by the environment and that they are, in a sense, fulfilling an ecological function. I further proposed that their influence on the environment is similar to that of acupuncture needles, in that they contribute towards the relaxation of space itself. And because the environment does not have hands to make these objects, She needs us to make them manifest. She needs our hands, our tools, to scoop them out of potentiality and *therefore* plants the urge to create within us. Artists then communicate with the ideal that the environment called forth and try to approximate it with their doings.

Because of this worldview, I attest that whatever comes forth as a result of this process manifests itself for a reason. That each work born out of such an orientation has an ecological function. And this ecological function lies beyond what one can comprehend by rational thought alone.

That is why I do not concern myself with the meaning of my artworks but seek to make way for whatever wants to manifest itself through me. The meaning, the societal critique, the message will always find its way into the work in sideway fashion and does not need to be imposed from the outside. It is for this reason that I regard notions of content, critique, story and so forth as mere by-products and not as central to the creative process.

My artworks exhibit a meaning that I cannot express in words. Because if there is something I would like to say, I will say it. Using words. And for whatever I cannot put into words, I use sculpture as a vehicle to "pass over in silence," as Wittgenstein put it, what I cannot say. I allow the artwork to speak for itself and have it transpose a meaning I cannot fully comprehend myself. "If a composer could say what he had to say in words," Gustav Mahler once said fittingly, "he would not bother trying to say it in music."

Also, when I am free of aspirations, politically or otherwise, the meaning, the content, the critique that finds itself into the work will speak much more convincingly than any message introduced by me ever could.

This is because whatever manifests itself out of the unknown is a direct expression of the *Unus Mundus* and thus miles ahead compared to my best idea.

All works revealed in this way within a given period then come to constitute a zeitgeist.[24] The mind can never know the zeitgeist it is in because something can never know what it is made of in itself. "No man can surpass his own time, for the spirit of his times is also his own spirit," Hegel once said. So about all one can do is try to feel and express it, as I have tried to do in writing this book.

The underlying archetypes through which these shifting "spirit of the times" are expressed remain constant over time. Only the forms change. So a sculptor remains a sculptor, no matter what time they are in. But what they do, what forms they make, what images they reveal, how they relate to the material, is renegotiated for each time anew.

That is why all approaches grounded in the past, such as attempts to revivify Greek or Renaissance sculpture, are a priori doomed to fail to bring forth anything of artistic value; what they revealed was an expression of their zeitgeist, not ours.[25]

So only when one is true to one's feeling sense, which is always rooted in the present, can one birth a work of art. Anything whose underlying drive was rooted in the past is apt to be *mere aping*, as Kandinsky put it, because it is no longer in sync with time itself. And because *all* thinking is rooted in the past, no artwork whose meaning was defined by thought can ever come to represent itself. "Art exists to be a way of operating that does not involve ideas." Jean Dubuffet once said: "When it is mixed with ideas, art becomes oxidized and worthless."[26]

Every true work of art is, in that way, simultaneously a reflection and a constituent part of an ongoing zeitgeist. Or, as Mondrian put it: "It is the spirit of the times that determines artistic expression, which, in turn, reflects the spirit of the times."[27]

But there is more. There is a persisting intuition that works of art do not just constitute an ongoing zeitgeist but that they are, in fact, anticipating the future.[28]

If there is something to that eerie intuition that art is foreshadowing what is about to come, one is, when looking across the contemporary art world, not presented with a particularly hopeful picture. Many so-called artists still seek to triumph over each other in terms of being more disturbing, weird, ugly, unintelligible and so forth. In defense of this argument that art foreshadows the future, some might claim that such works mirror and anticipate cultural downfall, environmental catastrophes, deterioration of health and so forth.

But to me, such works aren't works of art at all; they aren't artifacts discovered in the deep waters of the unknown but products of the linear mind. At best, they are stuck halfway. For what the (sick) minds behind these works overlook is that chaos tends to organize itself when it is left to itself. They overlook that if chaos is allowed to ensue, order arises. And not just any order, but a beautiful one.

Because whenever I start a new project, the sculpture also, sometimes for a very long time, takes on seemingly undefined and random forms. After a few sessions, someone might equally interpret my sculpture to be anticipating an incoming environmental crisis. I might even get a phone call from a contemporary art museum because they want to exhibit my disturbing piece. But when I keep taking one step at a time, the process will soon reveal an intrinsic order.

All chaotic systems, mathematics and the natural world have taught us, will eventually reveal a dynamic order when they are left to themselves. When order arises, or what this order will look like cannot be anticipated from the starting conditions, however. It only arises after the system has run for a while, which is to say: after one has taken one step at a time for a while in sculpture. The order revealed this way is, therefore, not an order defined top-down but an order that reveals itself from the bottom-up. It is, in fact, a natural order.

Whatever forms arise by themselves consistently bear a certain quality that makes them recognizable as artifacts of nature itself. If we observe feathers, crystals, leaves, or whatever else that simply occurs on its own, we notice a consistency of quality that resides below the multitude of forms. Whatever carries this quality, we call *beautiful, natural, healthy, alive.*

Most contemporary sculptures do not emit that flavor. It is difficult to define why they do not, but they miss this quality that nature always hits:

Either they are too rigid, or not rigid enough; too straight, or not straight enough; too complex, or not complex enough; too smooth, or not smooth enough. One can sense that someone was trying instead of letting loose. One can sense that their makers weren't considering the lilies in the field. . .

Whenever I go into an intact forest —that is: whenever I go into a forest that was not interfered with, that was not managed or controlled, but which was allowed to grow wild— I find this spontaneous order that nature always hits: The way the grass grows with the ferns, the way the ferns grow with the bushes, the way the bushes grow with the trees, all *makes sense* and gives rise to a beautiful whole. Even the distances between the trees, the width of the deer's path, the location of the anthill —all seem exactly *right*. So, even though nobody mapped the forest, decided where the trees must grow, where the deer must walk, where the ants must build their hill, everything seems perfectly integrated with everything else. And I can choose any lens of magnification and this order will persist: From above, I can see how the greens of the forest fade towards the river, how the river cooperates its way around a rock formation. . . From below, I can see how the spider's web builds perfectly into the branches, how the moss blends nicely with the browns of the tree. . . All but what men tries to control is distinguished by this divine perfection.

Whenever I encounter such an unspoiled ecosystem, I experience a feeling of depth, richness and mystery. I might not see the birds nesting on the top of the trees, or the mycelium working below my feet, but I can *feel* that life is thriving here. I can feel that I am in a healthy ecosystem. And I can feel its healing effects on *me*. And it is this same healing effect that I have felt emitted by Nirman's sculptures. For they come from the same place, are organized according to the same principles, are governed by the same laws.

This is a very different feeling I know from standing in front of a monoculture field or before a conceptual sculpture that was vomited out of a diseased mind. There, my breath gets more shallow, my thoughts more anxious. A kind of dissociation occurs. I am alienated from myself and the natural world. Sickness spawns.

So, as long as someone seeks to control any element of their work independently —such as its meaning or parts of its form— they is bound to remain within the confines of the intellect and removed from the intelligence of nature. And just like every attempt to control nature is bound to create ever more problems, approaches to sculpture that are targeted at controlling any one element individually are equally bound to result in ever more complications. That is because a sculpture, just like a forest, is simply too complex, comprised of too many parts, linked in too many ways, so that, no matter how much one knows, how good one's technique is, how much one has studied, one will never be able to control all aspects simultaneously. Like in an ecosystem, every part within a sculpture is connected to every other part, and by moving one aspect, the whole moves with it.[29] And no intellect can keep up with that, for its relationships are, on top of being infinite in number, connected non-linearly, spontaneously and chaotically.

Sculptors who do not allow this spontaneous organization of chaotic parts to occur will thus forever remain afraid of the material, anxiously hoping it will obey their will. And as a result of their subordinating act, their sculptures will, just like a monoculture field, spawn sickness.

If sculptors can find the courage to give up control, on the other hand, their sculptures will, just like a forest, find a dynamic equilibrium all of their own. I say dynamic because there can be earthquakes, volcanic eruptions, landslides, asteroid impacts, or pandemics, all of which can temporarily cause a great imbalance in the form. But if they go with them, such impacts can open up new ecological niches and allow new forms (of life) to move in. After some time then, a new dynamic equilibrium is found with different forms marking the landscape.

As a matter of fact, nature's ability to heal can be witnessed in this approach to sculpture: Whenever something brute happens in nature, everything immediately begins to reassemble itself so that it soon appears as if the broken part has always been integral to its surroundings. And so in sculpture, whenever something unintentional happens, the thread will always find a way to incorporate the happening into the becoming of the form. But not only is one returned to the baseline: One is led deeper, higher, to places one has never been before, to places one would not have traveled otherwise.

So the conviction that nature thrives when it is allowed to organize itself is what underlies this approach to sculpture. And when the body, which is part of nature, is allowed to partake in this process of self-organization, a sculpture will, all on its own, begin to take on the same quality as a healthy ecosystem. It will become an artifact of nature: it will come alive.

Acknowledgments

Thomas Butzlaff.
Viktoria Scherübel.
Nirman Cain.

Appendix

Thomas Butzlaff, who contributed greatly to this book, kindly allowed me to include his characterization of Nirman's approach to teaching and sculpture.

A Search for Dynamic Silence | Thomas Butzlaff

He [Nirman] introduces others to sculpture in the same way that he himself meets the stone. First comes his love for the material - the feeling; the technique is secondary.

He can spend hours circling the stone and looking, before a single blow with hammer and chisel is struck. He must feel in tune. In terms of art history, one could classify him loosely as a neo-romantic. Loosely this means, when looking at the world, or the stone, if nothing stirs within then forget about sculpting.

For a more graphic description: Nirman's attitude to his work introduces sculpture as a living, jazz-like element. As soon as the feeling between the two musicians, the stone and the artist is 'right,' the improvisation can begin. The sculpture evolves over the course of many, many sessions. When the feeling isn't there, he again circles around the figure, waiting and listening. Seeing is an intrinsic part of the process, hence the title of one of his works - Wait and See. This intuitive dialogue with the stone requires a relaxed patient way of working as well as intimate handwork. This is what makes his sculptures so precious. They take their own time until they are both finished.

The mind, of course, also plays its part. The questioning and often insecure mind steps in with a vengeance whenever the artist cannot access his intuitive improvisation: 'Why does it falter? Am I still working on what was intended? What does the material want?' To ponder and clarify these questions can be helpful. But what really gets him going again is, in fact, what he keeps telling his students. 'The breakthrough often comes when you just let go and risk.' This isn't always easy. Imagine you have invested many months of hard work in a statue, parts of it have even been polished already, but you feel that something is not yet right. Suddenly you grasp the hammer and in a fit of wild resolution you completely blast off a carefully honed corner. The standing figure has become a lying one. Yet you still don't know whether you will achieve the hoped-for improvement or just ruin the sculpture for good. Was this the right thing to do?

This is the way he works.

His students in the sculpting studio may take their time in understanding this very emotional and intuitive way of working. But by and by it dawns on them that, apart from sculpting techniques, they are being given a valuable insight: a timeless approach to art.

When he draws or paints, Nirman works fast, impulsively, and non-figuratively. For him, paint plays a subservient role. His theme is expressive tracks of black and white. Here, too, he has to wait for the right moment. What always counts is the moment. The moment of utmost awareness and spontaneity. Then it is either succeed – or fail. One cannot improve, only start afresh.

Nirman Cain's work as a sculptor follows the tradition of modern classicism. What interests him in his art is anything authentic, real, archetypal – the concentration on the essential in a form. In this way, he is far from Rodin, or Michelangelo but very close to Brancusi, or Cycladic sculptors. He lets himself be inspired by nature, but what comes out is non-representational. If his subject matter is a tree, the sculpture will show his dialogue with the tree rather than its literal image.

Jean Arp is the only forerunner I can think of with whom he shares the same love for sculpting vegetational shapes in stone. The artists of modern classicism did not want to depict reality; they were after something essential behind the incidental outer phenomena. No wonder then, that

Nirman loves the Dutch painter Piet Mondrian. Yet my feeling is that he is closer to Kandinsky or Paul Klee's apparently musical approach.

To date, Nirman has created two cycles of sculptures. The second has evolved out of the first, with an increasing degree of abstraction.

The first cycle of stones is characterized by an uprising, dynamic theme. The stones of the second cycle rest in themselves.

Nirman always lets himself be inspired by nature, giving it a synthesizing spin. No matter what the details may be, he is always aware of the whole form of his subject matter. The empty gaps become an essential part of the sculpture and in the cycle of the dynamic stones, this is clear. The lotus and the Palm leaf are immediately recognizable as a plant, even though the actual theme is the energy that makes it grow and unfold. They rise from a narrow base, expanding upwards in an effort to overcome gravity.

In the later cycle of the restful stones, that which originally inspired him is hardly recognizable anymore. They are very self-contained. On the level of plants, they are seeds. They seem to harbour a second form, another sculpture within, quietly waiting for the day when they will open up and give birth.

These two themes of dynamic unfolding and quiet waiting are expressions of two opposite poles, the male and the female, and two sides of Nirman's nature. They are the visible traces of his real work — the search for the dynamic restfulness of Nirman Cain.

Endnotes

Overture

[1] Schoenberg, *Theory of Harmony*, 417

[2] Schoenberg, *Theory of Harmony*, 1

[3] Putnam, *The Sculptor's Way*, xx

Part I: On Art

[1] Klee, *The Thinking Eye*, 17

[2] Nicolaides, *The Natural Way to Draw*, 151

[3] Steinbeck, *Cannery Row*, 2

[4] Klee, *On Modern Art*, 19

[5] Cited in Merill, *Brancusi*, 4

[6] Auguste Rodin writes equally dismissive about approaches rooted in copying: "Oh, doubtless a mediocre man copying nature will never produce a work of art; because he really looks without seeing, and though he may have noted each detail minutely, the result will be flat and without character." Rodin, Gsell, *Art by Auguste Rodin*, 33

[7] Malevich, *The Non-Objective World*, 48

[8] Arp, *On My Way, 122*

[9] Cited in Chipp, *Theories of Modern Art, 570*

[10] Malevich, *The Non-Objective World*, 34

[11] Stafford, *Writing the Australian Crawl*. 48

[12] The drawing can be seen on Nirman's homepage. Visit nirmancain.com and navigate to the *Comments* section.

[13] Eric Berne tells a similar story in Games People Play: 'A little boy sees and hears birds with delight. Then the "good father" comes along and feels he should "share" the experience and help his son "develop." He says: "That's a jay, and this is a sparrow." The moment the little boy is concerned with which is a jay and which is a sparrow, he can no longer see the birds or hear them sing. He has to see and hear them the way the father wants him to. Father has good reasons on his side, since few people can go through life listening to the birds sing, and the sooner the boy starts his "education" the better. Maybe he will be an ornithologist when he grows up. A few people, however, can still see and hear in the old way. But most of the members of the human race have lost the capacity to be painters, poets, or musicians, and are not left the option of seeing and hearing directly even if they can afford to; they must get it secondhand.' (Berne, *Games People Play*, 178)

[14] Goethe, *The Essential Goethe*, 959

232

[15] From this, I shall not conclude that art historians are to be the most ignorant, however. It can be beautiful to study art history and criticizing art can be an art in-and-of-itself. When good art critics speak about an artwork, they always remain spontaneous and do not introduce anything from the past in their assessment. They might have a great knowledge of art, but in the moment they are in front of the artwork, they drop it all. So, because no artwork ever presents itself in the same way twice, their critique will also differ each time.

[16] Dubuffet, *Crude Art Preferred to Cultural Art*, 595

[17] Nicolaides, *The Natural Way to Draw, 48*

[18] Henry David Thoreau wrote about this in relation to studying the natural world, for which the same applies: "It is only when we forget all our learning that we begin to know. I do not get nearer by a hair's breadth to any natural object so long as I presume that I have an introduction to it from some learned man. To conceive of it with a total apprehension I must for the thousandth time approach it as something totally strange. If you would make acquaintance with the ferns you must forget your botany. You must get rid of what is commonly called knowledge of them. Not a single scientific term or distinction is the least to the purpose, for you would fain perceive something, and you must approach the object totally unprejudiced. You must be aware that nothing is what you have taken it to be. . . Your greatest success will be simply to perceive things as they are." Thoreau, *Autumn, 67*

[19] Nicolaides, *The Natural Way to Draw*, 151

[20] Nicolaldes, *The Natural Way to Draw*, 100

Part II: Hammer on the Rock

[1] Nicolaides, *The Natural Way to Draw*, 221

[2] Cited in Adams, *Barbara Hepworth: a life told in six works*, The Guardian, 07.06.2015

[3] Nietzsche, *Thus Spoke Zarathustra*, 239

[4] Krenov, *The Fine Art of Cabinetmaking*, 59

[5] One exception might be the bottom which I sometimes like to preserve before I commit to a lying sculpture. Another reason I sometimes leave the bottom untouched is for safety. I once developed a sculpture in which I never decided where the bottom was and the stone punished me for not having grounded it. Because it did not have a base, it fell from the sculpting table and broke into pieces.

[6] For more on such aspects inherent to language, I recommend Lakoff and Johnson's *Metaphors We Live by.*

[7] Cited in West, *Delayed Trane: John Coltrane's Lost Album*, Jazztimes.com

[8] Cited in Becks-Malorny, *Cezanne*, 21/24

[9] Nicolaides, *The Natural Way to Draw*, 16

[10] Nicolaides, *The Natural Way to Draw*, 99

[11] Cummings, *E.E. Cummings*, 335

[12] Goethe, *Scientific Studies*, 39

[13] Nicolaides, *The Natural Way to Draw*, 5

[14] Cited in Jaffe, *Symbolism in the Visual Arts*, 310

[15] Thoreau has this beautiful quote in *Walden:* "The oldest Egyptian or Hindoo philosopher raised a corner of the veil from the statue of the divinity; and still the trembling robe remains raised, and I gaze upon as fresh a glory as he did, since it was I in him that was then so bold, and it is he in me that now reviews the vision. No dust has settled on that robe; no time has elapsed since that divinity was revealed. That time which we really improve, or which is improvable, is neither past, present, nor future." (Thoreau, *Walden*, 97)

[16] Buhner, *Plant Intelligence and the Imaginal Realm*, 305

[17] Read, *The semiotic aspect of Alfred Korzybski's general semantics*, 16

[18] Stegner, *One Way to Spell a Man*, 13

[19] Goethe, *Scientific Studies*, 64

[20] Stafford, *Writing the Australian Crawl*, 25f

[21] Stafford, *Writing the Australian Crawl*, 43

[22] Buhner, *Ensouling Language*, 96

[23] This sentence is inspired by a line in Thomas Butzlaff's essay *A Search for Dynamic Silence*. He kindly allowed me to attach it in the *Appendices*.

[24] Goethe, *Conversations of Goethe*, 153

[25] Stafford, *Writing the Australian Crawl*, 4

[26] Berger, *John Berger on Ways of Seeing, being an artist, and Marxism (2011)*, min. 03:00

[27] He got it from John Crowley, who popularized it in his novel *Little, Big*.

[28] Cited in Chipp, *Theories of Modern Art*, 564

[29] Buhner, *Ensouling Language*, 181

[30] Cited in Chipp, *Theories of Modern Art*, 541

[31] Kandinsky in Lindsay and Vergo, *Kandinsky: Complete Writings on Art*, 210

[32] Cited in Chipp, *Theories of Modern Art*, 548

[33] Osho, *Walk Without Feet, Fly Without Wings and Think Without Mind*, Chapter 7

[34] Cited in Coats, *Living Energies*, 299

[35] Klee, *Form und Gestaltungslehre (Transl. John Sallis)*, 269

[36] Klee, *The Thinking Eye*, 17

[37] Goethe, *Scientific Studies*, 41

[38] Klee, *On Modern Art*, 54

[39] Nicolaides, *The Natural Way to Draw*, 96

[40] See, for example: *Alberto Giacometti (1901-1966)*, Archive.org

[41] Goethe, *Scientific Studies*, 45

[42] Arp, *On My Way*, 70

[43] Also, just because I have spent months refining subtle aspects, this shall not mean that a sculpture must take a long time to finish. The mind likes to believe that something meaningful must have taken a long time to make or that it must have sprung out of a struggling process. But those are just ideas, not actualities: I've made a sculpture in a single session that lacks nothing compared to sculptures I have worked on for more than half a year.

[44] Cited in Chipp, *Theories of Modern Art*, 564

[45] Wittgenstein, *Culture and Value*, 22e

[46] Henry Moore, for example, writes: "... Certainly it [sculpture] is more difficult than the arts which involve appreciation of flat forms, shape in only two dimensions [painting, drawing]." (cited in Chipp, *Theories of Modern Art*, 594)

Part III: Inhabiting Stone

[1] Obviously, most people don't get that, and they believe that it is the story or the cultural context that gives the book its value. As a result, most editions in circulation are chopped-up versions of the original, in which editors flattened out these very nuances, not realizing that it was them that made the book come alive in the first place.

[2] Emerson, *The Complete Essays and Other Writings*, 166

[3] Gospel of Thomas: 70

[4] Campbell, *The Power of Myth*, 149

[5] Cited in Tiger, *Isamu Noguchi*, 51

[6] Krenov, *A Cabinetmaker's Notebook*, 127

[7] Viktor Frankl writes in the introduction to *Man's Search for Meaning*: "Don't aim at success—the more you aim at it and make it a target, the more you are going to miss it. For success, like happiness, cannot be pursued; it must ensue, and it only does so as the unintended side-effect of one's dedication to a cause greater than oneself or as the by-product of one's surrender to a person other than oneself. Happiness must happen, and the same holds for success: you have to let it happen by not caring about it. I want you to listen to what your conscience commands you to do and go on to carry it out to the best of your knowledge. Then you will live to see that in the long run—in the long run, I say!—success will follow you precisely because you had forgotten to think of it." (Frankl, *Man's Search for Meaning*, 12f)

[8] Krenov, *A Cabinetmaker's Notebook*, 126

[9] Cited in Maclagan, *Outsider Art*, 53

[10] This provides another example of how topsy-turfy the popular conception of art is. Because if you insist on calling anything *Outsider* Art, then it should be the other way around...

[11] Cited in Maclagan, *Outsider Art*, 10

[12] Rodin, Gsell, *Art by Auguste Rodin*, 46f

[13] Cited in Goodall, *Italian artists sells 'invisible art' for €15,000*, The Boar, 04.07.2021

[14] Dostoyevsky, *The Brothers Karamazov*, 48

[15] Arp, *On My Way*, 70

[16] Buhner, *Ensouling Language*, 25

[17] Rodin, Gsell, *Art by Auguste Rodin*, 168

[18] Schoenberg, *Theory of Harmony*, 416

[19] The Kalahari Bushmen, for example, kept their societal structure in check by putting each other down. See, for example, *Affluence without Abundance* by James Suzman

[20] Cited in Chipp, *Theories of Modern Art*, 593

[21] Some of the Greeks, Goethe, Thoreau, Luther Burbank, Viktor Schauberger, Rudolf Steiner, Stephen Buhner all touched on this notion in some of their writings. Goethe, for example, writes: "Nature understands no jesting; she is always true, always serious, always severe; she is always right, and the errors and faults are always those of man. The man incapable of appreciating her she despises; and only to the apt, the pure, and the true, does she resign herself and reveal her secrets." (*Conversations of Goethe with Eckermann and Soret*, 1829)

[22] Buhner, *The Secret Teaching of Plants*, 247

[23] Other than humans, which are generally agreed as to have something akin to a soul; other than animals, which are generally agreed as to have some kind of awareness; and other than plants or trees, which are generally agreed to be alive, stone is often rendered as an innate material at the bottom of the hierarchy of Being. I would, however, be careful with making such hasty conclusions without having worked with stone. Because to me, stone has always presented itself not as a lower form of matter but, if anything, as the highest, most intelligent form of matter, not only in its perceived quality but also in its behavior.

[24] The term *metaphysical background* was coined by Gottfried Benn. Stephen Buhner uses it extensively in his writing. The original quote by Benn reads as follows: "[For the Western model] reality is simply raw material, but its metaphysical background remains forever obscured." as quoted in Hofmann in *LSD: My Problemchild*, Chapter 11

[25] John Ralston Saul expressed a somewhat similar conception in *Voltaire's Bastards: The Dictatorship of Reason in the West*: "The structures of argument have been co-opted so completely by those who work for the system that when an individual reaches for the words and phrases which he senses will express his case, he finds that they are already in active use in the service of power. This now amounts to a virtual dictatorship of vocabulary." (Saul, *Voltaire's Bastards*, 36)

[26] Sturgeon, *Slow Sculpture*, 73

[27] Baudelaire, *The Painter of Modern Life*, 2

[28] Buhner, *Ensouling Language*, 64

[29] In Vipassana meditation, a Sankara is understood as a positive or negative attachment to a sensation which is stored in one's body. By staying equanimous to incoming sensations, no new Sankaras are formed and old ones are continuously cleared out.

[30] Nicolaides, *The Natural Way to Draw*, 2 | And in which life looks at you, I might add.

[31] Nicolaides, *The Natural Way to Draw*, 221

[32] Blake, *The Marriage of Heaven and Hell*, 42

[33] Steinbeck, *Steinbeck: A Life in Letters*, 289

[34] Cited in Chipp, *Theories of Modern Art*, 161

[35] Wassily Kandinsky once made a similar comparison in *The Art of Spiritual Harmony,* in which he reasoned that classical music must not mimic sounds of Nature (such as the chittering of birds or the splashing of a waterfall) but should focus on developing its own language. (Kandinsky, *The Art of Spiritual Harmony,* 42)

[36] David Maclagan wrote a book about this tension, or should I say: about this contradiction. The title is *Outsider Art: From the Margins to the Marketplace*.

[37] Jaffé, *Symbolism in the Visual Arts*, 310

[38] Herrigel, *Zen in the art of archery*, 88

[39] Buonarotti, Symonds, *The Sonnets of Michelangelo*, 46f

[40] Saslow, *The Poetry of Michelangelo,* Poem 151

[41] I owe this observation to Tobias Ballaty.

[42] Cited in *Symbolism in the Visual Arts*, 293

[43] Wilde, *The Picture of Dorian Gray, 21*

[44] Cited in *Symbolism in the Visual Arts*, 307

[45] Cited in Chipp, *Theories of Modern Art*, 330

[46] Tobler, *Nature!*, 3-5

Part IV: Sculptural Ecology

[1] This reflects the Tolstoian viewpoint in which art is worth to the degree it is able to "infect other people." See *What is art?* by Leo Tolstoy.

[2] Quoted in Hervier, Jünger, *The Details of Time*, 56

[3] Klee, *The Thinking* Eye, 15

[4] Eliot, *Tradition and the Individual Talent*, 39

[5] Cited in Chipp, *Theories of Modern Art*, 548

[6] Schoenberg, *Theory of Harmony*, 430

[7] Orwell, *Selected Essays*, 231

[8] Stephen Buhner wrote extensively about this intuition. He writes in *Plant Intelligence and the Imaginal Realm:* "Then they [writers, artists or all kind] struggle to get certain words to go along with those tones and the feelings they possess. They don't know why, they just know they have to. They keep at it because something in them says they must. The part of them that says they must is what some ancient Greeks called the daemon (or daimon). It is an outside force placed in living beings at birth that continually urges them towards their life purpose. From another perspective it could be considered the thing that directs human beings to fulfil their ecological purpose." (Buhner, *Plant Intelligence and the Imaginal Realm*, 382)

[9] P.D. Ouspensky seems to have been guided by a similar intuition when he concluded in *Tertium Organum*: "It is indeed probable that by the spur of love, Eros, humanity is aroused to the fulfillment of its principal function, of which we know nothing, but only at times glimpses hazily perceive." (Ouspensky, *Tertium Organum*, 141)

[10] Buhner, *Plant Intelligence and the Imaginal Realm*, 372

[11] From this, I shall not conclude that everyone should give up their job and start hammering on stone. I think it was Siddhartha who said that one person meditating per village is enough, so one person exploring form in stone might be enough for one village too. Artists have always been the salt of society and too much of it spoils

the dish. In tiny proportions, however, it makes the dish taste by complementing, supporting and bringing forth the different tastes encapsulated within the other ingredients. Societies that deprive themselves of them because they render them useless, unproductive, or even spiteful commit the same fallacy as those who do not add salt to a dish because they assess that salt does not taste in and of itself.

[12] An understanding of time that seems compatible with the implications of this conception was portrayed in Christopher Nolan's movie *Tenet*. The move draws from the Novikov self-consistency conjecture, which can be interpreted as follows: If you traveled backwards in time, you could not change any events in the past as they happened, but you would come to realize that your choices made whilst traveling backwards in time were necessary constituents of the unfolding present you started to travel backwards in time from. So anything done on your way backwards in time must have been part of the past all along. To make this more clear, the conjunction present a solution to the *Grandfather Paradox,* which asks what would happen if you traveled backwards in time and killed your grandfather, so that your existence would become impossible. According to the conjecture, you, if you traveled backwards in time to kill your grandfather, would, in the end, not end up killing him, no matter how strong your motivation was to do so. Some yet unforeseeable event, which took place in the past, would stop you from killing him; otherwise, the very reality from which you traveled backwards in time from would not have unfolded.

In a way, Christopher Nolan offers a deterministic view of reality in which we are stuck in some sort of loop, suggesting that, even though we might be under the impression of having free will, we actually aren't. But the movie's view on time does not have the bitter undertone that such worldviews usually suffer from because, albeit it might be so, it does not make a difference. The movie portrays how lives, actions and relationships still have as much meaning, or even more, than if it weren't for such philosophical implications. This is because, in such a universe, one's actions aren't just random chance but part of a greater whole in which each and everyone plays an essential part.

Such a view on time has far-reaching conclusions and can be used to make sense of many longstanding questions, such as providing an answer to whether the laws of physics were discovered or invented? Both, the obvious answer would be! They are invented —which is to look at time from the perspective of the past— as well as discovered —which is to look at time from the perspective of the future. Looking at time before $E=MC^2$ was known, it appears as if the equation was invented.

Looking back in time from the viewpoint of today, it seems as if it was discovered. The same can be said for the "discovery" of perspective in art, the "discovery" of zero in mathematics, the "discovery" of the unconscious, or the "discovery" of the Americas. All these existed long before they were "discovered," but only after they were assimilated into our culture, we became aware of their existence.

[13] Gardner, *On Becoming a Novelist*, 119ff

[14] Lovelock, *Healing Gaia*, 17

[15] In music, the composer Arnold Schoenberg can be credited with having initiated a similar shift: Driven by the motivation —or shall I say: by the necessity— to remove the outside, the exterior motive out of music, he sought to free music from the demands that were previously put on it, namely that it ought to sound *like* something, stand for something, or be *for* something. His search to allow music to *be* something for itself led him to compose atonal music, which he thought to be the next logical step in music's evolution. He was, in fact, under the sense that music has a will of its own, and he saw himself only as a mouthpiece to grant music its natural progression.

Following his work, it was no longer music's purpose to please the human ear, but its right to exist was made intrinsic. One reads that the twelve-tone technique, serial music and even electronic music would subsequently emerge from his work.

[16] Klee, *On Modern Art*, 15

[17] Malevich, The Non-Objective World, 38

[18] Sontag, *Against Interpretation*, 17

[19] Sontag, *Against Interpretation*, 17

[20] Cited in Chipp, *Theories of Modern Art*, 563

[21] Klee, *On Modern Art*, 49

[22] cited in Shanes, *Constantin Brancusi*, 106

[23] Auguste Rodin wrote about this process: "Without doubt, very fine works of art are appreciated only by a limited number; and even in galleries and public squares they are looked at only by a few. But, nevertheless, the thoughts they embody end by filtering through to the crowd. Below the men of genius there are other artists of less scope, who borrow and popularize the conceptions of the masters: writers are influenced by painters, painters by writers; there is a continual exchange of thought between all the brains of a generation—the journalists, the popular novelists, the illustrators, the makers of pictures bring within the reach of the multitude the truths discovered by the powerful intellects of the day. It is like a

spiritual stream, like a spring pouring forth in many cascades, which finally meet to form the great moving river which represents the mentality of an era." (Rodin and Gsell, *Art by Auguste Rodin*, 238ff)

[24] A zeitgeist is a fabric of values, forms and ways of expression that permeates all of society within a given era.

[25] Kandinsky writes about this in *The Art of Spiritual Harmony:* "Every work of art is the child of its age and, in many cases, the mother of our emotions. It follows that each period of culture produces an art of its own which can never be repeated. Efforts to revive the art-principles of the past will at best produce an art that is still-born. It is impossible for us to live and feel, as did the ancient Greeks. In the same way those who strive to follow the Greek methods in sculpture achieve only a similarity of form, the work remaining soulless for all time. Such imitation is mere aping." (Kandinsky, *The Art of Spiritual Harmony*, 5)

[26] Dubuffet, *Crude Art Preferred to Cultural Art*, 594

[27] Mondrian, *Mondrian*, 7

[28] Teilhard de Chardin, for example, wrote that "… art represents the area of furthest advance around man's growing energy, the area in which nascent truths condense, take on their first form, and become animate, before they are definitively formulated and assimilated." (cited in Shlain, *Art & Physics*, 387f)

[29] The Japanese Farmer Masanobu Fukuoka, for example, writes: "The causal relationship between factors in nature are just too entangled for man to unravel through research and analysis. Perhaps science succeeds in advancing one slow step at a time, but because it does so while groping in total darkness along a road without end, it is unable to know the real truth of things. This is why scientists are pleased with partial explications and see nothing wrong with pointing a finger and proclaiming this to be the cause and that the effect. The more research progresses, the larger the body of scholarly data grows. The antecedent causes of causes increase in number and depth, becoming incredibly complex, such that, far from unraveling the tangled web of cause and effect, science succeeds only in explaining in ever greater detail each of the bends and kinks in the individual threads. There being infinite causes for an event or action, there are infinite solutions as well, and these together deepen and broaden to infinite complexity." (Fukuoka, *The Natural Way of Farming*, 88)

Bibliography

Adams, Tim. 2015. *Barbara Hepworth: a life told in six works.* June 06. Accessed Last accessed: 19/07/2022. https://www.theguardian.com/artanddesign/2015/jun/07/barbara-hepworth-life-in-six-works-tate-retrospective-exhibition-sculpture-for-a-modern-world.

Arp, Jean. 1948. *On my way; poetry and essays, 1912-1947.* N.Y.: Wittenborn Schultz Inc. .

Baudelaire, Charles-Pierre. 2010. *The Painter of Modern Life.* London: Penguin.

Becks-Malorny, Ulrike. 2006. *Paul Cézanne.* Köln: Taschen.

Berger, John, interview by Gavin Esler. 2011. *John Berger on Ways of Seeing, being an artist, and Marxism (2011)* Accessed August 30, 2022. https://www.youtube.com/watch?v=b5y7QRt2bws&ab_channel=BBCNewsnight.

Berne, Eric. 1964. *Games People Play.* N.Y.: Grove.

Blake, William. 2010. "The marriage of Heaven and Hell." In *William Blake: Poems*, by William Blake, edited by James Fenton, 34-42. London: Faber and Faber.

Bly, Robert. 2009. *Reaching Out to the World: New and selected prose poems.* White Pine Press.

Buhner, Stephen H. 2010. *Ensouling Language: on the art of nonfiction and the writer's life.* Rochester: Inner Traditions.

—. 2014. *Plant Intelligence and the Imaginal Realm.* Rochester: Bear & Company.

—. 2004. *The Secret Teachings of Plants.* Rochester: Bear & Company.

Buonarotti, Michelangelo. 1950. *The Sonnets of Michelangelo.* Translated by J.A. Symonds. London: Vision.

Campbell, Joseph. 1988. *The Power of Myth.* N.Y.: Doubleday.

Chipp, Herschel B. 1968. *Theories of Modern Art.* LA: University of California Press.

Coats, Callum. 2991. *Living Energies: Viktor Schauberger's Brilliant Work with Natural Energy Explained.* Gill.

Crowley, John. 1942, 1990. *Little, big.* NY: Bentam Book .

Cummings, E. E. 1965. *E.E. Cummings: a miscellany revised.* NY: October House.

Dostoyevsky, Fyodor. 1900. *The Brothers Karamazov.* Translated by Constance Garnett. NY: The Modern Library.

Dubuffet, Jean. 1992. "Crude art preferred to cultural art." In *Art in Theory, 1900-1990*, edited by Charles Harrison and Paul Wood, 593-595. Oxford: Blackwell.

Eliot, T.S. 1982. "Tradition and the Individual Talent." *Perspecta,* Vol. 19: 36-42.

Emerson, Ralph Waldo. 1921. *Essays and poems.* N.Y.: Harcourt.

—. 1950. *The Complete Essays and Other Writings of Ralph Waldo Emerson.* N.Y.: Random House.

Frank, Anne. 1995. *The Diary of a Young Girl: The Definitive Edition.* Edited by Otto H. Frank and Mirjam Pressler. Translated by Susan Massotty. Doubleday.

Frankl, Viktor. 1984. *Man's Search for Meaning: An Introduction to Logotherapy.* NY: Simon & Schuster.

Fukuoka, Masanobu. 1985. *The Natural Way of Farming.* Tokyo: Japan Publications.

Gardner, John. 1985. *On Becoming a Novelist.* N.Y.: Harper & Row.

Goethe, Johann Wolfgang. 1953, 1963. *Maximen und Reflexionen.* Hamburg: Christian Wegner Verlag.

—. 1983. *Scientific studies.* Edited by Douglas Miller. N.Y.: Suhrkamp.

—. 2018. *The Essential Goethe.* Edited by Matt Bell. Princeton University Press.

Goethe, Johann Wolfgang, and Johann Peter Eckermann. 1850. *Conversations of Goethe with Eckermann and Soret.* Translated by John Oxenford. Vol. 1. 2 vols. London: Smith, Elder & Co.

Goodall, Reece. 2021. *Italian artist sells 'invisible art' for €15,000.* July 1. Accessed July 2022. https://theboar.org/2021/07/invisible-art/.

Herrigel, Eugen. 1971. *Zen in the art of archery.* N.Y.: Vintage Books.

Hervier, Julien, and Ernst Jünger. 1995. *The Details of Time: Conversations with Ernst Jünger.* Marsilio.

Hesse, Hermann. 2012. *Das Glasperlenspiel: Versuch einer Lebensbeschreibung des Magister Ludi Josef Knecht samt Knechts hinterlassenen Schriften.* Suhrkamp.

—. 1974. *Der Steppenwolf.* Berlin: Suhrkamp .

Hofmann, Albert. 2005. *LSD: My Problem Child.* MAPS.

Huxley, Aldous. 1942. *The Art of Seeing: An Adventure in Re-education.* N.Y.: Harper.

Jaffé, Aniela. 1978. "Symbolism in the Visual Arts." In *Man and his Symbols*, by Carl G. Jung, Franz Joseph Henderson, Jolande Jacobi and Aniela Jaffé, edited by Aniela Jaffé, 255-323. London: Pan Books.

Kandinsky, Wassily. 1914. *The Art of Spiritual Harmony.* London: Constable and Company.

Klee, Paul. 1970. *Form- und Gestaltungslehre.* Edited by Jürg Spiller. Schwabe Verlag.

—. 1966. *On Modern Art.* Translated by Paul Findlay. London: Faber.

—. 1961. *The Thinking Eye. The Notebooks of Paul Klee.* Edited by Jürg Spiller. Translated by Ralph Manheim. Vol. 1. London: Lund Humphries.

Krenov, James. 2000. *A Cabinetmaker's Notebook.* Fresno, CA: Linden.

—. 1977, 1992. *The Fine Art of Cabinetmaking.* Fresno, CA: Linden Publishing Inc.

Lakoff, George, and Mark Johnson. 2003. *Metaphors We Live By.* University of Chicago Press.

Lamott, Anne. 1994. *Bird by Bird.* N.Y.: Pantheon.

Lindsay, Kenneth, and Peter Vergo. 1994. *Kandinsky: Complete Writings on Art.* Boston: G.K. Hall.

Lovelock, James. 1991. *Healing Gaia: Practical Medicine for the Planet.* NY: Harmony Books.

Maclagan, David. 2009. *Outsider Art: From the Margins to the Marketplace.* London: Reaktion Books.

Malevich, Kazimir. 1971. *Essays on Art, 1915-1933.* 2nd Edition. Edited by Glowacki-Prus and Troels Andersen. London: Rapp & Whiting.

—. 2003. *The Non-Objective World: the manifesto of suprematism.* Dover Publications.

Merill, Flora. (3 October, 1926). "Brancusi, the Sculptor of the Spirit, would build "Infinite Column" in Park." *New York World* (New York World).

Mondrian, Piet. 1970. *Mondrian.* London: Hamlyn.

Nicolaides, Kimon. 1969. *The Natural Way To Draw.* Boston: Houghton Mifflin Company.

Nietzsche, Friedrich. 2006. *Thus Spoke Zarathustra: A Book for All and None.* Edited by Adrian Del Caro and Robert. B. Pippin. Translated by Adrian Del Caro. N.Y.: Cambridge University Press.

Orwell, George. 2021. *Selected Essays.* Edited by Stefan Collini. Oxford University Press.

Osho. 1976. *Get out of your own way.* Pune, India: Opensource.

—. 2000. *Walk Without Feet, Fly Without Wings and Think without Mind.* Full Circle Publishing Ltd.

Ouspensky, P. D. 1922, 2016. *Tertium Organum: The Third Canon of Thought.* London: Aziloth Books.

Putnam, Brenda. 2003. *The Sculptor's Way: A guide to modelling and sculpture.* Dover: Watson-Guptill.

Read, Allen Walker. 1983. "The Semiotic Aspect of Alfred Korzybski's General Semantics." *ETC: A Review of General Semantics* 16-21.

Rodin, Auguste, and Paul Gsell. 1912. *Art by Auguste Rodin.* Boston: Small, Maynard & Co.

Saslow, James M. 1991. *The Poetry of Michelangelo: An Annotated Translation.* London: New Haven.

Saul, John Ralston. 1992. *Voltaire's Bastards: The dictatorship of reason in the West.* N.Y. : Free Press.

Schoenberg, Arnold. 1978. *Theory of Harmony.* Translated by Roy E. Carter. Berkeley and Los Angeles: University of California Press.

Shanes, Eric. 1989. *Constantin Brancusi.* Abbeville Press.

Shlain, Leonard. 1991. *Art & Physics: Parallel Visions in Space, Time, and Light.* N.Y.: Quill.

Sontag, Susan. 1969. *Against Interpretation.* NY: Dell Pub. Co. .

Stafford, William. 1978. *Writing the Australian Crawl.* University of Michigan Press.

Stegner, Wallace. 1982. *One Way to Spell Man.* Garden City: Doubleday.

Steinbeck, John. 1945. *Cannery Row.* Penguin Books.

—. 1975. *Steinbeck: A Life in Letters.* Edited by Elaine Steinbeck and Robert Wallsten. NY.: Viking Press.

Sturgeon, Theodore. 1971. "Slow Sculpture." In *Sturgeon is Alive and Well*, by Theodore Sturgeon, 57-79. N.Y. : Putnam.

Suzman, James. 2017. *Affluence Without Abundance: The Disappearing World of the Bushmen.* N.Y.: Bloomsbury.

The Brummer Gallery. 1926. *Brancusi.* NY: The Brummer Gallery.

Thoreau, Henry D. 1892. *Autumn: from the Journal of Henry D. Thoreau.* Boston: Boston Houghton, Mifflin.

—. 2004. *Walden: A fully annotated edition.* Yale University Press.

Tiger, Caroline. 2007. *Isamu Noguchi.* N.Y.: Chelsea House.

Tobler, Georg Christoph. 1983. "Nature!" In *Scientific Studies*, by Johann Wolfgang Goethe, edited by Douglas Miller, 3-5. N.Y.: Suhrkamp.

Tolstoy, Leo. 2005. *What is Art?* Translated by Richard Pevear and Larissa Volokhonsky. London: Penguin.

Wilde, Oscar. 1992. *The Picture of Dorian Gray.* Wordsworth.

Wittgenstein, Ludwig. 1980. *Culture and Value.* Edited by G.H. Von Wright. Translated by Peter Winch. Oxford: Basil Blackwell Publisher.

—. 2013. *Tractatus Logico-Philosophicus.* Routledge.